THE TIES THAT BIND US

U.S.-Mexico Contemporary Perspectives Series, 23
Center for U.S.-Mexican Studies
University of California, San Diego

The TIES THAT BIND US

MEXICAN MIGRANTS IN SAN DIEGO COUNTY

Edited by Richard Kiy &
Christopher Woodruff

LA JOLLA, CALIFORNIA
CENTER FOR U.S.-MEXICAN STUDIES, UCSD

Printed in the United States of America

Cover photographs courtesy of Tamara Kay
Cover design by UCSD Publications Office

Library of Congress Cataloging-in-Publication Data

The ties that bind us : Mexican migrants in San Diego County / edited by
Richard Kiy & Christopher Woodruff.
    p. cm. – (U.S.-Mexico contemporary perspectives series ; 23)
    ISBN 1-878367-53-6
    1. Mexicans—California—San Diego County—Social conditions. 2.
Immigrants—California—San Diego County—Social conditions. 3.
Mexicans—Employment—California—San Diego County. 4. Immigrants—
Employment—California—San Diego County. 5. Transnationalism. 6. San
Diego County (Calif.)—Social conditions. 7. San Diego County (Calif.)—
Economic conditions. 8. San Diego County (Calif.)—Emigration and
immigration. 9. Tijuana (Baja California, Mexico)—Emigration and
immigration. I. Kiy, Richard. II. Woodruff, Christopher. III. University of
California, San Diego. Center for U.S.-Mexican Studies. IV. Series.

F868.S15T54 2005
306.868'72'097948'021—dc22
                                                     2005050757

CONTENTS

Preface

Spurred by the introduction of the Bracero Program in 1942 and sustained by the United States' seemingly unrelenting demand for unskilled workers, Mexican labor migration to the United States has become a way of life for Mexican families in search of economic opportunity and a better quality of life. Although the influx of migrants from Mexico was initially confined to the border counties of the U.S. Southwest, today's migration flows are undergoing an unprecedented transformation, extending well beyond the border region to communities throughout the heartland of America, from Washington State to New York, from Illinois to Florida.

Today, as migrants' destinations are multiplying, only 1.6 percent of would-be migrant workers coming from Mexico identify San Diego as their preferred destination.[1] Yet San Diego County's proximity to the border and its high demand for unskilled labor for its agricultural, hospitality, construction, and service industries have driven a steady rise in in-migration from Mexico since 1970. As a result, there are now nearly 630,000 residents of Mexican descent living in San Diego County and accounting for over 22 percent of the region's population. Among the Mexicans residing in San Diego County, nearly one in three is undocumented, and these undocumented residents account for some 6.5 percent of the county's population.

In the past, the members of San Diego's Mexican community came principally from neighboring Baja California and the traditional migrant-sending states of Jalisco and Guanajuato in central Mexico. Today's migration patterns are changing, driven by growing social inequalities and rural poverty in Mexico's southern and central regions. As a consequence, nearly a quarter of San Diego County's migrant

---

[1] This according to a 2003 survey by El Colegio de la Frontera Norte (COLEF) in Tijuana.

workers arriving since 1990 have come from two of Mexico's poorest and most economically deprived states, Oaxaca and Guerrero. Increasingly, these new migrants are members of indigenous populations.

For would-be migrants from impoverished Mexican states, the northbound trek is often chosen as the best of a dwindling number of survival options, despite the emergence of new obstacles to undocumented border crossing since the September 11, 2001, terrorist attacks. For those who successfully navigate the hazards and reach San Diego County, economic opportunities do indeed improve, but the combination of the area's high living costs and the ongoing challenges of life in the shadows of undocumented status means that they will be severely underserved in the areas of housing, education, and health services. As just one example, Bonnie Bade notes (in her chapter in this volume) that 72 percent of migrant children fail to apply for school breakfast programs even though they would otherwise qualify. Although one can debate the politics of providing social services to the region's undocumented workforce and their families, the fact remains that for a growing number in San Diego's Mexican migrant community, the poverty they hoped to leave behind continues to oppress them. The growing ranks of Mexican migrants living below the poverty line have helped place San Diego sixth among major metropolitan areas in the United States in terms of the rate of increase in poverty among its population.

U.S. census data indicate that children of foreign-born residents across the United States are twice as likely to be living in poverty as are children of native-born parents. Research highlighted in this volume indicates that similar challenges confront children and youths within San Diego County's Mexican foreign-born population. A growing number of Mexican immigrant families are living with ten to twelve people to a household in order to cope with San Diego County's escalating housing costs. The high mobility of San Diego's migrant workforce presents unique challenges for these workers' children, contributing to their poorer academic performance and higher-than-average school dropout rates.

As San Diego's Mexican immigrant community continues to grow, so too do its health challenges. A growing number of Mexican migrant workers and their families are uninsured. The region's migrant workforce has a higher susceptibility to HIV/AIDS and tuberculosis than does the rest of the population. Migrants also have a higher prevalence of otherwise preventable diseases, such as cervical cancer, diabetes, and obesity. Thousands of Mexican migrants are living in migrant worker camps in San Diego County that lack basic utilities and access to potable water, which converts, in turn, to higher occupational and other public health risks.

Given these many challenges—the hazards of border crossing, poverty in the United States that belies the migrants' hopes for economic advancement, and the lack of services available to them—why do these migrants remain in San Diego? The answer is clear: a population of this size would not remain if it did not have gainful employment. And this fact is linked to three other considerations: (1) the Mexican immigrant community is making enormous contributions to the San Diego regional economy; (2) there is a relationship of codependence between these migrants and many of the region's major employers; and (3) through their remittances, the immigrants are providing ongoing financial support to their communities of origin in Mexico. These considerations speak to the clear and crucial need for a better understanding of San Diego's Mexican immigrant community and its requirements.

Toward this end, the International Community Foundation—in collaboration with the University of California, Los Angeles, California State University, San Marcos, and El Colegio de La Frontera Norte—embarked on an eighteen-month research initiative to better comprehend the situation of San Diego County's Mexican immigrant community. This initiative led to a November 2003 research seminar sponsored by the University of California, San Diego's Center for U.S.-Mexican Studies and ultimately to the publication of this anthology. The research was made possible through the financial support of the Rockefeller Foundation's Working Communities Program.

The work that is presented here is significant in many ways. David Runsten offers the first detailed analysis of Mexican *matrícula consular* data, providing a precise mapping of migrants' places of origin in Mexico and of residence in San Diego County. This has important implications for the delivery of education and social and health services to this population; for efforts at binational cooperation; and for services, such as transportation and the sending of remittances, that relate to migration from specific points in Mexico. When matched with the 2000 U.S. census, *matrícula consular* data for San Diego show a positive correlation between areas in the county that are experiencing increases in poverty and those that show high concentrations of Mexican migrant workers.

Bonnie Bade discusses conditions where the migrants live in San Diego County—in migrant camps and overcrowded apartments—along with the related impacts on these individuals' health. Konane Martínez, David Runsten, and Alejandrina Ricárdez highlight other key needs within the transnational Mexican migrant community, including the need for more trained staff in culturally and linguistically appropriate services, particularly for indigenous migrants. These authors note that, absent a change in federal immigration policy, it will be very difficult to addaress at the local level the problems that are associated with recent immigrants. Legalization of this labor force would resolve many prevailing issues and make cost-effective cross-border social service alternatives more accessible to this segment of the population.

Several chapters analyze the population of individuals who cross the Tijuana–San Diego border, sometimes daily, to work and to access services. Drawing on data from the Survey of Migration at Mexico's Northern Border (EMIF) conducted between 1993 and 2001, Rafael Alarcón characterizes the migrants coming to Tijuana from elsewhere in Mexico and those entering and returning from the United States. Consistent with the characteristics of migrants residing in San Diego County that Runsten describes, Alarcón finds that Mexico's southern and southeastern regions account for a substantial share of migrants who arrive in Tijuana intending to cross into the United States. María Eugenia Anguiano Téllez provides a demographic and economic profile of the population resident in Tijuana. And Luis Escala Rabadán and Germán Vega Briones document the extent to which the San Diego–Tijuana border has become blurred as a huge "commuter population" crosses the border on a daily or weekly basis and people who work in San Diego find affordable housing in Tijuana.

Collectively, these chapters document the growing economic differences that are emerging between transnational Mexican migrants in San Diego and trans-border residents who can move freely between the

United States and Tijuana. The level of economic prosperity among Tijuana's cross-border commuters has increased steadily, as evidenced in their rising rates of home ownership; this is in stark contrast to San Diego's transnational migrant residents, who are contributing to the ranks of the area's working poor.

Finally, Naoko Kada and I highlight the emergence of the cross-border provision of social services to the Mexican migrant community in San Diego County and the importance of looking beyond existing social service agencies to address the community's growing unmet education and health needs.

Through these contributions, the International Community Foundation hopes to give civic leaders and elected officials in San Diego County and throughout the United States a deeper understanding of the unique challenges faced by the Mexican immigrants in their communities. We hope these chapters will highlight the need for expanded philanthropy and outreach to the major migrant-sending regions in Mexico. And finally, we hope that this collective research will help to better inform local, state, and federal elected officials as they seek to enact and enforce immigration policies, policies that will have profound impacts on the immigrant population across the breadth of this nation.

—Richard Kiy
President and CEO, International Community Foundation

Part I

The Mexican Immigrant Community in San Diego County

1

Origins and Characteristics of Mexican Immigrants in San Diego: Evidence from the *Matrículas Consulares*

David Runsten

San Diego had been the principal entry point for Mexican undocu-mented workers for thirty years before Operation Gatekeeper shifted the traffic out into the deserts. One local tomato grower interviewed in the early 1990s described the migration as "a great wave washing over us, headed north." In interviews with Oaxacan farmworkers around the United States, we found that many had worked for farmers Harry Singh or the Ukegawa Brothers in San Diego. But who comes from Mexico to live in San Diego? Is San Diego just like the rest of the United States—or even like the rest of California—or is it more like other towns along the border?

Thanks to Nabil Kamel and Jaron Waldman for preparing the maps that corre-spond to this chapter, and to Nicolas Navarro, Paula Castro, and Abigail Ro-lon Santoscoy for data assistance. The NAID Center is especially grateful to Rodolfo Figueroa, the Mexican consul in San Diego at the time, for providing the *matrícula* data. We also thank the current consul, Luis Cabrera, for his con-tinuing support. Consulate staff who assisted us included Felipe U. Cuéllar Sánchez and Luis F. Gómez-Duarte. I also want to thank Raúl Hinojosa and Richard Kiy for envisioning the analysis of these data and making it happen. Finally, thanks to Chris Woodruff for helpful comments on an earlier draft. Errors and omissions are, of course, mine.

Cornelius (1992) reviewed the evidence on the composition of migration to the United States from the San Diego and California perspectives. In his view, a more generalized pattern of migration from Mexico to the United States had existed through the 1920s, but following the Great Depression, it was refocused on agriculture through the Bracero Program, which operated from 1942 until 1965. During this program's later years (after the cotton and sugarbeet harvests were mechanized in the 1950s) this guestworker program was mainly used by California fruit and vegetable producers, and it tended to focus migration on California. Since it mainly recruited workers from west-central Mexico, it established patterns of migration from these states (principally Jalisco, Michoacán, Guanajuato, and Zacatecas) to California that persisted after the Bracero Program's termination. Even in other states with minor participation in the program, such as Oaxaca, interviews with migrants later revealed that subsequent undocumented migration networks usually began with former braceros (Runsten and Kearney 1994).

Cornelius (1992) identified a number of new migration patterns that were emerging: more migrants were coming from urban areas (especially Mexico City) as well as regions that had not sent migrants previously; Oaxaca was rising as an important origin point; more women were migrating; there was increased settlement in the United States, prompted in part by the amnesty provisions of the Immigration Reform and Control Act of 1986 (IRCA); and Mexican migrants had entered more and more nonagricultural sectors of the economy. Mexico's National Population Council (CONAPO) also found these to be the principal trends in the 2000 Mexican census data they analyzed (CONAPO 2002: 29). We focus only on the migrants' origins and characteristics in the discussion that follows, but in retrospect we can see that the spreading out of Mexican immigrants in the United States, both geographically and occupationally, was occurring at a much greater rate than anyone imagined. The National Agricultural Worker Survey showed that Mexican immigrants had been employed in agriculture all across the country; the 2000 census reported similar results on the settlement of Mexican immigrants. And the spreading out of migration origins in Mexico was also occurring more rapidly than imagined, as the data presented in this chapter show.

This essay looks at a new source of data to assess the origins and makeup of the Mexican migrants in the San Diego region of California. Where previously relatively small samples of immigrants or apprehended border crossers were mined for their origins (Dagodag 1975; Jones 1984; Cornelius 1992), now we are beginning to get the endpoints for a much larger group. This pilot analysis of the *matrícula* (consular registration card) data shows that though the traditional sending states, such as Jalisco and Michoacán, are less important as sources of migrants than they once were, they nevertheless continue to send migrants that end up living relatively close to the border in San Diego, likely having gained access to better job niches through their networks. However, the migrant population portrayed in the San Diego matrículas is increasingly dominated by people from southern and central Mexico, their origins are more urban, and there are more women (44 percent), just as Cornelius (1992) suggested.

MATRÍCULAS CONSULARES

Migration researchers have always had a difficult time judging the origins, destinations, and composition of the flow from Mexico to the United States. Data on border apprehensions have been analyzed, surveys in villages extrapolated, surveys conducted at the border, and census questionnaires altered to produce better data. Now the Mexican government is engaged in a significant effort to provide documents to Mexican citizens in the United States. These *matrículas*, issued by the consulates, contain data on place of birth, age, gender, and current residence of the applicants, thus providing a new source of data on the origins, destinations, and composition of Mexicans in the United States. The Mexican consul in San Diego made these data available as a pilot project to test their usefulness for public policy research.

This chapter explores the data from the *matrículas consulares* of the Mexican consulate in San Diego for the years 1995–2002. There were over 63,000 matrículas issued in San Diego during this period. Table 1.1 shows their issuance by year. One can see that about 70 percent were issued after 2000, and the rate of growth of their issuance has been rising, increasing 110 percent between 2001 and 2002.

Table 1.1. Matrículas Issued by Year, Mexican Consulate in San Diego, 1995–2002

Year	Number of Matrículas Issued	Percent of Matrículas Issued, 1995–2002
1995	3,616	5.7%
1996	4,884	7.7
1997	1,242	2.0
1998	2,364	3.7
1999	7,267	11.5
2000	8,512	13.4
2001	11,452	18.0
2002	24,138	38.0
Total	63,475	100.0%

Source: Mexican Consulate in San Diego.

More migrants have been obtaining matrículas because their usefulness has increased. In the early years they were seen as a form of identification for migrants returning to Mexico. In more recent years they have become a form of identification in the United States, accepted in many instances by law enforcement, banks, and other institutions, and their security features have improved. They have been promoted by the Mexican government, so it is not simply a matter of more migrants seeking them.

Who obtains a matrícula? Clearly, not all Mexicans in San Diego have a use for a matrícula. Anyone who has a passport would not need it, so the wealthy and professionals would not be included. On the other hand, very recent immigrants and those in marginal and isolated situations, such as farmworkers in rural encampments, might have so little contact with institutions that the matrícula would appear of no use. It is most likely those immigrants who have been in the United States for a while, and have a job and a place to live, who seek to obtain the matrícula. Of an estimated 300,000 Mexicans in San Diego County, by the end of 2002 only some 60,000, or about 20 percent, are represented by these matrícula data. As with the data on apprehensions by the U.S. Border Patrol, there are difficulties in interpreting the meaning of these data, since their numbers are susceptible to bureaucratic effort and they are not a random sample. However, unlike the apprehensions data, these are unique individuals, and the data link the endpoints of migration in a way that was not previously available.

Of the 63,475 matrículas issued over the eight years from 1994 to 2002, only 200 were issued to people who did not claim a California residence. Of the 63,275 matrículas issued to people reporting a California address, 62,195 (or over 98 percent) had an address in San Diego County. Most of the non–San Diego residents were living in neighboring areas of Imperial, Riverside, or Orange counties and may well have been working in San Diego. They are included in the analysis of Mexican sending regions, but non-California residents are excluded.

SOURCES OF MEXICAN IMMIGRANTS TO SAN DIEGO: STATES AND REGIONS

Table 1.2 shows the breakdown of the San Diego matrículas by state of birth in Mexico. The top ten states account for 75 percent of the immigrants, and we focus mainly on these states in the analysis that follows.

The leading sending states are Oaxaca and Guerrero, in southeastern Mexico, which together account for almost a quarter of all matrículas. They are followed by Jalisco and Michoacán, two of the "traditional" migrant-sending states of western Mexico; similar states—Guanajuato and Nayarit—are also in the top ten. Baja California is fifth and Sinaloa eighth, representing northwestern Mexico. Finally, the Federal District (DF) is sixth and México State ninth, demonstrating that the Mexico City area, the main urban region of Mexico, is a major contributor of migrants to San Diego.

CONAPO has analyzed the 10 percent sample of the 2000 Mexican population census and derived various indicators of migration. If we take the percentage of households receiving remittances as a fairly uniform indicator of migration to the United States, then multiplying this by the number of households yields an absolute number of households receiving remittances, which can be compared across states. Table 1.3 shows the Mexican states ranked by this indicator. Assuming the probability of finding a migrant in the United States is proportional

Table 1.2. San Diego Matrículas, 1995;nd2002, by State of Birth[a]

State	Number	Percent	Cumulative Percent
Oaxaca	7,397	11.7%	11.7%
Guerrero	6,837	10.8	22.5
Jalisco	6,377	10.1	32.6
Michoacán	5,966	9.4	42.0
Baja California	5,223	8.3	50.3
Federal District	4,664	7.4	57.6
Guanajuato	3,178	5.0	62.7
Sinaloa	2,710	4.3	67.0
México State	2,561	4.1	71.0
Nayarit	2,495	3.9	74.9
Querétaro	1,908	3.0	78.0
Morelos	1,856	2.9	80.9
Puebla	1,714	2.7	83.6
Zacatecas	1,396	2.2	85.8
San Luis Potosí	1,286	2.0	87.8
Hidalgo	1,189	1.9	89.7
Veracruz	1,189	1.9	91.6
Sonora	1,097	1.7	93.3
Durango	1,036	1.6	95.0
Colima	593	0.9	95.9
Chihuahua	524	0.8	96.7
Chiapas	446	0.7	97.4
Tlaxcala	382	0.6	98.1
Aguascalientes	279	0.4	98.5
Coahuila	272	0.4	98.9
Nuevo León	226	0.4	99.3
Tamaulipas	165	0.3	99.5
Baja California Sur	97	0.2	99.7
Yucatán	89	0.1	99.8
Tabasco	66	0.1	99.9
Campeche	27	0.04	99.9
Quintana Roo	15	0.02	100.0%
Total	63,260		

Source: Mexican Consulate in San Diego.

[a] There are an additional 220 matrículas issued to people born in the United States. We have excluded them from this analysis.

to the size of this number, then table 1.3 expresses a ranking of the likelihood that we would find a matrícula from a given state of Mexico if we were looking at all matrículas in the United States. Thus México State and the Federal District, which are ranked 25th and 27th out of 32 in *rate* of migration, are, because of their large populations, 4th and 9th in absolute numbers of households receiving remittances. If migration were uniform across the United States, then tables 1.2 and 1.3 should be the same. The differences are indications of the very particular and cumulative manner in which migration occurs via networks. The case of Oaxaca is especially noteworthy in San Diego and is the result of stage migration to work in northwest Mexican agriculture. Since these matrícula data were taken over a number of years, it is interesting to look at trends in the shares of the different states. Though it is possible that outreach efforts by the consulate to particular groups might skew these data in any one year, in general we would expect the people seeking matrículas to be particular types of immigrants and not necessarily from particular states of Mexico. Figure 1.1 shows the matrículas issued to the top ten sending states to San Diego for the period 1995–2002. The most striking trends are the falling share of Jalisco, which is about halved, and the rising shares of Oaxaca and Guerrero. Jalisco received the most matrículas until 2000, after which the southeastern states became more prominent.

If we look more closely at the ten states that contribute 75 percent of the matrículas in San Diego, we see that they are a varied group. Table 1.4 presents data for all Mexican states on marginality (a Mexican government welfare measure; see chapter appendix A), the proportion of households receiving remittances, and the level of migration from the entity. It is ordered the same as table 1.2.

- The leading two states sending migrants to San Diego—Oaxaca and Guerrero—are, along with Chiapas, considered the poorest states in Mexico, with marginality indices of 1 (the lowest). Guerrero has almost twice the rate of migration and remittances as Oaxaca.

- The next two states—Jalisco and Michoacán—with the other "traditional" sending states of western Mexico (here Guanajuato and Nayarit) are characterized by much higher levels of migration

Table 1.3. Mexican States Ranked by Absolute Number of Households Receiving Remittances

State	Total Number of Households	Percent of Households Receiving Remittances	Number of-Households Receiving Remittances	Index of Migration Intensity	CONAPO Migration Ranking
Jalisco	1,457,326	7.70	112,199	0.888	High
Michoacán	893,671	11.37	101,630	2.060	Very high
Guanajuato	990,602	9.20	91,090	1.366	Very high
México State	2,978,023	2.11	62,764	-0.747	Low
Guerrero	677,731	7.86	53,280	0.428	High
Veracruz	1,649,332	2.74	45,208	-0.707	Low
San Luis Potosí	509,582	8.20	41,776	0.673	High
Zacatecas	306,882	13.03	39,979	2.584	Very high
Federal District	2,203,741	1.72	37,929	-0.910	Very low
Puebla	1,098,409	3.28	36,059	-0.423	Medium
Chihuahua	767,679	4.32	33,196	-0.001	Medium
Durango	331,242	9.70	32,143	1.090	Very high
Oaxaca	762,517	4.13	31,516	-0.264	Medium
Sinaloa	586,245	.4.60	26,958	-0.266	Medium
Hidalgo	507,225	5.06	25,645	0.397	High
Tamaulipas	690,067	3.64	25,132	-0.430	Medium
Baja California	613,602	4.02	24,694	-0.001	Medium

Morelos	376,140	6.44	24,233	0.519	High
Nuevo León	925,493	2.46	22,735	-0.666	Low
Nayarit	222,714	9.64	21,476	1.270	Very high
Coahuila	555,793	3.38	18,790	-0.480	Medium
Sonora	539,528	3.16	17,049	-0.639	Low
Aguascalientes	207,327	6.69	13,878	1.039	High
Querétaro	311,896	3.71	11,570	-0.042	Medium
Colima	136,926	7.34	10,055	0.803	High
Chiapas	832,111	0.76	6,339	-1.246	Very low
Yucatán	387,434	1.41	5,476	-1.082	Very low
Tlaxcala	203,259	2.24	4,558	-0.738	Low
Tabasco	426,653	0.64	2,742	-1.271	Very low
Quintana Roo	219,671	0.99	2,166	-1.146	Very low
Campeche	163,451	1.02	1,665	-1.193	Very low
Baja California Sur	107,536	1.08	1,159	-0.864	Low

Source: CONAPO 2000.

Table 1.4. Migration Intensity, Remittances, and Marginality: Mexican States, 2000

State	Marginality Index[a]	Total Number of Households	Percent of Households Receiving Remittances	Index of Migration Intensity	Degree of Migration Intensity
Oaxaca	1	762,517	4.1	-0.264	Medium
Guerrero	1	677,731	7.9	0.428	High
Jalisco	4	1,457,326	7.7	0.888	High
Michoacán	3	893,671	11.4	2.060	Very high
Baja California	6	613,602	4.0	-0.001	Medium
Federal District	7	2,203,741	1.7	-0.910	Very low
Guanajuato	3	990,602	9.2	1.366	Very high
Sinaloa	4	586,245	4.6	-0.266	Medium
México State	6	2,978,023	2.1	-0.747	Low
Nayarit	4	222,714	9.6	1.270	Very high
Querétaro	4	311,896	3.7	-0.042	Medium
Morelos	4	376,140	6.4	0.519	High
Puebla	2	1,098,409	3.3	-0.423	Medium
Zacatecas	3	306,882	13.0	2.584	Very high
San Luis Potosí	2	509,582	8.2	0.673	High
Hidalgo	2	507,225	5.1	0.397	High
Veracruz	2	1,649,332	2.7	-0.707	Low

Sonora	6	539,528	3.2	− 0.639	Low
Durango	4	331,242	9.7	1.090	Very high
Colima	4	136,926	7.3	0.803	High
Chihuahua	6	767,679	4.3	−0.001	Medium
Chiapas	1	832,111	0.8	−1.246	Very low
Tlaxcala	4	203,259	2.2	− 0.738	Low
Aguascalientes	6	207,327	6.7	1.039	High
Coahuila	6	555,793	3.4	− 0.480	Medium
Nuevo León	6	925,493	2.5	− 0.666	Low
Tamaulipas	6	690,67	3.6	− 0.430	Medium
Baja California Sur	6	107,36	1.1	− 0.864	Low
Yucatán	4	387,434	1.4	−1.082	Very low
Tabasco	2	426,653	0.6	−1.271	Very low
Campeche	2	163,451	1.0	−1.193	Very low
Quintana Roo	5	219,671	1.0	−1.146	Very low

Source: CONAPO n.d.; INEGI 2000.

[a] The marginality index is graded from 1 to 7, with 1 being the most marginal and 7 the least. See chapter appendix A.

(high and very high) and remittances (8–11 percent of households), and more moderate poverty (3–4 on the marginality scale).

- The northern states of Baja California and Sinaloa are a bit better off (6 and 4 on the marginality scale) and have medium levels of migration, similar to Oaxaca's.

- Finally, the area around Mexico City (the Federal District and México State) has even higher welfare levels (7 and 6) and quite low rates of migration and remittances, given the large population.

As Alarcón (this volume) notes, CONAPO has divided Mexico into just four regions for purposes of studying migration: the Southeast, the "traditional" West, the North, and the Central region.[1] Table 1.5 compares the distribution of San Diego matrículas grouped into these regions to Dagodag's (1975) sample of apprehensions by the Border Patrol in the Chula Vista sector in 1973, Alarcón's data on migration to Tijuana and the United States from the Northern Mexico Migration Survey (EMIF), and to the Banco de México's reported remittances for 1995 and 2003.

First, the 1973 apprehensions data (Dagodag 1975) are included to show the predominance in California of migration from the "traditional" western Mexican sending states. All of the more recent data show just how much this dominance has been eroded by migration from the Southeast of Mexico and the area around Mexico City. The 2002 San Diego matrículas suggest that the latter two regions are now comparable sources of migrants to San Diego. Second, the San Diego matrícula data are much more comparable to the EMIF migrants who were headed to Tijuana than they are to general groups of migrants headed somewhere else in the United States. That is, the origins of the migrants in San Diego and Tijuana are more alike than different. The idea that the San Diego–Tijuana region functions as a single urban la-

---

[1] "Traditional" *West*: Aguascalientes, Colima, Durango, Guanajuato, Jalisco, Michoacán, Nayarit, San Luis Potosí, and Zacatecas; *North*: Baja California, Baja California Sur, Coahuila, Chihuahua, Nuevo León, Sinaloa, Sonora, Tamaulipas; *Central*: Federal District, Hidalgo, México State, Morelos, Puebla, Querétaro, Tlaxcala; *Southeast*: Campeche, Chiapas, Guerrero, Oaxaca, Quintana Roo, Tabasco, Veracruz, Yucatán.

bor market would be supported by this finding. Finally, the remittance data, from all of the United States to all of Mexico, show a continued dominance by the traditional sending states, whose migrants have doubtless found more employment away from the border. However, the change in the data over the past ten years similarly indicates the tremendous growth in migration from the Central and Southeast regions of Mexico.

As with the individual states of origin, we can also look at the matrícula data grouped into these four regions over time. Figure 1.2 shows that the "traditional" sending states' share of the San Diego matrículas fell from 45 percent in the 1990s to 30 percent by 2002. The North's share also fell (from 24 percent to 15 percent), while the Central (from 16 percent to 26 percent) and Southeast (from 16 percent to 29 percent) regions gained steadily.

SOURCES OF MEXICAN IMMIGRANTS TO SAN DIEGO: *MUNICIPIOS*

One of the advantages of the matrícula data is that they attempt to establish the *municipio* (basically equivalent to a U.S. county) of birth of the migrants. In the data we were given, only 57 percent of the records had the name of a municipio that corresponded to the listed state, so the following discussion is based on that reduced set of records (36,395).

Figure 1.3 shows the Mexican states of origin of the San Diego immigrants. Though migrants come from all parts of Mexico, the most important states are those along the Pacific Coast. The "traditional" sending states of Jalisco and Michoacán have been joined by the states along the coast to the south, Guerrero and Oaxaca. The Mexico City region and the Tijuana region of Baja California are the other major sources of San Diego immigrants.

We mapped the top ten states of origin for the San Diego matrículas, highlighting the principal muncipios of origin of the migrants. Some of the notable aspects are the following:

- The striking aspect of the Oaxaca map (figure 1.4) is the large swaths of the state sending few or no migrants (light pink and green areas). Migration to San Diego is highly concentrated in a

Table 1.5. Region of Origin of Mexican Migrants

Migrant-Sending Region in Mexico	Chula Vista Apprehensions, 1973	EMIF: Tijuana Is Destination, 1993–2001	EMIF: U.S. Is Destination, 1993–2001	Remittances to Mexico (all U.S.), 1995	Remittances to Mexico (all U.S.), 2003	San Diego Matriculas, 1995–2002	San Diego Matriculas, 2002 only
Traditional	72.4 %	38.0 %	59.4 %	53.1 %	42.1 %	35.7 %	29.7 %
North	17.8 %	13.5 %	7.5 %	10.6 %	8.7 %	16.3 %	15.0 %
Central	6.1 %	25.9 %	16.0 %	22.6 %	29.0 %	22.6 %	26.4 %
Southeast	3.7 %	22.2 %	17.1 %	13.7 %	20.3 %	25.4 %	28.9 %
N	3,204	5,433	2,532			63,256	24,138

Sources: Column 1: Dagodag 1975; columns 2 and 3: Alarcón, this volume; columns 4 and 5: Banco de México 2004; columns 6 and 7: Mexican Consulate in San Diego

few regions: the Mixteca to the west, the Central Valleys (Oaxaca City and Ejutla, Zimatlán, and Ocotlán to the south), and a couple areas in the Sierra Juárez to the north (Ixtlán and San Juan del Estado). Of course Oaxaca is broken into 570 municipios, and if the other states were similarly divided we might see such specificity there as well. Oaxacan workers came to San Diego in large numbers via contract labor in northwestern Mexican agriculture, where they are still the dominant labor force in such places as Baja California, Sinaloa, and Sonora (Zabin et al. 1993).

- The Guerrero map (figure 1.5) shows migration concentrated in and around Acapulco and to the west. The eastern area bordering on Oaxaca tends to send migrants to New York. Only 13 of the 76 municipios of Guerrero did not have matrículas in San Diego.

- The Jalisco map (figure 1.6) shows migrants in San Diego from all but 9 of the 124 municipios of Jalisco. There is a large concentration of people from Guadalajara (41 percent).

- The Michoacán map (figure 1.7) similarly shows migrants from virtually every muncipio. There is no obvious pattern to the migration other than larger numbers from some of the larger towns, such as Morelia and Uruapan.

- Baja California (figure 1.8) has few municipios. Most of the matrículas are issued to people from the larger population centers on the border: Tijuana and Mexicali.

- In Guanajuato (figure 1.9), with the exception of traditional migration municipios in the south of the state, most of the migrants are from the larger urban areas, such as León, Guanajuato, Irapuato, or Salamanca.

- The map of the Federal District (figure 1.10) shows that the migrants are from its northern and eastern areas, which are some of the poorer areas.[2]

---

[2] We are less confident of this result, since our coverage of the Federal District is very poor. Only 8 percent of the Federal District matrículas contained an indication of which part of the city the holder was from.

- Sinaloa (figure 1.11) shows migrants from every part, with the main concentrations from cities (Culiacán, Mazatlán) or from commercial agricultural areas. Sinaloa, along with Sonora and Baja California, has long imported agricultural workers from southern Mexico. This has led to a form of stage migration to the United States (Runsten and Zabin 1994), which means that many of the immigrants born in these states could be members of families originally from such states as Oaxaca.

- The map of México State (rigure 1.12) shows that most of the migrants are coming from greater Mexico City, that is, the municipios surrounding the northern and eastern parts of the Federal District (Nezahualcoyotl, Ecatepec, Tlanepantla, Naucalpan). These areas are contiguous with the main sending areas of the Federal District. There are also some concentrations of migrants from Toluca and the southwest portion of the state.

- Finally, the map of Nayarit (figure 1.13) shows migrants from virtually everywhere, as was the case in the other traditional sending states of Jalisco and Michoacán. Migration is so extensive in these states that no area is untouched.

In order to explore the origins of San Diego immigrants, we looked at Mexican government data about the states and leading municipios of origin reported in the matrícula data. Table 1.6 reports the total number of households, a marginality index that is based on an array of factors (see chapter appendix A), the proportion of households receiving remittances, and some measure of migration intensity.

The first conclusion is that the states are considered more "marginal" than the principal municipios sending migrants to San Diego. Only some places in the Oaxacan Mixteca are considered as poor as the states of Oaxaca and Guerrero as a whole. In fact, 56 percent of the municipios considered have a score of 7, identifying them as among the least marginal places in Mexico; and 85 percent of the municipios scored 5 or more, or above average. The poorest places are not the main sources of migrants. This has often been remarked upon in the literature—that the poor are often too poor to afford the costs of migration to the United States (see, for example, Jones 1984; CONAPO 2002).

Figure 1.1. Mexican State Shares of San Diego Matrículas, 1995-2002

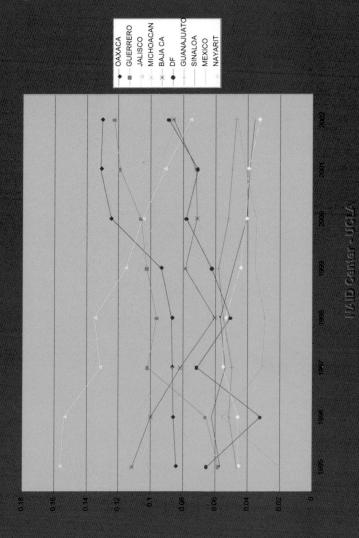

NAID Center – UCLA

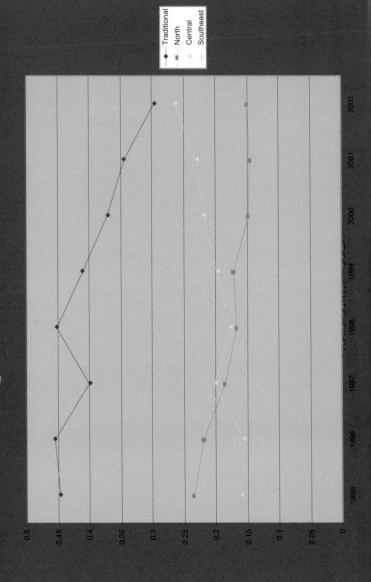

Figure 1.2. Mexican Migration Regions' Shares of San Diego Matrículas, 1995-2002

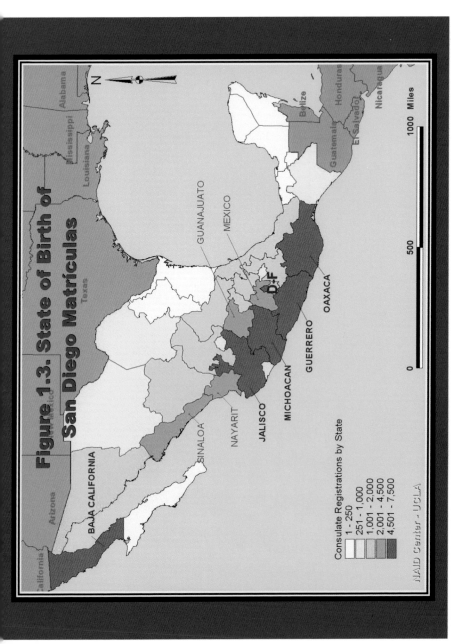

Figure 1.3. State of Birth of San Diego Matrículas

Consulate Registrations by State

- 1 - 250
- 251 - 1,000
- 1,001 - 2,000
- 2,001 - 4,500
- 4,501 - 7,500

NAID Center - UCLA

BAJA CALIFORNIA
SINALOA
NAYARIT
JALISCO
MICHOACAN
GUERRERO
OAXACA
GUANAJUATO
MEXICO
D.F.

California
Arizona
New Mexico
Texas
Louisiana
Mississippi
Alabama

Belize
Guatemala
Honduras
El Salvador
Nicaragua

0   500   1000 Miles

N

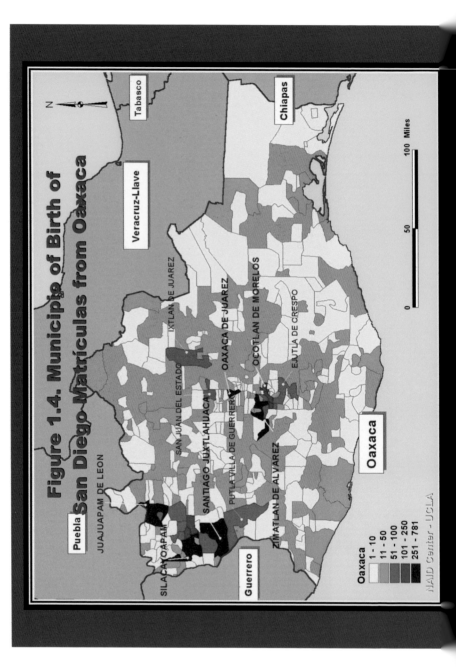

Figure 1.4. Municipio of Birth of San Diego Matrículas from Oaxaca

Puebla

JUAJUAPAM DE LEON

SILACAYOAPAM

Guerrero

SAN JUAN DEL ESTADO

SANTIAGO JUXTLAHUACA

PUTLA VILLA DE GUERRERO

ZIMATLAN DE ALVAREZ

IXTLAN DE JUAREZ

OAXACA DE JUAREZ

OCOTLAN DE MORELOS

EJUTLA DE CRESPO

Veracruz-Llave

Tabasco

Chiapas

Oaxaca

N

Oaxaca
- 1 - 10
- 11 - 50
- 51 - 100
- 101 - 250
- 251 - 781

NAID Center - UCLA

0   50   100 Miles

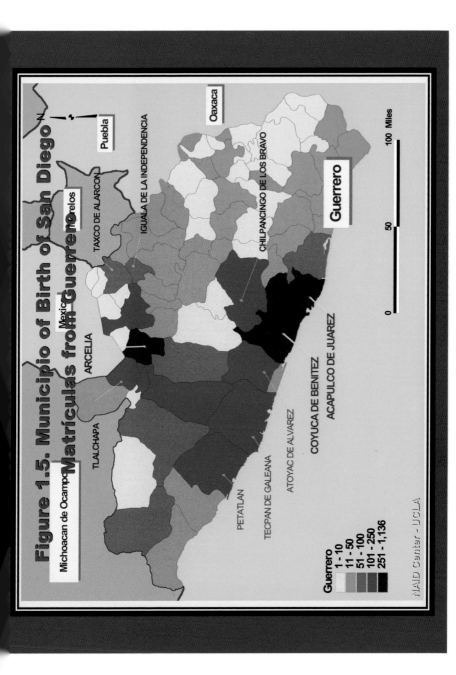

Figure 1.5. Municipio of Birth of San Diego Matrículas from Guerrero

Guerrero
1 - 10
11 - 50
51 - 100
101 - 250
251 - 1,136

NAID Center - UCLA

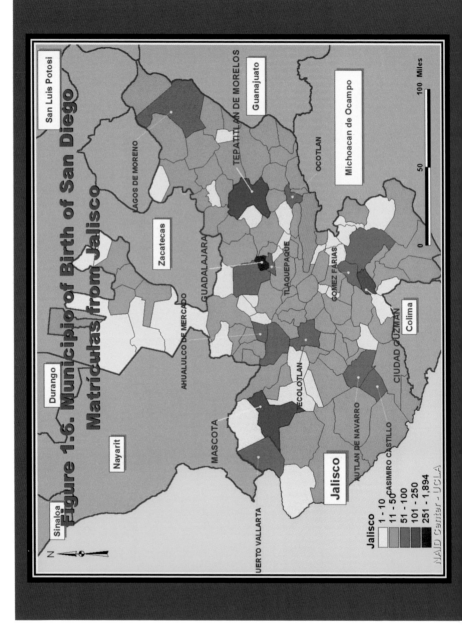

Figure 1.6. Municipio of Birth of San Diego Matrículas from Jalisco

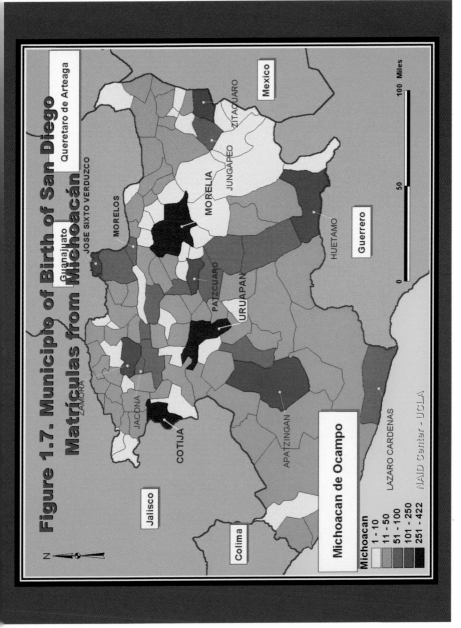

Figure 1.7. Municipio of Birth of San Diego Matrículas from Michoacán

Guanajuato
Queretaro de Arteaga
JOSE SIXTO VERDUZCO
ZAMORA
MORELOS
MORELIA
JUNGAPEO
ZITACUARO
Mexico
PATZCUARO
URUAPAN
HUETAMO
Guerrero
JACONA
COTIJA
APATZINGAN
Michoacan de Ocampo
LAZARO CARDENAS
NAID Center - UCLA

Jalisco
Colima

Michoacan
- 1 - 10
- 11 - 50
- 51 - 100
- 101 - 250
- 251 - 422

N

0   50   100 Miles

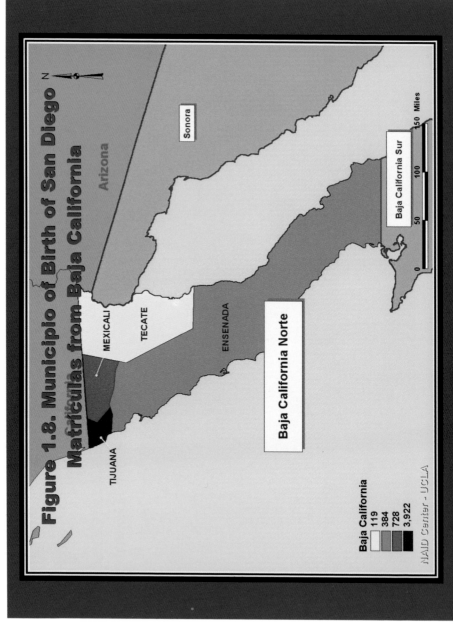

Figure 1.8. Municipio of Birth of San Diego Matrículas from Baja California

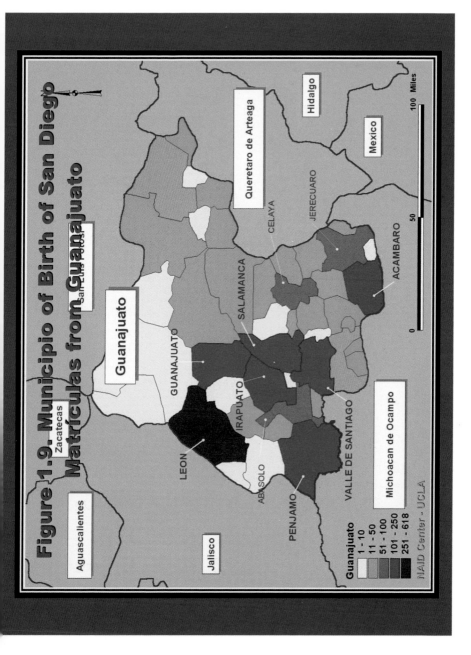

Figure 1.9. Municipio of Birth of San Diego Matrículas from Guanajuato

Aguascalientes

Zacatecas

Guanajuato

Jalisco

Querétaro de Arteaga

Hidalgo

Mexico

Michoacan de Ocampo

LEON
GUANAJUATO
IRAPUATO
ABASOLO
PENJAMO
VALLE DE SANTIAGO
SALAMANCA
CELAYA
JERECUARO
ACAMBARO

San Diego

Guanajuato
- 1 - 10
- 11 - 50
- 51 - 100
- 101 - 250
- 251 - 618

0   50   100 Miles

NAID Center - UCLA

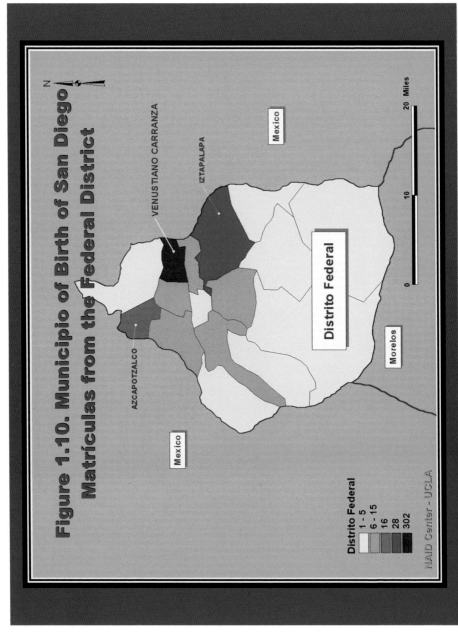

Figure 1.10. Municipio of Birth of San Diego Matrículas from the Federal District

VENUSTIANO CARRANZA

IZTAPALAPA

AZCAPOTZALCO

Mexico

Mexico

Morelos

Distrito Federal

Distrito Federal
1 - 5
6 - 15
16
28
302

NAID Center - UCLA

N

0   10   20 Miles

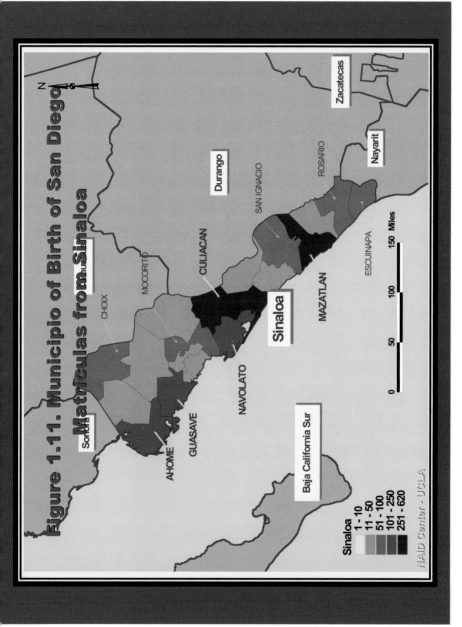

Figure 1.11. Municipio of Birth of San Diego Matriculas from Sinaloa

Sinaloa
1 - 10
11 - 50
51 - 100
101 - 250
251 - 620

Sonora
CHOIX
MOCORITO
AHOME
GUASAVE
CULIACAN
NAVOLATO
SAN IGNACIO
Durango
Sinaloa
MAZATLAN
ROSARIO
ESCUINAPA
Nayarit
Zacatecas
Baja California Sur

N

0   50   100   150 Miles

NAID Center - UCLA

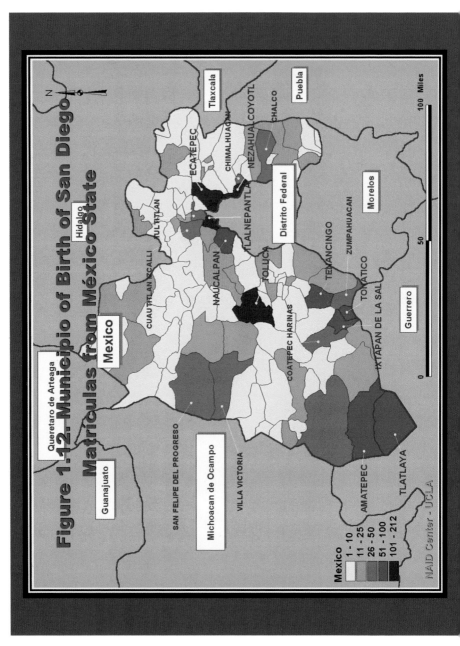

Figure 1.12. Municipio of Birth of San Diego Matriculas from México State

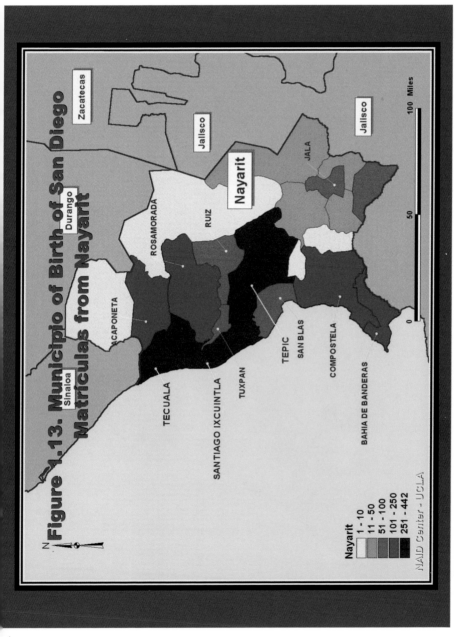

Figure 1.13. Municipio of Birth of San Diego Matrículas from Nayarit

NAID Center - UCLA

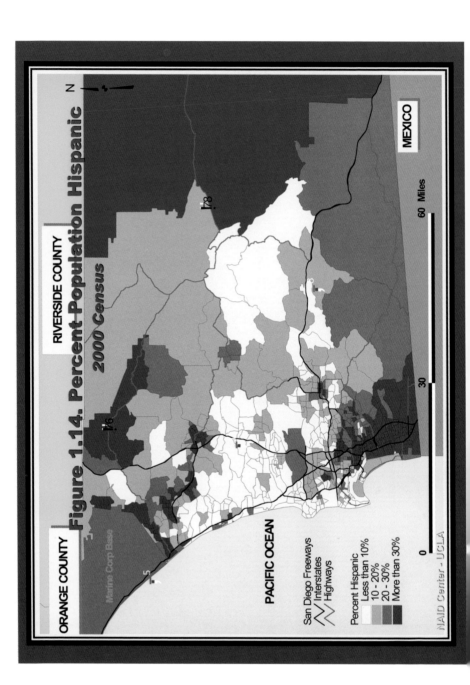

Figure 1.14. Percent Population Hispanic
2000 Census

ORANGE COUNTY

RIVERSIDE COUNTY

N

Marine Corp Base

I-5

I-76

I-84

PACIFIC OCEAN

MEXICO

San Diego Freeways
Interstates
Highways

Percent Hispanic
Less than 10%
10 - 20%
20 - 30%
More than 30%

0   30   60 Miles

NAID Center - UCLA

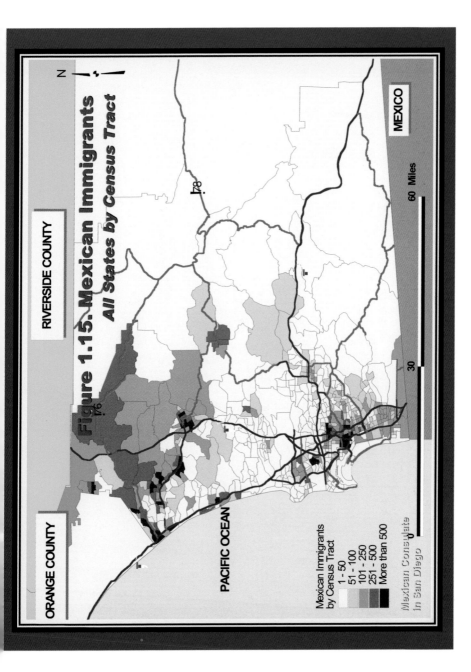

Figure 1.15. Mexican Immigrants
All States by Census Tract

ORANGE COUNTY

RIVERSIDE COUNTY

N

I-76

I-78

PACIFIC OCEAN

MEXICO

60 Miles

30

Mexican Immigrants
by Census Tract

1 - 50
51 - 100
101 - 250
251 - 500
More than 500

Mexican Consulate
in San Diego

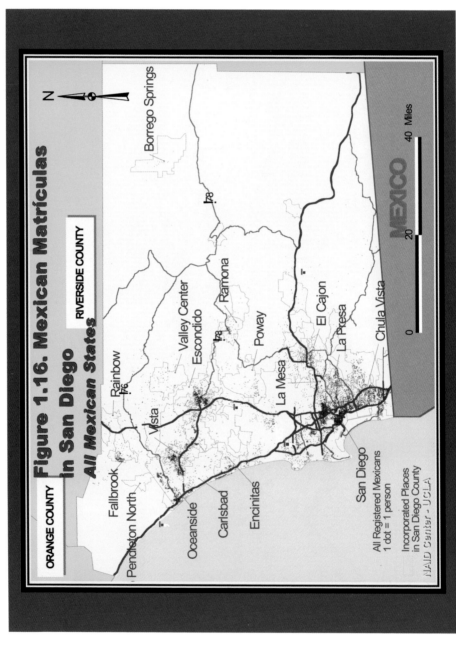

Figure 1.16. Mexican Matrículas in San Diego

All Mexican States

ORANGE COUNTY

RIVERSIDE COUNTY

N

Borrego Springs

Rainbow

Fallbrook

Pendleton North

Vista

Oceanside

Carlsbad

Encinitas

Valley Center

Escondido

Ramona

Poway

La Mesa

El Cajon

La Presa

Chula Vista

San Diego

MEXICO

All Registered Mexicans
1 dot = 1 person

Incorporated Places
in San Diego County

NAID Center - UCLA

0   20   40   Miles

Figure 1.17. Mexican Matrículas: Oaxaca

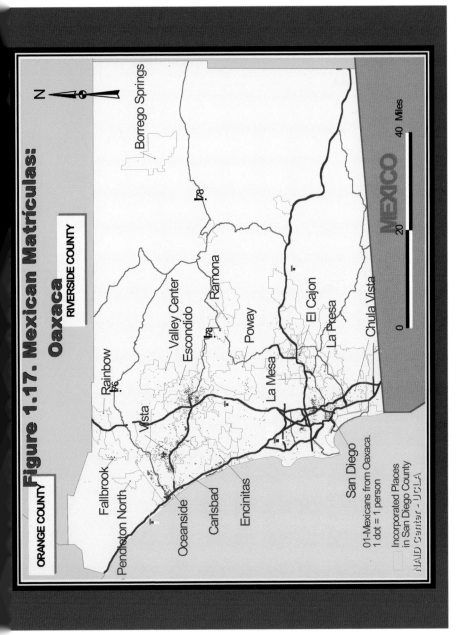

ORANGE COUNTY

RIVERSIDE COUNTY

MEXICO

N

Borrego Springs

Rainbow

Vista

Fallbrook

Pendleton North

Oceanside

Carlsbad

Encinitas

Valley Center

Escondido

Ramona

Poway

La Mesa

El Cajon

La Presa

Chula Vista

San Diego

01-Mexicans from Oaxaca.
1 dot = 1 person

Incorporated Places
in San Diego County

NAID Center - UCLA

0   20   40 Miles

Figure 1.18. Mexican Matrículas: Guerrero

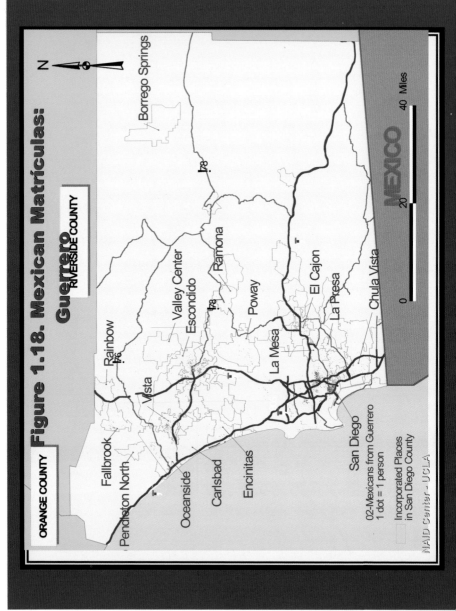

RIVERSIDE COUNTY
ORANGE COUNTY

N

Borrego Springs

Rainbow

Vista

Valley Center

Escondido

Ramona

Poway

La Mesa

El Cajon

La Presa

Chula Vista

Fallbrook

Pendleton North

Oceanside

Carlsbad

Encinitas

San Diego

02-Mexicans from Guerrero
1 dot = 1 person

Incorporated Places
in San Diego County

MEXICO

0   20   40   Miles

NAID Center - UCLA

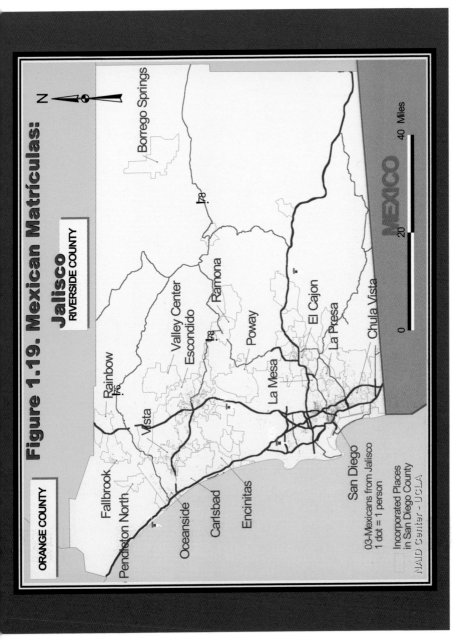

Figure 1.19. Mexican Matrículas:
Jalisco

ORANGE COUNTY

RIVERSIDE COUNTY

N

Borrego Springs

Fallbrook

Pendleton North

Rainbow
76

Vista

Oceanside

Carlsbad

Encinitas

Valley Center

Escondido

Ramona

78

Poway

La Mesa

San Diego

El Cajon

La Presa

Chula Vista

MEXICO

78

0   20   40 Miles

03-Mexicans from Jalisco
1 dot = 1 person

Incorporated Places
in San Diego County

NAID Center - UCLA

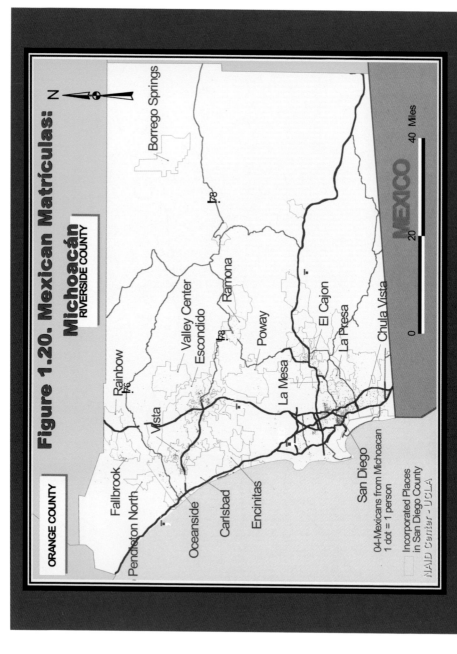

Figure 1.20. Mexican Matrículas:
Michoacán
RIVERSIDE COUNTY

ORANGE COUNTY

Fallbrook

Pendleton North

Rainbow
I-76

Vista

Oceanside

Carlsbad

Encinitas

Valley Center

Escondido
I-78

Ramona

Poway

La Mesa

El Cajon

La Presa

Chula Vista

San Diego

Borrego Springs

I-78

MEXICO

N

04-Mexicans from Michoacan
1 dot = 1 person

Incorporated Places
in San Diego County

0   20   40 Miles

NAID Center - UCLA

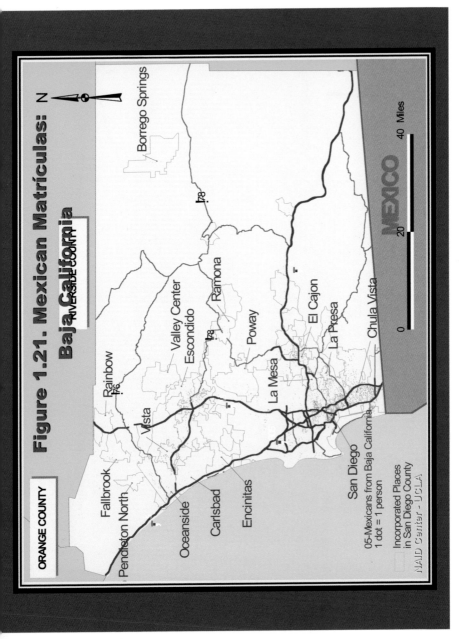

Figure 1.21. Mexican Matrículas: Baja California

ORANGE COUNTY

RIVERSIDE COUNTY

Pendleton North
Fallbrook
Rainbow
I-76
Vista
Oceanside
Carlsbad
Encinitas
Valley Center
Escondido
I-78
Ramona
Poway
La Mesa
San Diego
El Cajon
La Presa
Chula Vista
Borrego Springs
I-78

MEXICO

N

05-Mexicans from Baja California
1 dot = 1 person

Incorporated Places
in San Diego County

NAID Center - UCLA

0   20   40 Miles

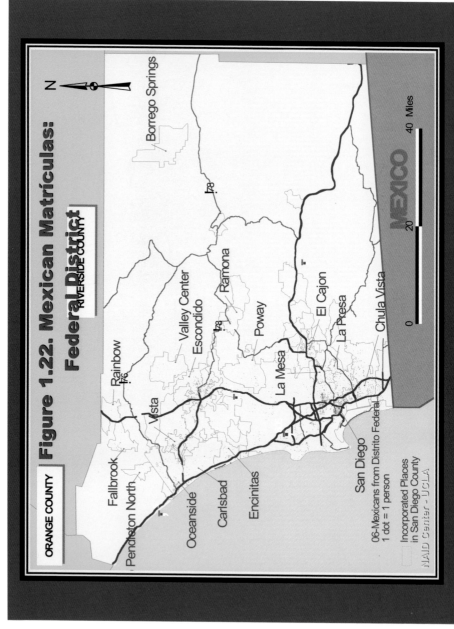

Figure 1.22. Mexican Matriculas: Federal District

ORANGE COUNTY

RIVERSIDE COUNTY

N

Borrego Springs

Pendleton North

Fallbrook

Rainbow

Vista

Valley Center

Escondido

Ramona

Oceanside

Carlsbad

Poway

Encinitas

La Mesa

El Cajon

La Presa

San Diego

Chula Vista

MEXICO

Incorporated Places
in San Diego County

06-Mexicans from Distrito Federal
1 dot = 1 person

NAID Center - UCLA

0   20   40   Miles

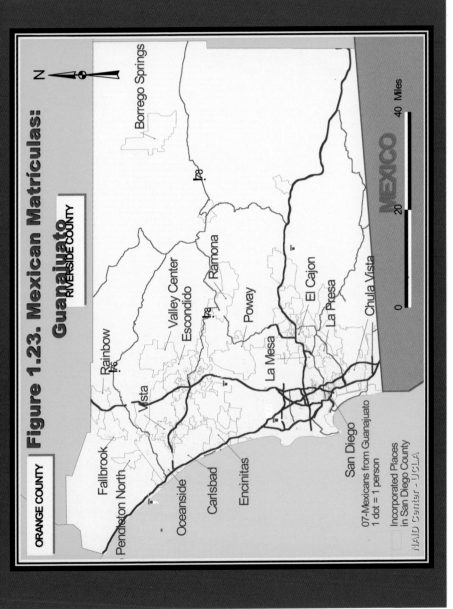

ORANGE COUNTY

Figure 1.23. Mexican Matrículas: Guanajuato

RIVERSIDE COUNTY

N

Borrego Springs

I-78

Rainbow
I-76

Fallbrook

Pendleton North

Vista

Valley Center

Escondido

I-78

Ramona

Oceanside

Poway

Carlsbad

La Mesa

El Cajon

La Presa

Encinitas

Chula Vista

San Diego

MEXICO

☐ Incorporated Places
   in San Diego County

07-Mexicans from Guanajuato
1 dot = 1 person

NAID Center - UCLA

0   20   40 Miles

Figure 1.24. Mexican Matrículas:
Sinaloa
RIVERSIDE COUNTY

ORANGE COUNTY

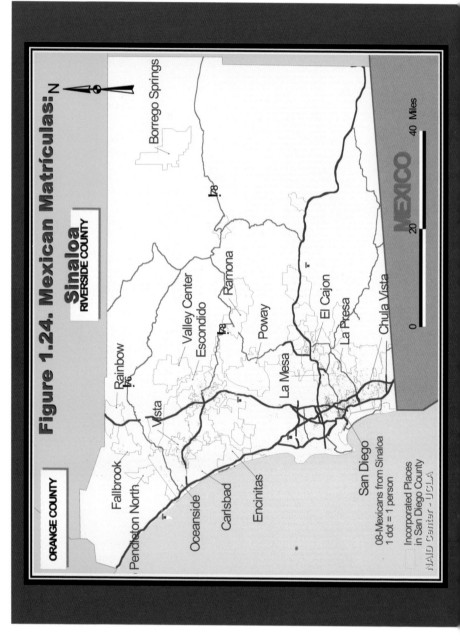

N

Borrego Springs

Rainbow

Vista

Fallbrook

Pendleton North

Oceanside

Carlsbad

Encinitas

Valley Center

Escondido

Ramona

Poway

La Mesa

El Cajon

La Presa

San Diego

Chula Vista

MEXICO

08-Mexicans from Sinaloa
1 dot = 1 person

Incorporated Places
in San Diego County

NAID Center - UCLA

0   20   40 Miles

Figure 1.25. Mexican Matrículas: México State

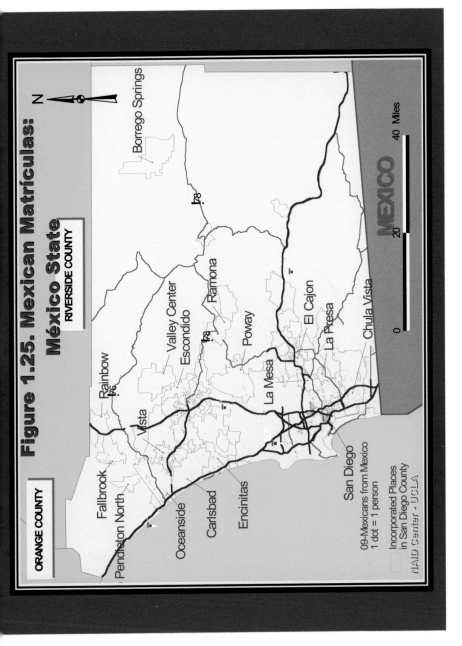

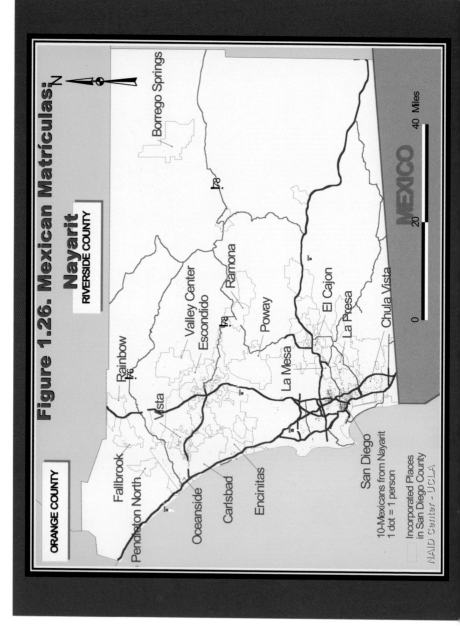

Figure 1.26. Mexican Matrículas: Nayarit

RIVERSIDE COUNTY

ORANGE COUNTY

Borrego Springs

I-78

Rainbow

Valley Center

Escondido

Ramona

I-78

Vista

Poway

Fallbrook

Pendleton North

La Mesa

El Cajon

Oceanside

La Presa

Carlsbad

Encinitas

Chula Vista

San Diego

MEXICO

10-Mexicans from Nayarit
1 dot = 1 person

Incorporated Places
in San Diego County

NAID Center - UCLA

N

0   20   40 Miles

Figure 3.1.
San Diego County Percent Hispanic (Census Tract Level)

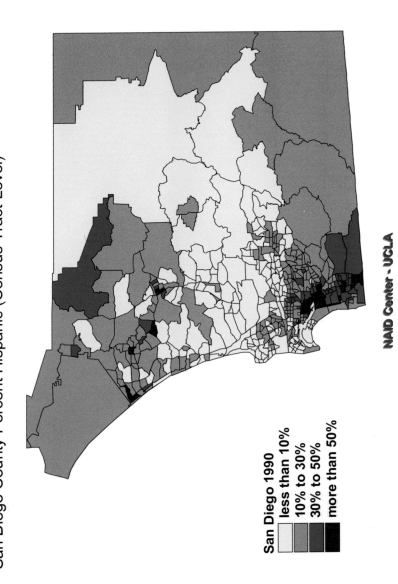

San Diego 1990
less than 10%
10% to 30%
30% to 50%
more than 50%

NAID Center - UCLA

Figure 3.2.
San Diego County Percent Hispanic (Census Tract Level)

San Diego 2000
less than 10%
10% to 30%
30% to 50%
more than 50%

NAID Center - UCLA

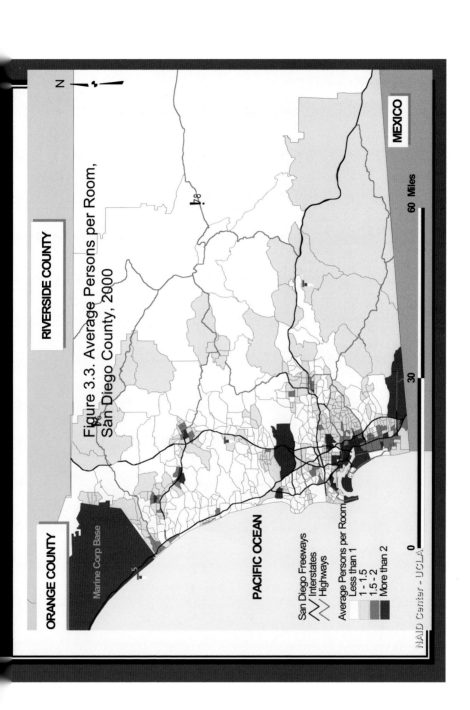

Figure 3.3. Average Persons per Room, San Diego County, 2000

ORANGE COUNTY

RIVERSIDE COUNTY

MEXICO

Marine Corp Base

PACIFIC OCEAN

San Diego Freeways
Interstates
Highways

Average Persons per Room
Less than 1
1 - 1.5
1.5 - 2
More than 2

0   30   60 Miles

N

NAID Center - UCLA

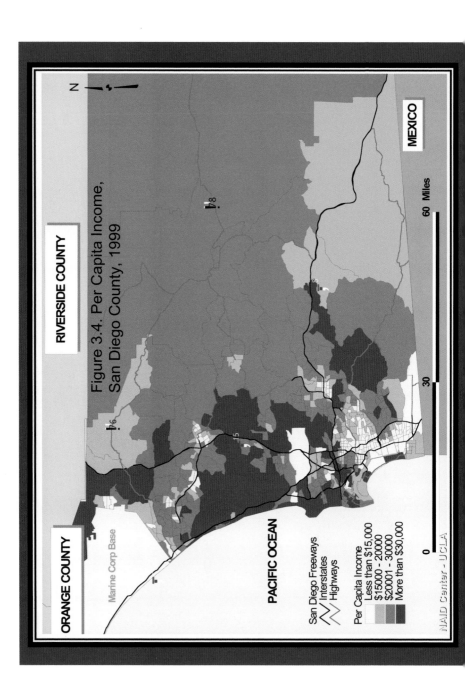

ORANGE COUNTY

RIVERSIDE COUNTY

Figure 3.4. Per Capita Income,
San Diego County, 1999

Marine Corp Base

PACIFIC OCEAN

MEXICO

San Diego Freeways
Interstates
Highways

Per Capita Income
Less than $15,000
$15000 - 20000
$20001 - 30000
More than $30,000

N

0   30   60 Miles

NAID Center - UCLA

Second, and in line with the first observation, many of the birthplaces of the migrants are urban areas: Oaxaca City, Acapulco, Guadalajara, Morelia, Tijuana, León, Mexico City, Toluca, Mazatlán, Tepic. There are many rural areas as well, but the cities tend to be the biggest sources of migrants in the different states (see table 1.6). Cornelius (1992) noted this growing urbanization of U.S.-bound migration, and the data show it clearly here.

Finally, the share of households receiving remittances in these municipios varies from one percent to 23 percent, and measures of migration intensity vary from very low to very high. Smaller muncipios tend to have greater dependency on remittances, but this is not strictly true.

Table 1.7 re-ranks the sending municipios in two states, Jalisco and Guerrero, by intensity of migration, as represented by the San Diego matrículas as a share of a municipio's population. In Jalisco, Guadalajara falls from first to nineteenth and Tepatitlán from second to twentyfifth. In Guerrero, Acapulco falls from first to tenth. Mascota in Jalisco and Arcelia in Guerrero remain high on both lists. These municipios have a high intensity of migration to San Diego.

Turning to some characteristics of the people from the sending regions, table 1.8 shows the gender breakdown and average age of migrants at the time they acquired a matrícula. Overall, of the 63,000 matrículas, 56 percent were requested by males and 44 percent by females. The states with the highest proportion male are Oaxaca (61 percent) and Guanajuato (60 percent). In contrast, Baja California matrículas are only 47 percent male. The migration life-cycle begins with single male migrants and then moves on to women and families as migration evolves and the network finds stable employment in the United States. The appearance of women and children usually denotes some form of settlement. The high proportion of women in the Baja California group is indicative of this state's proximity to San Diego and the consequent ability of people to shift their residence across the border without having to abandon their families and friends. There may also be a significant number of women born in Tijuana who marry migrants from elsewhere in Mexico and end up living in San Diego.

At the municipio level, there are a number of individual muncipios among the top ten states that have high proportions of male migrants: Juxtlahuaca (65 percent) and Huahuapan de León (64 percent) in Oaxaca,

Table 1.6. Migration Intensity, Remittances, and Marginality: Selected Municipios with High San Diego–Bound Migration, 2000

State and Municipality	Municipio's Share of State's San Diego Matrículas (%)	Marginality Index[a]	Total Number of Households	Percent of Households Receiving Remittances	Index of Migration Intensity	Degree of Migration Intensity
Oaxaca	19.8	**1**	**762,517**	**4.10**	**−0.26**	**Medium**
Zimatlán de Álvarez	19.8	3	3,481	4.22	−0.15	Low
Silacayoapam	16.6	2	1,492	12.20	0.38	Medium
Santiago Juxtlahuaca	8.4	1	5,270	4.52	−0.41	Low
Huajuapan de León	6.6	5	11,878	9.77	0.70	Medium
Oaxaca de Juárez	6.6	7	63,942	3.26	−0.43	Low
Guerrero		**1**	**677,731**	**7.90**	**0.42**	**High**
Acapulco	30.5	7	175,202	5.45	−0.28	Low
Arcelia	9.8	5	6,746	21.32	1.02	High
Coyuca de Benítez	8.5	3	15,546	7.06	0.00	Medium
Jalisco		**4**	**1,457,326**	**7.70**	**0.89**	**High**
Guadalajara	41.2	7	390,643	4.58	−0.24	Low
Tepatitlán de Morelos	2.4	5	25,200	7.67	0.85	High
Mascota	2.2	6	3,136	18.65	0.89	High
Michoacán		**3**	**893,671**	**11.40**	**2.06**	**Very high**
Morelia	12.4	7	147,857	5.85	−0.04	Low
Cotija	10.9	4	4,880	23.05	2.30	Very high
Uruapan	7.5	7	60,145	7.04	0.18	Medium
Baja California		**6**	**613,602**	**4.00**	**−0.001**	**Medium**
Tijuana	83.3	7	295,773	3.56	−0.17	Low

Guanajuato		3	990,602	9.20	1.37	**Very high**
León	30.2	7	235,598	4.07	-0.29	Low
San Francisco del Rincón	13.8	5	19,632	10.35	0.45	Medium
Irapuato	10.7	7	96,165	6.63	0.05	Medium
Valle de Santiago	6.7	5	27,509	12.74	0.56	Medium
Acambaro	5.7	5	26,367	20.98	2.19	Very high
Federal District		7	2,203,741	1.70	-0.91	**Very low**
Venustiano Carranza	77.2	7	120,824	1.37	-0.69	Very low
Iztapalapa	7.2	7	427,592	1.81	-0.62	Very low
Azcapotzalco	4.1	7	114,182	1.28	-0.68	Very low
Sinaloa		4	586,245	4.60	-0.27	**Medium**
Culiacán	35.9	7	169,658	5.79	-0.24541	Low
Mazatlán	21.2	7	94,680	2.46	-0.57934	Low
Novolato	9.4	6	32,832	3.43	-0.49427	Low
México State		6	2,978,023	2.10	-0.75	**Low**
Nezahualcoyotl	16.2	7	292,281	2.41	-0.46297	Low
Ecatepec	8.7	7	377,877	2.19	-0.54995	Low
Toluca	8.2	7	149,398	1.42	-0.68246	Very low
Tlalnepantla	6.9	7	177,711	1.68	-0.61715	Very low
Nayarit		4	222,714	9.60	1.27	**Very high**
Tepic	26.1	7	74,227	6.39	0.04	Medium
Santiago Ixcuintla	16.4	6	24,838	8.87	0.32	Medium
Tecuala	15.4	6	10,190	12.60	0.40	Medium

Sources: CONAPO n.d.; INEGI 2000.

[a] The marginality index is graded from 1 to 7, with 1 being the most marginal and 7 the least. See chapter appendix A.

Table 1.7. Leading Municipios of Jalisco and Guerrero for San Diego Matrículas, by Rate of Migration

JALISCO MUNICIPIOS	Total Population (2000 Census)	San Diego Matrículas	Matrículas as % of Total Population	GUERRERO MUNICIPIOS	Total Population (2000 Census)	San Diego Matrículas	Matrículas as % of Total Population
Mascota	13,873	101	**0.728**	**Arcelia**	32,818	381	**1.161**
San Marcos	3,497	15	0.429	Tlalchapa	12,942	84	0.649
Ejutla	2,155	8	0.371	**Coyuca de Benítez**	69,059	332	**0.481**
Villa Guerrero	5,938	12	0.202	Benito Juárez	15,448	38	0.246
Tolimán	9,277	17	0.183	Ajuchitlán del Progreso	41,266	85	0.206
Chimaltitán	3,926	7	0.178	Coahuayutla de JM Izazaga	15,372	28	0.182
Guachinango	4,769	8	0.168	Técpan de Galeana	60,313	107	0.177
Valle de Guadalupe	5,958	9	0.151	Petatlán	46,328	79	0.171
Tecolotlán	16,074	24	0.149	Tlapehuala	22,677	38	0.168
San Juanito de Escobedo	8,610	12	0.139	**Acapulco de Juárez**	722,499	1,133	**0.157**
Ayutla	13,135	18	0.137	San Miguel Totolapan	28,986	39	0.135

Municipality	Population	Migrants	Rate		Municipality	Population	Migrants	Rate
Pihuamo	14,115	19	0.135		Tlalixtaquilla de Maldonado	6,699	8	0.119
Quitupan	11,528	15	0.130		Teloloapan	53,950	59	0.109
San Diego de Alejandría	6,384	8	0.125		Cuetzala del Progreso	9,869	10	0.101
La Huerta	22,827	28	0.123		San Marcos	48,782	49	0.100
Valle de Juárez	5,758	7	0.122		Atoyac de Álvarez	61,736	56	0.091
Gómez Farías	12,705	15	0.118		Cocula	15,666	14	0.089
El Limón	6,026	7	0.116		Atenango del Río	8,504	7	0.082
Guadalajara	**1,646,319**	**1,894**	**0.115**		Buenavista de Cuéllar	12,619	10	0.079
Juchitlán	5,831	6	0.103		Cuajinicuilapa	25,641	20	0.078
Mixtlán	3,938	4	0.102		Coyuca de Catalán	46,172	32	0.069
Villa Corona	15,936	16	0.100		Azoyú	32,400	22	0.068
Tenamaxtlán	7,179	7	0.098		Copala	13,060	8	0.061
Atoyac	8,697	8	0.092		Taxco de Alarcón	100,245	43	0.043
Tepatitlán de Morelos	**119,197**	**109**	**0.091**		Pilcaya	10,851	4	0.037
All others	4,348,350	872	0.020		All others	1,565,747	233	0.015
State total	**6,322,002**	**6,377**	**0.101**		**State total**	**3,079,649**	**6,837**	**0.222**

Sources: Consulate of Mexico in San Diego; INEGI.

Table 1.8. Demographics of Leading Sending States and Municipios, San Diego Matrículas, 1995–2002

State	Municipio	Municipio's Share of State's Matrículas (%)	Percent Male	Percent Female	Mean Age
Oaxaca	**all municipios**		**60.9**	**39.1**	**34**
	Zimatlán de Álvarez	19.8	56.2	43.8	34
	Silacayoapam	16.6	55.9	44.1	34
	Santiago Juxtlahuaca	8.4	64.6	35.4	31
	Huajuapan de León	6.6	64.2	35.8	35
	Oaxaca de Juárez	6.6	54.2	45.8	32
Guerrero	**All municipios**		**55.3**	**44.7**	**34**
	Acapulco	30.5	53.0	47.0	31
	Arcelia	9.8	52.5	47.5	33
	Coyuca de Benítez	8.5	58.7	41.3	33
Jalisco	**All municipios**		**53.7**	**46.3**	**41**
	Guadalajara	41.2	49.4	50.6	37
	Tepatitlán de Morelos	2.4	58.7	41.3	40
	Mascota	2.2	54.5	45.5	49
Michoacán	**All municipios**		**57.1**	**42.9**	**38**
	Morelia	12.4	56.4	43.6	35
	Cotija	10.9	60.2	39.8	40
	Uruapan	7.5	53.8	46.2	36
Baja California	**All municipios**		**46.6**	**53.4**	**34**
	Tijuana	83.3	47.2	52.8	34

Guanajuato	**All municipios**		**60.1**	**39.9**	**37**
	León	30.2	57.9	42.1	34
	San Francisco del Rincón	13.8	55.7	44.3	37
	Irapuato	10.7	63.0	37.0	36
	Valle de Santiago	6.7	72.5	27.5	43
	Acambaro	5.7	56.9	43.1	37
Federal District	**All delegaciones**		**54.9**	**45.1**	**35**
	Venustiano Carranza	77.2	55.5	44.5	45
	Iztapalapa	7.2	60.7	39.3	28
	Azcapotzalco	4.1	56.3	43.8	33
Sinaloa	**All municipios**		**50.1**	**49.9**	**39**
	Culiacán	35.9	52.9	47.1	36
	Mazatlán	21.2	45.2	54.8	40
	Navolato	9.4	54.0	46.0	44
México State	**All municipios**		**56.9**	**43.1**	**34**
	Nezahualcoyotl	16.2	57.1	42.9	27
	Ecatepec	8.7	63.2	36.8	28
	Toluca	8.2	52.3	47.7	33
	Tlalnepantla de Baz	6.9	50.5	49.5	29
Nayarit	**All municipios**		**52.3**	**47.7**	**37**
	Tepic	26.1	51.8	48.2	34
	Santiago Ixcuintla	16.4	46.9	53.1	37
	Tecuala	15.4	55.4	44.6	37
All matrículas			**55.9**	**44.1**	**36**

Source: Mexican Consulate in San Diego.

Cotija (60 percent) in Michoacán, Irapuato (63 percent) and Valle de Santiago (73 percent) in Guanajuato, Iztapalapa (61 percent) in the Federal District, and Ecatepec (63 percent) in México State. For the Oaxacan locations and the areas around Mexico City, the argument that they are relatively early in the migration life-cycle makes sense, but how to explain Valle de Santiago, where people have been migrating for a very long time?

Turning to the age data, we see that the mean age of all the matrículas is 36 years. In general, migrants from the traditional sending states have an average age of late 30s or early 40s, those from Oaxaca and Guerrero are in their early 30s, and the youngest group—late 20s on average—is coming from the municipios in México State around Mexico City. Once again, since the people who get matrículas are likely to be somewhat established in San Diego, these age differences are more likely a measure of a network's time in San Diego. Young people continue to migrate from all of the states, but the networks with the least time in San Diego have the youngest average age.

Table 1.9 breaks the age data into cohorts for all of the states. For each age cohort, the first column shows the number of San Diego matrículas in that cohort for each state, the second column shows the row percentage (that is, the share of a state's San Diego matrículas accounted for by that age cohort), and the third column shows the column percentage (the percent of the age cohort accounted for by each state).

Looking first at the 15–24 age cohort—the group coming of working age in Mexico—Oaxaca and Guerrero account for the largest shares. However, where Oaxaca accounted for 11.7 percent of all matrículas and Guerrero 10.8 percent, here their shares are 15 percent and 12.1 percent, respectively. In contrast, Jalisco accounts for 10.1 percent of all matrículas but only 4.8 percent of this age cohort. Michoacán accounts for 9.4 percent overall and 8.6 percent here. Added together, the Federal District and México State account for about 13.5 percent of this age cohort. Looking at the row percentages, this age cohort accounts for 27.5 percent of the Oaxacan matrículas, 24.1 percent of the Guerrero matrículas, 19.6 percent of the Michoacán matrículas, and only 14 percent of the Jalisco matrículas. Oaxacans are twice as likely as Jaliscienses to fall into this age group; southeastern and central Mexico are supplanting the traditional western states among the young migrants.

Looking at the next older age group, 25–39, Guerrero accounts for the largest number (12.3 percent), followed by Oaxaca (11.9 percent), Michoacán (8.9 percent), and Jalisco (8.6 percent). Overall, this age cohort represents about half of all matrículas. It accounts for 55.7 percent of the Guerrerenses, 50 percent of the Oaxacans, 46.5 percent of the Michoacanos, and 42 percent of the Jaliscienses.

Finally, the numbers turn around when we examine the 40–59 age cohort. Jalisco accounts for 14 percent of these matrículas, followed by Michoacán (10.8 percent), Oaxaca (9.4 percent), and Guerrero and Baja California (8.1 percent each). This age group accounts for 32.3 percent of the Jaliscienses, 26.5 percent of the Michoacanos, 18.7 percent of the Oaxacans, 17.4 percent of the Guerrerenses, and 22.7 of Baja California matrículas. For the group 60 years of age and over, Jalisco accounts for about 22 percent and Michoacán, 12 percent. There is an aging population of immigrants from the traditional western Mexican states.

Thus the age data show clearly that Jaliscienses are the oldest group of migrants, followed by Michoacanos. Migration of young people continues from all states, but young age groups are increasingly dominated by migrants from southern Mexico and the region around Mexico City.

PLACES OF RESIDENCE IN SAN DIEGO

Mexican immigrants in San Diego are spread throughout the county, according to the matrícula data. Table 1.10 shows their distribution as reported on the matrículas. Table 1.11 lists the top ten places of residence. The City of San Diego—which includes a variety of places, including La Jolla and San Ysidro—accounted for over 40 percent of the matrículas, followed by several North County cities (Escondido, Oceanside, and Vista).

In table 1.11 the share of a city's matrículas is compared to its share of the 2000 census count of the Hispanic population in the county. The North County cities (Escondido, Oceanside, Vista, San Marcos, Fallbrook, Encinitas) are all overrepresented in the matrículas by this measure, whereas South County locations (Chula Vista, National City, San Ysidro) are all underrepresented. The mid-county places (City of

Table 1.9. San Diego Matrículas by Age Cohort

State	Age <15			Age 15–24			Age 25–39		
	N	Share of Matrículas from State (%)	Share of <15 (%)	N	Share of Matrículas from State (%)	Share of 15–24 (%)	N	Share of Matrículas from State (%)	Share of 25–39 (%)
Aguascalientes	5	2	1	40	14	0	119	43	0
Baja California	218	4	28	1,144	22	8	2,548	49	8
Baja Calif. Sur	1	1	0	23	24	0	28	29	0
Campeche	0	0	0	10	37	0	15	56	0
Chiapas	3	1	0	47	17	0	111	41	0
Chihuahua	5	1	1	115	20	1	297	50	1
Coahuila	3	1	0	114	26	1	249	56	1
Colima	2	0	0	51	10	0	192	37	1
Federal District	59	1	7	1,137	24	8	2,328	50	8
Durango	7	1	1	152	15	1	423	41	1
Guanajuato	36	1	5	652	21	5	1,504	47	5
Guerrero	53	1	7	1,641	24	12	3,798	56	12
Hidalgo	12	1	2	294	25	2	659	56	2
Jalisco	54	1	7	890	14	7	2,675	42	9
México State	31	1	4	687	27	5	1,291	51	4

Michoacán	62	1	8	1,166	20	9	2,770	47	9
Morelos	32	2	4	571	31	4	980	53	3
Nayarit	18	1	2	437	18	3	1,276	51	4
Nuevo León	3	1	0	56	25	0	101	45	0
Oaxaca	102	1	13	2,033	28	15	3,695	50	12
Puebla	11	1	1	464	27	3	831	49	3
Querétaro	33	2	4	475	25	4	1,007	53	3
Quintana Roo	0	0	0	4	27	0	10	67	0
San Luis Potosí	6	1	1	238	19	2	670	52	2
Sinaloa	14	1	2	427	16	3	1,285	48	4
Sonora	10	1	1	125	11	1	487	44	2
Tabasco	0	0	0	18	28	0	32	49	0
Tamaulipas	2	1	0	27	17	0	78	48	0
Tlaxcala	1	0	0	115	30	1	190	50	1
Veracruz	6	1	1	236	20	2	682	57	2
Yucatán	1	1	0	7	8	0	28	32	0
Zacatecas	2	0	0	197	14	1	600	43	2
Total all states	**792**	**1**	**100**	**13,593**	**22**	**100**	**30,959**	**49**	**100**

Table 1.9 continued (San Diego Matrículas by Age Cohort)

State	Age 40nd59			Age 60 and over			State Total
	N	Share of Matrículas from State (%)	Share of 40–59 (%)	N	Share of Matrículas from State (%)	Share of 60 and over (%)	
Aguascalientes	94	34	1	20	7	1	278
Baja California	1,183	23	8	123	2	4	5,216
Baja Calif. Sur	26	27	0	18	19	1	96
Campeche	2	7	0	0	0	0	27
Chiapas	83	31	1	27	10	1	271
Chihuahua	134	23	1	39	7	1	590
Coahuila	74	17	1	6	1	0	446
Colima	203	39	1	74	14	2	522
Federal District	931	20	6	204	4	6	4,659
Durango	349	34	2	101	10	3	1,032
Guanajuato	821	26	6	160	5	5	3,173
Guerrero	1,190	17	8	141	2	4	6,823
Hidalgo	189	16	1	33	3	1	1,187
Jalisco	2,054	32	14	693	11	22	6,366
México State	474	19	3	74	3	2	2,557
Michoacán	1,577	27	11	382	6	12	5,957

Morelos	258	14	2	11	1	0	1,852
Nayarit	626	25	4	131	5	4	2,488
Nuevo León	43	19	0	22	10	1	225
Oaxaca	1,382	19	9	172	2	5	7,384
Puebla	354	21	2	52	3	2	1,712
Querétaro	346	18	2	46	2	2	1,907
Quintana Roo	1	7	0	0	0	0	15
San Luis Potosí	316	25	2	51	4	2	1,281
Sinaloa	754	28	5	228	8	7	2,708
Sonora	352	32	2	122	11	4	1,096
Tabasco	14	22	0	1	2	0	65
Tamaulipas	41	25	0	15	9	1	163
Tlaxcala	65	17	0	10	3	0	381
Veracruz	219	18	2	45	4	1	1,188
Yucatán	31	35	0	22	25	1	89
Zacatecas	447	32	3	148	11	5	1,394
Total all states	**14,633**	**23**	**100**	**3,171**	**5**	**100**	**63,148**

Source: Mexican Consulate in San Diego.

Table 1.10. San Diego Places of Residence and Numbers of Matrículas, 1995–2002

Locations within the City of San Diego and Number of Matrículas for Each	
City Heights	2
Clairemont	2
Clairemont Mesa	4
Encanto	3
La Jolla	206
Linda Vista	4
Mira Mesa	5
Mission Valley	1
Normal Heights	1
North Park	1
Ocean Beach	3
Otay Mesa	1
Pacific Beach	18
Rancho Bernardo	3
Rancho Penasquitos	1
San Diego	23,803
San Ysidro	1,204
Total City of San Diego	**25,262**

Locations within the County of San Diego and Number of Matrículas for Each

Location	Number	Location	Number	Location	Number
Alpine	72	Imperial Beach	322	Rainbow	5
Bonita	240	Jacumba	1	Ramona	648
Bonsall	173	Jamul	64	Ranchita	1
Borrego Springs	31	Julian	29	Rancho Santa Fe	68
Campo	3	La Mesa	253	San Luis Rey	64
Cardiff by the Sea	227	Lakeside	221	San Marcos	2,912
Carlsbad	976	Lemon Grove	267	Santa Ysabel	20
Chula Vista	3,424	Leucadia	63	Santee	107
Coronado	71	Mesa Grande	3	Solana Beach	400
Del Mar	47	National City	1,922	Spring Valley	704
Descanso	5	Oceanside	5,526	Sunnyside	1
Dulzura	12	Pala	61	Tecate	14
El Cajon	1,717	Palomar	4	Valley Center	438
Encinitas	1,060	Pauma Valley	167	Vista	4,973
Escondido	7,627	Pine Valley	4	Warner Springs	10
Fallbrook	1,465	Potrero	14	**Total San Diego City and**	
Guatay	9	Poway	488	**County**	**62,195**

Source: Mexican Consulate in San Diego.

Table 1.11. Top Ten Places in San Diego County Reported as Residences by Matrículas, 1995–2002

Place	Number of Matrículas	Share of All San Diego Matrículas	2000 Hispanic Population	Share of All Hispanics in San Diego County
San Diego City	25,262	40.6 %	310,752	41.4 %
(includes San Ysidro)	(1,204)	(1.9 %)	(23,998)	(3.2 %)
Escondido	7,627	12.3 %	51,693	6.9 %
Oceanside	5,526	8.9 %	48,691	6.5 %
Vista	4,973	8.0 %	34,990	4.7 %
Chula Vista	3,424	5.5 %	86,073	11.5 %
San Marcos	2,912	4.7 %	20,271	2.7 %
National City	1,922	3.1 %	32,053	4.3 %
El Cajon	1,717	2.8 %	21,313	2.8 %
Fallbrook	1,465	2.4 %	11,894	1.6 %
Encinitas	1,060	1.7 %	8,584	1.1 %
Total top ten	55,888	89.9 %	626,314	83.4 %

Sources: Mexican Consulate in San Diego; U.S. Department of Commerce, U.S. Bureau of the Census.

Table 1.12. City of Oceanside: Mexican Matrículas, 1995–2002, by Zip Code and State of Birth

State of Birth	Zipcode				State Total	State's Share
	92054	92056	92057			
Oaxaca	1,200	137	413		1750	33.0%
Michoacán	261	111	114		486	9.2%
Jalisco	277	78	76		431	8.1%
Guerrero	254	46	85		385	7.3%
Federal District	221	44	70		335	6.3%
México State	175	17	89		281	5.3%
Guanajuato	97	28	69		194	3.7%
Nayarit	84	29	38		151	2.8%
Baja California	86	18	33		137	2.6%
Sinaloa	52	17	33		102	1.9%
Subtotal top 10 sending states	**2,707**	**525**	**1,020**		**4,252**	**80.1%**
Puebla	116	20	49		185	3.5%
Hidalgo	93	24	12		129	2.4%
Veracruz	89	19	20		128	2.4%
Morelos	69	13	20		102	1.9%
Other states (with <100 matrículas)	296	91	126		513	9.7%
Total	**3,370**	**692**	**1,247**		**5,309**	**100.0%**
Zip code's share	63.5%	13.0%	23.5%			

Source: Mexican Consulate in San Diego.

San Diego and El Cajon) have similar shares in both measures. The immigrants who seek matrículas from the consulate are more likely to live in North County than South County, which is to say that there are likely more undocumented immigrants in North County. South County has a more long-term, settled Latino population, with many U.S. citizens and permanent residents. The City of San Diego seems to be big enough to harbor both groups.

This relationship can be seen visually in Figures 1.14 and 1.15. Figure 1.14 shows the 2000 census counts of Hispanics by census tract. The largest concentration is in South County. In contrast, figure 1.15 shows the San Diego matrículas by census tract, where the greatest concentrations are in North County cities and the City of San Diego.

We also mapped the actual street addresses of the matrículas with dots. Figure 1.16 shows these locations for all of the San Diego matrículas. The concentration of immigrants in the City of San Diego (Barrio Logan, East San Diego) is the most pronounced, with concentrations in the North County cities and in the South County between Interstate Highways 5 and 805.

Figures 1.17 through 1.26 show the same type of dot mappings for each of the ten leading sending states as represented in the San Diego matrículas.

- The Oaxacans are concentrated in North County and in the central city. They have the least dispersion of any of the groups; even though they have the most dots, it does not look that way because the dots lie right on top of one another.

- The Guerrerenses are heavily concentrated in the City of San Diego, with smaller groups in North County. Migrants from México State and Nayarit have similar patterns.

- In contrast, immigrants from Jalisco are much more spread out, covering virtually all of the areas seen in figure 1.16. The other traditional sending states—Michoacán and Guanajuato—have similar patterns as Jalisco's, only with fewer matrículas.

- Immigrants from Baja California are clustered in the City of San Diego and on south to the border. The groups of Baja California–born persons in North County could well be the children of migrants from other states who came to Baja California, such as the Mixtec from Oaxaca who came as farmworkers to San Quintín. The same pattern appears for Sinaloa.

- The group from the Federal District shows more dispersion, as with the traditional sending states. They exhibit one of the heaviest concentrations in the City of San Diego proper.

One potential future use of the matrícula data would be to look more closely at smaller jurisdictions and the sources of immigrants to them. Table 1.12 presents data on the breakdown of matrículas for people reporting a residence in the City of Oceanside. Oaxacans are the largest group by far, and two-thirds of the Oaxacans are in zip code 92054, as are two-thirds of all Mexican immigrants. One could then break down the Oaxacan group by municipio of origin at the Mexican end or by some smaller area in Oceanside: census tracts, public school boundaries, or even city blocks.[3] This analysis could lead to a much better understanding of the origins of immigrants in a variety of institutions, such as schools, clinics, or community services. It might lead to more sensible "sister-city" relationships or projects by service organizations (such as the Kiwanas) or churches in relevant sending villages in Mexico. It would allow binational health and education projects to function in the most efficient manner. The Mexican consulate added 24,000 matrículas in 2002 and even more in 2003. These data will soon cover a large share of the Mexican immigrants in San Diego, and their analysis could provide significant new knowledge for localities.

CONCLUSION

The San Diego matrícula data provide new information on Mexican immigrants in the region. They allow us to identify the precise origins of the population, which the U.S. census does not. They allow us to pinpoint the residential location of the immigrants in San Diego and tie this to the origins and characteristics of the immigrants. Since there is a vast literature arguing that such immigrants operate on the basis of

---

[3] We have not done this here, both for confidentiality reasons and because the data would require more extensive cleaning.

networks tied to their place of origin, these data open up the possibility of understanding the location of such networks in the United States. This has important implications for the delivery of social services, education, and health care to the population, for efforts at binational cooperation, and for services such as transportation and remittances that are related to migration from specific places.

The matrícula data indicate that many of the trends Cornelius noted in 1992 have in fact continued: there are more women; the origins of the migrants are increasingly urban; and the source of migrants has spread out, with the southeastern states and the Mexico City region having become major sources of migrants to San Diego. The data also confirm another piece of received wisdom on this migration—namely, that the migrants are generally not coming from the poorest parts of their states. These trends are generally reflective of overall migration trends in Mexico (CONAPO 2002).

The matrículas are overrepresented in the northern part of San Diego County and underrepresented in the southern part, suggesting that this document is more useful to the more undocumented population in the north. The various Mexican sending states have differing settlement patterns in San Diego, with, for example, Oaxacans concentrated in North County, Baja Californians in South County, and Guerrerenses in between, in the City of San Diego.

Reviewing these data, the role of networks in channeling migrants is clear. Though the migrants come from many places, most come from a relatively small number of easily identifiable cities or villages. Greater knowledge of these places could assist government officials, service providers, and the general population in San Diego to understand the origins and culture of the immigrants in their midst. Rather than viewing immigrants as anonymous "aliens," perhaps people's perceptions could be changed if they had more information about these groups. This is especially true of the indigenous migrants from Oaxaca, who often live and work in the most difficult conditions in San Diego, but who have a rich history and culture to offer the society.

References

Banco de México. 2004. "Ingresos por remesas familiars." Press release, February 3. Available at http://www.banxico.org.mx/fBoletines/Boletines/FSBoletines.html.

CONAPO (Consejo Nacional de Población). 2002. *Índices de intensidad migratoria México–Estados Unidos*. Mexico City: CONAPO.

———. n.d. "Índices de densidad migratoria." Spreadsheet. Mexico City: CONAPO.

Cornelius, Wayne A. 1992. "From Sojourners to Settlers: The Changing Profile of Mexican Immigration to the United States." In *U.S.-Mexico Relations: Labor Market Interdependence*, edited by Jorge A. Bustamante, Clark W. Reynolds, and Raúl A. Hinojosa Ojeda. Stanford, Calif.: Stanford University Press.

Dagodag, W. Tim. 1975. "Source Regions and Composition of Illegal Mexican Immigration to California," *International Migration Review* 9.

INEGI (Instituto Nacional de Estadística, Geografía e Informática. 2000. "Niveles de bienestar en México, Censo 2000." Available at http://www.inegi.gob.mx/prod_serv/contenidos/espanol/niveles/jly/nivbien/nacional.asp?c=126.

Jones, Richard C., ed. 1984. *Patterns of Undocumented Migration: Mexico and the United States*. New Jersey: Rowman & Allenheld.

Runsten, David, and Michael Kearney. 1994. *A Survey of Oaxacan Village Networks in California Agriculture*. Davis: California Institute for Rural Studies.

Runsten, David, and Carol Zabin. 1994. "A Regional Perspective on Mexican Migration to Rural California." Paper presented at the conference "The Changing Face of Rural America," Asilomar, California, June 12–14.

Zabin, Carol, Michael Kearney, Anna García, David Runsten, and Carole Nagengast. 1993. *Mixtec Migrants in California Agriculture: A New Cycle of Poverty*. Davis: California Institute for Rural Studies, May.

Appendix A. Marginality Index

Variables	Grade Indicator							
	Grade 1	Grade 2	Grade 3	Grade 4	Grade 5	Grade 6	Grade 7	National
% population < 15 years old	**44.5**	40.8	38.4	36.6	36.4	34.6	31.2	34
% population born in another state	**2.1**	4.4	6.2	7.8	8.8	13.1	26.3	18.5
% population >= 5 years that in 1995 lived in another state	1	1.9	2.2	3.1	3	4	6	4.6
Literacy rate among population 6 to 14 years old	68.9	80.6	82.5	86.3	85.6	88.5	91.2	87.3
Literacy rate among population >= 15 years old	61	76.2	81.5	86.3	86.9	90.8	95.4	90.5
% population attending school, 6 to 11 years old	**85.7**	92.4	92.4	94.5	93.3	94.9	95.7	94.2
% population attending school, 12 to 14 years old	**74.2**	80.4	81.3	75.3	80.9	84.7	89.9	85.3

% population attending school, 15 to 19 years old	**28.1**	32.8	37.5	28.3	39.7	41.1	54.2	46.5
Average years of education	**3.5**	4.6	5.4	5.3	6.3	6.7	8.7	7.5
Average live births of women > 12 years old	**3.2**	3.3	3	3.2	2.8	2.8	2.2	2.5
Average live births of women 12 to 19 years old	**0.2**	0.1	0.1	0.1	0.1	0.1	0.1	0.1
% population economically active	**44.6**	40.7	43.6	37.8	46.2	46.4	52.9	49.3
% population working in the public sector	**1**	2	3.5	3.5	5.1	5.1	6.8	5.8
% population working in retail	**3.2**	5.6	8.3	9.5	12.4	10.2	14.3	12.5
% population economically active that works < 24 hrs/week	**14**	15.6	13.2	17.3	12.6	12.3	9.8	11.2
% households with dirt floors only (no other ground covering)	**69.9**	44.4	30.4	15.3	16.1	11.5	4.5	13.2

Variables	Grade 1	Grade 2	Grade 3	Grade 4	Grade 5	Grade 6	Grade 7	National
Number of rooms per household	**2.4**	2.8	2.9	3.5	3.4	3.5	3.9	3.6
% households with sewerage connections	**20.9**	30.9	50.4	63.8	72.7	75.2	91.5	78.1
% households with water lines	**59.8**	62.3	73.9	88.4	85.9	89.7	95.2	88.8
% households with electricity	**69.4**	82.6	89.2	94.3	94.5	95.8	98.4	95
% rural population	**92.5**	92.8	66.6	82.5	41.2	54.6	7.2	31.2
% urban population	**2**	1.4	8.6	4.2	53.3	3.8	90.2	60.7
% population with postprimary education	**15.3**	23.3	32	28.1	40.6	44.2	63.4	51.8
% population working in the primary sector	**71.7**	57.1	43.6	40.7	24	25.9	3.6	15.9
% population working in the tertiary sector	**14.9**	23.2	34.2	32.5	45.8	41.5	63	53.4
% population working <33 hrs/week	**23.5**	25.2	22.3	27.4	20.6	20	16.1	18.3
% households with only one room	**17.9**	11.6	15.2	5.6	11	9.1	8.1	9.5

% households using wood/coal for cooking	**88.6**	71.3	50.6	25.4	21.6	15.4	2.7	17.2
% population without social security	**90.6**	88.5	80.9	81.5	69.3	62	44.7	58
% population that works in a familiy business without pay	**14.4**	14.7	8.7	10.4	5.1	4.4	1.7	4.1
% households without bathroom	**37**	32.6	26.5	23.8	17.3	14.3	7.1	13.5
% households without refrigerator	**87.2**	72.9	61.4	39.3	40.8	34.6	16.7	30.6
% households without television	**69.4**	44.8	30.8	15	15.4	12.3	4.7	13.3

Source: INEGI 2000.

2

Farmworker Health in Vista, California

BONNIE BADE

At the end of a dirt road flanked by ornamental flower nurseries in Vista stands a forest of eucalyptus trees. By day this shady area is vacant; only the port-a-potty positioned behind a tree trunk betrays the fact that dozens of local farmworkers occupy a clearing in the trees. In the evening, workers arrive by carloads and set up camp for the night. Men reach into paper bags and pull out their dinners of burritos and tacos bought at a local Mexican drive-thru. Someone lights a fire, keeping it small so that it cannot be seen from the road. Some of the workers sleep in their cars; others unroll blankets and lie down on the eucalyptus leaves. All are careful not to make too much noise because the occupants of the million-dollar homes on the hillsides overlooking the clearing have complained about their presence in the past.

A million thanks to Don Villarejo, who cleaned and organized the data for Vista that are presented here. He warns that the physical examination data are "crude" in the sense that they are not adjusted for age and gender (as is scientifically rigorous) because there were too few subjects in Vista to present data in this form and, at the same time, provide statistically stable findings.

This essay is dedicated to the thousands of farmworkers living and working in San Diego County. Your hard work and hardships are not unrecognized. Thank you.

*In the morning, those individuals without steady jobs at the local
nurseries make their way to a place called "Strawberry Fields," a day
labor pickup point on Rancho Santa Fe Road. There they wait for local residents or business owners to pull up and offer them a day's labor weeding a garden or clearing debris from construction sites.*

AGRICULTURE IN SAN DIEGO COUNTY

San Diego's agricultural industry boasts more than $1.3 billion in sales
annually. The most lucrative crops are indoor flowering and foliage
plants, with a reported value for 2002 of $305,442,053 (County of San
Diego 2002). Other important crops in San Diego County are avocados,
mushrooms, citrus, strawberries, tomatoes, and cucumbers, as well as
specialty crops such as macadamia nuts and chili peppers, and apiary
products such as honey and bees wax. Over 226,665 acres of land are
devoted to agricultural production in the county. The San Diego
County Chamber of Commerce ranked agriculture, much of which
occurs in North County (the northern portion of San Diego County),
the area where Vista is located, as the fourth largest component of the
county's economy, behind manufacturing, tourism, and the defense
industry. San Diego ranks fifth in the state for production value for all
crops, contributing 5.5 percent to the state's total agricultural production (County of San Diego 2001). In addition, San Diego County ranks
number one in the state for organic farming, with 292 registered organic farms producing an estimated crop value of nearly $12 million
(County of San Diego n.d.).

The many reports lauding the production value of agriculture in
San Diego County never mention the area's farmworkers and the important role they play. No one seems to know how many farmworkers
are employed in the lucrative agriculture business of San Diego
County. Indeed, the seasonality of many of the jobs and the area's
proximity to the border further complicate estimates. There is no systematic method in existence that accounts for these individuals who
tend and harvest the food crops that make San Diego County rich.

However, Don Villarejo has developed a means to estimate the
population of farmworkers. He examined employer reports to the Department of Employment Development, which include quarterly pay-

roll totals and monthly reports of the number of persons on the payroll during the pay period that includes the twelfth day of that month. In the data for 2000, the maximum number of hired farmworker employment in San Diego County was 12,054, in June of that year; and the lowest monthly report was 9,459, for January. Thus the number of workers in 2000 was at least 12,054, and it was probably much higher given that many workers are employed on a seasonal basis. The annual payroll total in 2000 for hired farmworker employment in San Diego County was $210.6 million. If we assume that hired farmworker earnings averaged about $10,000 per year (average annual salaries for California farmworkers fall between $7,500 and 10,000; see Rosenberg et al. 1998; Villarejo et al. 2000), then these payroll data suggest that there were approximately 21,060 individual farmworkers employed. If annual earnings average just $7,500 per year, then this figure would rise to 28,080 individuals. If the annual average earnings are somewhere between $7,500 and $10,000, then it is reasonable to assume that the number of farmworkers also falls between 21,060 and 28,080; the midpoint would be 24,570. A reasonable conclusion would be that the number of farmworkers hired in San Diego County in 2000 was at least 12,054, very probably around 24,570, and possibly as high as 28,080.

CALIFORNIA AGRICULTURAL WORKER HEALTH SURVEY

This report presents the findings from the Vista portion of the first statewide, cross-sectional health survey of hired farmworkers to include a comprehensive physical examination. The California Agricultural Worker Health Survey (CAWHS), conducted during 1999, included 970 randomly selected hired farmworkers. The sample was statewide and cross-sectional in seven representative communities: Arbuckle, Calistoga, Cutler, Firebaugh, Gonzales, Mecca, and Vista.[1]

Vista became the Southern California Coastal regional site through a process of random selection. In Vista, as in the other sites surveyed in the CAWHS study, the research team enumerated all dwellings in the

---

[1] A previous report included findings on health status as obtained from physical examinations, insurance coverage, and recent health care visits. A detailed description of survey methods is presented in Villarejo et al. 2000: appendix I.

neighborhoods where farmworkers were found to reside and then randomly selected dwellings to contact. Physically walking the streets in the dwelling-enumeration process ensured that nonconventional housing—such as the trailers, shacks, backyard garages, and parked cars where the team found many farmworkers living—would be included in the study. In the case of Vista, which was the only urban agricultural site in the statewide study, the research team used census tract and census block data to locate concentrations of farmworker residences. Furthermore, the team consulted with local agencies, such as Migrant Education, and local farmworker organizations, such as the Coalition of Indigenous Communities of Oaxaca (COCIO), to discover where farmworkers were living, working, shopping, and sending their children to school. In Vista there were 127 CAWHS interviews completed, of which 102 were of residents of permanent dwellings and 25 with residents of outlying areas.

Individual participants were randomly selected through the enumeration of all eligible persons in each randomly selected dwelling, followed by random selection of one or more residents to be subjects. Eligible participants had to be 18 years old or older and have performed hired farmwork, including livestock and crop work of any type, in the previous twelve months. There were 167 eligible males and 48 eligible females in the dwellings surveyed in Vista, which suggests that the composition of the population aged 18 and older was 77.7 percent males and 22.3 percent females. To capture a more balanced representation of farmworker health, the CAWHS research team deliberately over-sampled females in Vista, bringing 6 more women (and, correspondingly, 6 fewer men) into the Vista sample beyond what a random sampling would have generated.[2]

The CAWHS study had a three-part focus: a 1-to-2-hour interview conducted in the participant's residence, a physical examination at a contracted local health clinic, and a risk-behavior instrument conducted in a private examination room in the clinic after the physical

---

[2] The item on eligible males and females in residence was not recorded for a few dwellings, so the 215 (167 males, 48 females) is technically an incomplete count of eligible males and females in the dwellings surveyed in Vista (CAWHS Vista Notes, October 18, 2000).

exam. The survey instrument included lengthy and detailed questions concerning housing conditions, income, and family structure, some of which were purposefully identical to those of the Census of Population and Housing.[3] An overall response rate of 83 percent was achieved.

The CAWHS team negotiated with local clinics in five of the city sites to provide the space and personnel for the physical examinations.[4] In the case of Vista, the researchers set up an office at the Vista Community Clinic (VCC). The VCC staff performed the physical exams, which documented biometric measures, dental condition, skin and body condition, screening, blood chemistry, and medical history. They also did follow-ups and provided treatment in cases where a discovered health condition coincided with the clinic's various grant-funded and illness-specific programs.

The hired farmworkers who participated in the study were brought to the clinic twice, once for the physical exam and once for a follow-up consultation. Farmworkers were transported to and from the clinic for the physical and follow-up exams by the CAWHS research team. At the other California research sites—Gonzales, Firebaugh, Culter, Calistoga, Arbuckle, and Mecca—the transportation that CAWHS provided to and from the clinic was crucial because of the lack of public transportation in the town. In Vista, although the VCC has a van service available to its patients, CAWHS did not use this service but rented a car and driver instead.

---

[3] Other components of the survey include household composition, personal demographics, health services utilization, self-reported health conditions, doctor-reported health conditions, work history, income and living conditions, workplace health conditions, protective equipment and safety training, working with pesticides in the United States, field sanitation, work-related injuries and injury module, and immigration status.

[4] In Arbuckle, which has neither a physician nor a clinic, California Institute for Rural Studies (CIRS) staff set up a storefront clinic. In Calistoga, CIRS contracted with the staff of a clinic in St. Helena to set up a temporary facility in the Calistoga high school.

VISTA RESULTS

The Vista portion of the CAWHS study yielded 127 interviews (34 with women, 93 with men) and 100 physical exams (27 female, 73 male).[5] One hundred percent of the farmworkers interviewed reported that they had been born in Mexico. The majority were from southern Mexican states with large indigenous populations, such as Oaxaca and Guerrero (see table 2.1). The high presence of indigenous Mexican farmworkers in the agricultural labor force of Vista is confirmed by the fact that 31 percent of those interviewed identified themselves as "indigenous." Those farmworkers reporting Oaxaca as their home state were primarily from the districts of Juxtlahuaca and Silacayoapan. Both of these districts are in the region of Oaxaca known as the Mixteca, which has been occupied by indigenous Mixtec-speaking people for thousands of years. The numbers indicate that, at least in the farm-labor sector, there is a significant Mixtec population in Vista.[6]

---

[5] Vista investigators include Bonnie Bade, site coordinator; Konane Martínez, research associate; and interviewers Héctor García, Enrique Parada, Alejandra Sánchez, Miriam Snyder, Berenice Suárez, and Aide Villalobos, all of whom are students at California State University San Marcos; as well as José Conde and Sofía Orta, VCC outreach workers. Consultants for Vista include Dorothy Luján, VCC assistant director; Fernando Sañudo, director of health promotions; Connie Crisman, registered nurse; Frances Cerda, medical assistant; Jesús Acevedo of COCIO; and the San Marcos/Vista Migrant Education Office.

[6] To date, the only systematic estimate of the Mixtec population was conducted in 1996 by David Runsten and Michael Kearney, who found 50,000 Mixtecs living in California. Current estimates of the Mixtec population in California are much greater, with at least 25,000 living in San Diego's North County and more than 100,000 in the Central Valley. However a true census is still lacking.

In San Diego the largest percentage (12 percent) of Mexican consular identifications (*matrículas consulares*) issued between 1995 and 2002 were issued to individuals from Oaxaca. Looking at Oceanside, a community in North County, we find that the majority of matrículas issued over this period were for individuals from Oaxaca (33 percent) (see Runsten, this volume). These findings point to a sizable population of Oaxacan migrants in the North County region.

Table 2.1. Vista Farmworkers' Place of Birth

State of Birth	N	Percent
Oaxaca	56	44%
Guerrero	11	9
Puebla	8	6
Michoacán	7	6
Zacatecas	6	5
Hidalgo	4	3
Veracruz	4	3
Other Mexican states	18	14
Not reported/Don't know	13	10

The CAWHS data revealed that 49 percent of the workers interviewed in Vista are undocumented and that their median educational attainment falls between 4th and 6th grade. The farmworker population of Vista is relatively young, with a median age of 27, and 45 percent report being married.

LIVING CONDITIONS

Jesús got in the passenger seat of the car, notebook in hand, and took off his baseball cap. "Por aquí," he indicated; "I'll show you where almost all the farmworkers in town live." We drove up Twin Oaks Valley Road, in the opposite direction from the new California State University on the hill. Up the road we passed the Buena Creek convenience store, with a line of workers forming out the door and into the parking lot. "The paisianos cash checks there," Jesús commented. The road narrowed and orange groves flanked us along one side. On the left the hills sloped upward to form a small ridge facing west. We pulled into a church parking lot and got out of the car. "Look up that hill. Don't you see the blue tarps?" Jesus asked. Sure enough, small flecks of blue could be seen among the sage and sumac of the chaparral. Three men walked up the road and into the parking lot as we stood there. Jesús knew them and introduced us to these gentlemen from Juxtlahuaca, Oaxaca. The men then ducked under the chain-link fence at the corner of the parking lot, each carrying a bag of food they had bought at the Buena Creek store, and began climbing up toward their homes in the brush.

In combination, Vista's lack of affordable housing and its low pay rates create situations in which farmworkers must share housing with many other individuals or live in unconventional accommodations, such as out in the open in orchards and fields, alongside creeks and rivers, on hillsides, or in their cars. Many live in labor camps; there are between 100 and 150 registered farm-labor camps in San Diego County and probably about the same number that are not registered (SANDAG 1999).[7] At the Rancho de Victor, off Highway 76, for example, Jesús warns us not to enter: "He [the owner] chases people off with a gun and won't let the men leave the ranch very often." Given that the intent of the CAWHS study is to give every farmworker in the selected region an opportunity to participate, the researchers decide to include pickup points in the sample, and they denote these populations as "outlying workers." Thus, in addition to the apartment complexes on West Los Angeles, Nevada, Santa Fe, and California streets, where most farmworkers live, the study included homeless workers who often live at or near a pickup point. The pickup points in Vista where day laborers wait in the mornings for contractors or private individuals to drive up and offer work include "Strawberry Fields" off East Vista Way, Sleeping Indian, Evergreen, and North Santa Fe Street at Melrose Avenue.

Crowded living conditions characterize the lives of farmworkers with housing in Vista. Rents at the apartments where the study found the largest concentrations of farmworkers ranged from $750 to $950 per month. Significant but not surprising was the finding that 87 percent of the dwellings in which individuals were interviewed were shared by

---

[7] The Regional Task Force on the Homeless in San Diego reports that "More than 7,000 resident day laborers/farmworkers live year-round under difficult conditions in perhaps 100 encampments on public and private property throughout the county. These camps are located in the canyons and hillsides of North County, along the coast, in northern San Diego City and adjacent to farming operations where the workers regularly seek day labor. The workers' tenuous living conditions and their geographical, linguistic and cultural isolation make it impossible to closely estimate their numbers." Available at http://www.co.san-diego.ca.us/rtfh/profile.html#farm%20workers.

two or more households.[8] It is difficult to find a precise definition of "overcrowding" in the literature, but it is generally assessed at a density of more than one person per room in a dwelling, excluding the bathrooms.[9] The CAWHS study found an average of 7.5 persons per room in Vista. This compares with an average of 4.3 persons per dwelling for all seven CAWHS communities. Significantly, 16 percent of those dwellings reported having no telephone.

As elsewhere in California, the lack of affordable housing in Vista creates situations in which local Native American reservations end up subsidizing the California agricultural industry by providing housing to farmworkers. San Pasqual, Pala, Pauma, Soboba, Jamul, and other Native American reservations in San Diego County rent land to farmworkers from Mexico on which families can park trailers.[10]

---

[8] Household is defined as a group in which individuals share the costs of food, clothing, health care, and other necessities.

[9] The term "overcrowding" is a subjective assessment applied to determinations of population densities in a dwelling, usually expressed in terms of persons per room (PPR). Data on dwelling densities are reported by the Census of Population and Housing, expressed as PPR. The census reports refer to room counts that exclude bathrooms. Thus kitchens are counted along with bedrooms, living rooms, and so on. Unlike fixed standards of housing quality, such as whether a dwelling has plumbing or electricity, the measure used for determining if a dwelling is overcrowded has been remarkably altered during the past half-century (Myers, Baer, and Choi 1996). Prior to 1950, the conventional standard for overcrowding was 2.0 PPR. It was lowered to 1.50 PPR in 1950, and then to 1.00 PPR in 1960, half the widely accepted value just two decades earlier.

Importantly, the Bureau of the Census does not define the terms "crowding" or "overcrowding." Rather, the Census of Population and Housing simply reports findings of residential density, allowing other agencies to apply whatever standard seems to make sense. More precisely, the Census 2000 Technical Report states, "Although the Census Bureau has no official definition of crowded units, many users consider units with more than one occupant per room to be crowded" (Summary File 3, Technical Documentation, 2000 Census of Population and Housing, Appendix 8, p. B-58, August 2002). Unfortunately, many authors incorrectly assume that the Census Bureau defines overcrowding as corresponding to more than 1.00 PPR and attribute this criterion to the Census.

[10] The CAWHS witnessed rental of land to hundreds of farmworkers at the Torres-Martinez Reservation in Riverside County, where the Health Depart-

Twenty-five participants in the CAWHS in Vista were termed "outliers" in the participant-enumeration process because they were contacted at worker pickup points and included persons who were homeless. Overall, 16 of 127 participants in Vista (13 percent) reported that they did not have full plumbing facilities. Seventeen percent of the unconventional dwellings had no plumbing facilities, and in these dwellings the self-reported prevalence of adverse health conditions, such as diarrhea, was more than six times greater than that found among residents of conventional dwellings with complete plumbing facilities.

HEALTH CONDITIONS, INSURANCE, AND SERVICE UTILIZATION

Tiburcio returned to the Vista Community Clinic for his follow-up exam. He had participated in the CAWHS study and had his first physical exam three weeks prior. At 54 years of age, he was an elder farmworker, and he shared an apartment on Nevada Street with eleven other men from Oaxaca. He told the site coordinator of the project that he frequently went to Tijuana for medicine. "They give me injections for my arthritis," he said. He worried about an eye infection and a sore wrist. The VCC medical assistant led him to an examination room, where she proceeded to relate the results of his physical. "He has high cholesterol, very high." She told him this, and when she saw the blank look on his face, she said, "Here, read this. You cannot eat so much grasa (fat)." She handed him an 8-1/2 x 11–inch paper printed from top to bottom in English in a very small font. I could make out a small drawing of tablespoons midway down the page. "Eat no more than two grams of grasa a day, señor," she said. At that moment the doctor called her to assist with another exam, so she excused herself. "What is she talking about?" Tiburcio asked me. "Why didn't she say anything about my eye? What about my wrist?" He shook his head and began walking toward the exit. "Wait," I said, "let's see that." So we sat down and read together the instructions for changing one's diet to lower cholesterol. Tiburcio spoke Spanish with

ment had closed down makeshift trailer parks in the town of Mecca and the surrounding non-Native American areas due to health code violations.

a heavy accent. He hadn't learned this language until he was an adult and began working in California in the 1980s. His roommates on Nevada Sreet. were from the same small town in Silacayoapan, and they all spoke Mixtec, the native language of the peoples in the Mixteca region of Oaxaca. Tiburcio's ancestors had built dynasties, kingdoms, huge palaces of stone. I tried to translate the piece of paper for him, but I realized the futility of this and pondered why it was me, and not a clinic employee, administering the medical advice. Tiburcio shares a kitchen and weekly dinner chores, so he has little control over the ingredients that go into the meals his roommates make. The "lonchera" at the corner sells mostly burritos and tacos, hardly the multigrain bread and mayonnaise substitute that this paper full of medical advice recommends. Tiburcio was upset that he had had no resolution on his wrist problem. "I plant seedlings in flats at the nursery," he said; "I thought they might be able to help the pain in my wrist with an injection or something." He left frustrated.

Consistent with conditions throughout the history of California agriculture, seasonally employed farmworkers normally do not have basic employee benefits, such as health insurance, job security, or sick leave. Access to health care resources is the most fundamental health need, and nearly all farmworkers in Vista are without health insurance. In 2000, 96 percent of the farmworkers interviewed in the CAWHS in Vista reported that they had no health insurance. The two individuals (out of 127 interviewed) who did have employer-provided health insurance stated that it only covered the worker, and not the worker's family. These numbers are slightly worse than those found statewide, where the CAWHS study found that 70 percent lacked any form of health insurance; of the 16.5 percent whose employers offered health insurance, only two-thirds stated they could afford the premiums or co-payments (Villarejo et al. 2000).

The opportunities for clinical health care available to individuals in an uninsured working sector of the population are limited to emergency/pregnancy-related care provided by Medi-Cal; disease-specific short-lived programs dependent on grant money, such as the Vista Community Clinic's "Proyecto Dulce" program for diabetes; or out-of-pocket payments at a local health clinic, which usually has sliding-scale payment options. The data presented in table 2.2 report the most recent visits to a doctor, dentist, and eye exam (in either Mexico or the United States) as reported by the 127 farmworkers surveyed in Vista.

Table 2.2. Most Recent Clinical Visit /Exam among Vista's Migrant Farmworkers

Recency of Last Visit	Doctor	Dentist	Eye Exam
Within the last 2 years	53%	19%	10%
Two years ago or more	18%	14%	4%
Never	28%	64%	85%

Source: CAWHS 2000.

More than half of the farmworkers interviewed indicated that they had been to a doctor within the last two years. The high number of individuals who reported having seen a doctor recently could be explained by Vista's proximity to Mexico; indeed, many more of the Vista farmworkers reported having visited a doctor in Mexico than did the farmworkers surveyed in more distant sites, such as Cutler, Firebaugh, Gonzales, Arbuckle, and Calistoga. Furthermore, reproductive health is a primary need among the farmworker population. A higher proportion of the women who participated in the CAWHS in Vista (27 women out of 349 in the study overall) were of childbearing age than was the case for women in the other survey sites. The emergency/pregnancy-related care provided by Medi-Cal and the effectiveness of the Vista Community Clinic's outreach to these women may also account for the frequency of recent visits to a clinic or doctor. In Vista, 28 percent of the participants reported never having been to a doctor, which is statistically consistent with the 32 percent of male subjects statewide who said they had never been to a doctor or clinic (Villarejo et al. 2000).

Dental care is the most glaring deficiency in farmworkers' health care. In Vista, 20 percent of the farmworkers who underwent a physical exam had decayed teeth; 18 percent also had missing or broken teeth; and 3 percent had gingivitis. Sixty-four percent of Vista farmworkers interviewed had never been to a dentist. Statewide, the CAWHS study found that 50 percent of male subjects and 40 percent of female subjects reported never having been to a dentist (Villarejo et al. 2000). Eighty-five percent of the study participants in Vista report having never had an eye exam.

Surprisingly, 33 percent of farmworkers in Vista (31 of 95) qualified as obese as measured by the Body Mass Index.[11] In the CAWHS study statewide, 81 percent of male subjects and 76 percent of female subjects had unhealthful weight, as measured by the Body Mass Index, with 28 percent of men and 37 percent of women obese (Villarejo et al. 2000). The incidence of obesity appears to be more extreme among indigenous farmworkers. In the statewide CAWHS, of those individuals who identified themselves as indigenous (83 of 970), 46.2 percent of the women and 24 percent of the men qualified as obese.

In Vista, 23 percent of the study participants (23 of 98) had high blood pressure, with a systolic measure above 140 or a diastolic measure above 90. This measurement can indicate that a significant number of farmworkers may be suffering from hypertension. In the statewide CAWHS study, both male and female participants show substantially greater incidence of high blood pressure as compared with the incidence of hypertension among U.S. adults (Villarejo et al. 2000).

Seven percent of the farmworkers who underwent physical exams in Vista had anemia, 4 percent had high serum cholesterol, and 2 percent had glucose higher than 200mg/dl. The blood chemistry results in Vista are consistent with the patterns the study uncovered elsewhere in California, where the CAWHS found that nearly one in five males (18 percent) had at least two of three risk factors for chronic disease: high serum cholesterol, high blood pressure, or obesity.

The concentration of indigenous farmworkers in Vista points toward greater incidence of ethnospecific illness in the region. Illnesses such as *susto* (fright), *corajes* (anger), and *nervios* (nervousness) ranked highest in incidence in the statewide study. Among indigenous participants, susto was reported by 18 percent, corajes by 18.1 percent, and

---

[11] The Body Mass Index (BMI) is defined as a person's weight divided by height. The higher the BMI, the more massive the person will be, as indicated by physical breadth. Persons with a BMI of 25 or more are considered overweight, while those with a BMI over 30 are obese (Villarejo et al. 2000).

nervios by 16.9 percent. The emotional nature of these ethnospecific illnesses indicates the probability of mental health problems among many of Vista's farmworkers. Difficulties with language, illegal political status, and crowded living conditions create situations in which farmworkers experience frustration, insecurity, and isolation from the larger society.

> *Rosario sat in the clinic's waiting room with her two-year-old on her lap. Her husband, a participant in the CAWHS study, was in one of the examination rooms receiving treatment for syphilis. We had encountered three other individuals with syphilis, but Rosario's husband was the only one whose wife was living in California with him. Fortunately, the clinic had a special program for sexually transmitted diseases, so the treatment was free. When Rosario's husband had come for his follow-up and discovered he had syphilis, we implored him to bring his wife in for treatment too. We were surprised he had actually done so because he, not she, was the source of the illness. Vanloads of sex workers arrive at various labor camps, arroyos, and secluded areas throughout Vista every Saturday evening to service the farmworkers, many of whom have wives and families in Mexico and are here for the seasonal agricultural employment. The clinic is well aware of the practice and can do nothing but make sure that free condoms are available, though they are seldom used. Rosario's husband came into the waiting room and took the child in his arms. "They want to see you now," he said to his wife. She looked down at the ground as she proceeded toward the waiting medical assistant.*

DISCUSSION

The health of farmworkers in Vista is characterized by chronic illness and lack of clinical care. Unhealthful body weights, high cholesterol, anemia, and elevated blood pressure all combine with crowed living conditions or homelessness and the lack of health insurance to create a workforce that is at high risk for severe health problems. Low rates of visitation to doctors or clinics, eye exams, or dental exams put this population at further risk. Local clinics, such as the Vista Community Clinic or the North County Health Services Clinic, provide invaluable service to the farmworker population through sliding-scale payment options, grant-funded programs for the homeless, or illness-specific programs, but without health insurance farmworkers will continue to suffer from chronic illness.

Crowded and unconventional living conditions constitute a major threat to farmworker health in Vista. Lack of plumbing facilities for farmworkers living outdoors correlates with increased rates of diarrhea and other communicable illnesses. Furthermore, Vista's farmworkers were found to share housing at an average rate of 7.5 persons per room, more than seven times the standard definition of overcrowding. And more than four-fifths of Vista farmworkers shared their dwellings with at least one other household. Clearly, if the lack of affordable housing for Vista's farmworkers is ignored, the health threats associated with overcrowded living conditions will persist. Surely it is time for the agricultural industry to support its workers in ways that allow them dignified housing and a decent living wage.

LOCAL SUPPORT

The health needs of farmworkers in Vista, California—access to health care, health insurance, dignified housing—have been addressed by various actors, including local health clinics, Migrant Education, and the transnational migrant population from Oaxaca living in California. Local coalitions have emerged throughout California in defense of Oaxacan indigenous interests. The Coalition of Indigenous Communities of Oaxaca, with bases in Vista, Oceanside, and Carlsbad, the Fresno and Central Valley–based Oaxacan Indigenous Binational Front (FIOB), and many other such organizations tied through regional affiliations in Oaxaca generate local activities in California related to workers' rights, legal rights, housing, health, and culture. The Guelaguetza festivals organized by Oaxacans living in California attract thousands of celebrants each year in San Marcos, Los Angeles, Fresno, Portland, and other farm- or service-related labor pockets in the United States.

Many local associations in California have obtained nonprofit 501(c)3 status and gotten funding to support outreach projects within the Oaxacan community in their region. These projects have included, among others, work on the 2000 census to document Mexican indigenous populations living in California (carried out by FIOB and affiliated organizations such as California Rural Legal Assistance and the Aguirre Group) and health education among Mixtec women living in the Central Valley (FIOB).

Local associations that do not have nonprofit status, which includes the majority of "Oaxacalifornian" hometown associations, fund cultural, religious, and sports activities, such as basketball tournaments, out of their own pockets. The COCIO, which has organized and presented the annual Guelaguetza in San Marcos and Oceanside for nearly ten years, has collaborated with student organizations at California State University San Marcos, principally the Movimiento Estudiantil Chicano de Aztlan (MEChA), to host the event at the university. This collaboration has had the result of connecting local farmworker families with the university community. More than five thousand people attend the Guelaguetza in San Marcos, where a message of cultural pride and self-reliance is all-pervasive.

The Mexican indigenous community in Vista, and throughout California more generally, has demonstrated the desire to nurture its populations living outside of Mexico by fostering cultural and social support and seeking collaborative engagement with health, legal, and local agencies. Examples include the hometown associations' negotiations with local and Mexican economic entities to facilitate the transfer of earnings remittances to families in Oaxaca, and the appointment of Mexican indigenous members to an advisory board for a project on farmworker mental health run by North County Health Services and funded by the California Endowment. Solutions regarding the health of farmworkers in Vista, California, must involve collaborations such as these among the farmworker community, local health clinics, educational agencies, and industry.

References

County of San Diego. 2001. "Summary of County Agricultural Commissioner's Reports." San Diego: University of California Cooperative Extension.
———. 2002. "San Diego County Crop Statistics & Annual Report." San Diego: County of San Diego Department of Agriculture, Weights and Measures.

————. n.d. "Regulatory Fact Sheet for Standards Enforcement—Organic Handler/Producer." San Diego: County of San Diego Department of Agriculture, Weights and Measures.

Myers, Dowell, William C. Baer, and Seong-Youn Choi. 1996. "The Changing Problem of Overcrowded Housing," *Journal of the American Planning Association* 62, no. 1 (Winter).

Rosenberg, Howard, Anne Stierman, Susan M. Gabbard, and Richard Mines 1998. *Who Works on California's Farms? Demographic and Employment Findings from the National Agricultural Workers Survey.* Agricultural and Natural Resources Publication 21583. Berkeley: Agricultural Personnel Management Program, University of California, Berkeley.

SANDAG (San Diego Association of Governments). 1999. *Regional Housing Needs Statement.* San Diego: SANDAG, June.

Villarejo, Don, David Lighthall, Daniel Williams III, Ann Souter, Richard Mines, Bonnie Bade, Steve Samuels, and Stephen McCurdy. 2000. *Suffering in Silence: A Report on the Health of California's Agricultural Workers.* Sponsored by the California Endowment. Davis, Calif. California Institute for Rural Studies.

3

Salir Adelante—Getting Ahead: Recent Mexican Immigrants in San Diego County

KONANE MARTÍNEZ, DAVID RUNSTEN, AND
ALEJANDRINA RICÁRDEZ

"Illegal aliens," "public charge," an "out-of-control border"—these are just a few of the images dominating public perceptions of immigrants in California today. But they are more than fleeting images; they are entrenched in the state's history and indicative of its future social relations. Immigration is a topic that can make or break political campaigns, local initiatives, and revenue drives.

Because San Diego County shares the border with Mexico, it magnifies the struggles surrounding the immigration issue in the state. This essay is the result of the combined efforts of the authors to address some of the pressing issues that newly arrived Mexican immigrants face in San Diego County. We discuss salient themes uncovered through field-based research conducted in the county, including the context that recent migrants face in regards to health services, housing, and civic participation.

Participants in our interviews told of their experiences and those of family, friends, and neighbors. Their experiences reflect a few of the myriad realities in which new immigrants find themselves in the post–

September 11 anti-immigrant environment of San Diego County. We argue that the marginalized position of new immigrants makes them susceptible to impoverishment and negatively affects their ability to access services and to participate in local civic and political movements that could potentially bring their perspective to the table. New immigrants, especially undocumented immigrants, have a limited voice in the county's planning efforts and little or no presence in the construction of "community" in the region. We show how, despite this intense marginalization, the Latino community finds alternative and positive strategies to create their lives in San Diego and to fulfill their goal to *salir adelante* (get ahead). We discuss these findings with an applied goal in mind: to outline a set of key findings and recommendations that can act as a guide to changing the current trajectory of political, social, and economic policies that are negatively impacting the health and well-being of recent Mexican immigrants in San Diego.

BACKGROUND

Ten years ago the Center for U.S.-Mexican Studies at the University of California, San Diego issued a monograph addressing the difficulties Mexican immigrants faced in San Diego's North County region (Eisenstadt and Thorup 1994). Titled *Caring Capacity versus Carrying Capacity*, the book was written after rapid population growth in North County in the 1980s had brought suburban development close to—and in conflict with—the camps of migrant farmworkers. Wholesale "camp abatement," where contractors evicted sometimes hundreds of people, had only begun in the late 1980s. The monograph discussed a number of important issues associated with immigrants in San Diego: day laborers congregating on streets and the efforts to create job centers for them; the rapid increase in limited-English-proficient students in the schools; strains on the health-care system; racist attacks on immigrants and a focus on their role in crime; and "the most acute problem ... the lack of adequate, sanitary, and inexpensive housing."

Eisenstadt and Thorup discussed these problems against the backdrop of reaction against the amnesty provisions of the Immigration Reform and Control Act of 1986 (IRCA). This large-scale legalization of undocumented immigrants, combined with family reunification provisions of immigration law, led to family settlement in places like San Diego and to a more open presence for many immigrants. The failure of the federal government to provide adequate funding to heavily impacted communities for health care, housing, education, and other services associated with this settlement fueled public resentment of immigrants and caused these individuals to be seen as a burden on local taxpayers.

Similarly, Leo Chávez's 1992 ethnography, *Shadowed Lives: Undocumented Immigrants in American Society*, details the invisibility of undocumented Mexican immigrants in "America's Finest City" (an identity to which San Diego lays claim). Chávez brings voice to this unacknowledged sector of San Diego residents, using life and migration histories to draw a picture of undocumented immigrants living in homeless camps surrounded by urban sprawl. He finds that despite the immigrants' positive economic and social contributions to the region, an atmosphere of exclusion and discrimination negatively shapes their incorporation in the region. Paul Espinoza's documentary film *Uneasy Neighbors* (1989) perhaps best illustrates this reality. Espinoza visually and ethnographically documents San Diego's "uneasy" and contradictory sentiments—and the resulting policies—regarding the presence of undocumented migrants.

Looking at these works in 2005, one is struck by how little has changed. If anything, the problems are now worse. Rapid increases in the Latin American immigrant population in San Diego County over the past decade have compounded the difficulties of providing adequate housing and services in a region notoriously reluctant to pay taxes. The federal government has not significantly improved funding to impacted regions,[1] and federal immigration policy (Operation Gatekeeper) has closed the San Diego border, dramatically increasing the cost and danger for migrants traveling to and from Mexico without documents. Estimates of the real cost (in 1983 dollars) of hiring a "coyote" to cross someone over the border have risen from $150 in 1990 and $525 in 1998 (Massey, Durand, and Malone 2002) to $1,500 in 2004 (Cornelius 2005). This has discouraged temporary return migration to

---

[1] Congress recently set aside $1 billion to reimburse states over four years for the health-care costs of treating undocumented immigrants (Kelly 2004).

Mexico and trapped increasing numbers of undocumented immigrants on the U.S. side of the border. There has been no further amnesty in the last eighteen years, and this has caused the number of undocumented Mexicans residing in the United States to increase steadily, by an estimated 150,000 to 300,000 per year.

At the same time that the number of immigrants in California was rising, the economic fortunes of the state were falling, producing a crisis in the state budget—and in county, city, and school district budgets as well—and prompting substantial numbers of California residents to place the blame on immigrants. The collapse of the stock market bubble in early 2000 exacerbated the situation. As investment shifted to real estate, there was rapid inflation in housing prices, and San Diego is now the least affordable area in Southern California, with only 10 percent of local households able to afford a median-priced home.[2] As Brad Wiscon noted at the conference from which this volume derived, "There is no affordable housing in North County San Diego."

The lack of affordable housing has contributed to the persistence of migrant camps despite continuing public demand for cities and the Border Patrol to force out their residents once and for all. Such anti-immigrant sentiment waxes and wanes, yet it always detrimentally affects immigrants' access to health and social services. Anti-immigrant sentiment is especially volatile in northern San Diego County, where conservative politicians and residents add to the already tense situation caused by the juxtaposition of upscale housing developments and immigrant camps. The post–September 11 focus on controlling the nation's borders has led local residents to call for more sweeps to rid the region of "illegal aliens" and to ballot initiatives being circulated in California in late 2004 to deny driver's licenses to undocumented immigrants and to limit the social services available to them.

In 2002, the International Community Foundation (ICF) commissioned the North American Integration Center (NAID) at the University of California, Los Angeles to gather information pertaining to the experience of new immigrants in San Diego. Data collection was complemented with focus groups and interviews with key informants in

---

[2] Data from California Association of Realtors, *Los Angeles Times*, September 19, 2004, p. K5.

three regions of the county: San Ysidro, Barrio Logan/East San Diego, and North County. We chose these areas as representative of the different realities facing immigrants in the southern, middle, and northern portions of San Diego County. The aim of the focus groups was to illuminate the concerns of recent (post-1986) Mexican immigrants in San Diego. Separate focus groups were held for men and women in order to collect a wider range of experiences and stories. Participants were recruited and engaged through the collaboration of key agencies targeting the immigrant community: Migrant Education in San Marcos, Town Site Community Center in Vista, Barrio Logan College Institute and Family Health Centers of San Diego in Barrio Logan, and Casa Familiar in San Ysidro. A focus group and a series of interviews with key informants were conducted with representatives from agencies servicing the immigrant community and with local elected officials within the selected regions. The questions for the focus groups were constructed by the team of researchers (some were borrowed from Eisenstadt and Thorup 1994), highlighting issues in the areas of health, housing, social services, and civic participation. The focus group data are complemented by Konane Martínez's five years of research on immigrant and farmworker health, examining the relationship between indigenous Oaxacan transnational communities and clinical health-care systems through work in North County clinics and ethnographic fieldwork (Martínez 2005).

In this chapter, we first examine the nature of the selected communities and relate some accounts that emerged from the focus groups. We then look at the demographic changes that occurred in the selected communities from 1990 to 2000. We next turn to the nature of the immigrant experience in San Diego, focusing on the problems immigrants confront in accessing health care and housing or participating more actively in civic life. We find that not only has there been little improvement in the past ten years, in many ways the current situation is worse, because the number of undocumented immigrants has risen and the border is now more difficult and costly to cross. Solutions to immigrants' everyday problems are constrained by the structural and political reality of their situation.

THE STUDY COMMUNITIES

A comparison of the 1990 and 2000 censuses reveals the rapid demographic growth and concentration of Latino immigrants in San Diego County. Figure 3.1 maps the data for percent of Hispanics by census tract for 1990; figure 3.2 maps the same data for 2000. These maps reveal the clustering of the Latino population in specific towns of North County, several central parts of the City of San Diego, and along the corridor that runs from central San Diego to the border, as well as a slight spreading out in the 1990s into other census tracts in North County. The communities chosen for this study reflect the diverse environments and conditions that new immigrants face in San Diego County as well as the demographic concentrations revealed in figures 3.1 and 3.2. The communities we selected are: Vista, Escondido, Oceanside, and San Marcos in North County (the cities in that area with the largest populations of Latinos); East San Diego and Barrio Logan in central San Diego; and San Ysidro in the south, by the U.S.-Mexico border.

San Ysidro

San Ysidro, the southernmost community of San Diego County, lies within the boundaries of the United States (and the City of San Diego), yet focus group participants in San Ysidro indicated that it is viewed by local residents as an extension of Tijuana. One participant noted that the town is often referred to as "San Ysidro, Tijuana." Residents living in San Ysidro related their life experience as one of movement back and forth across the border. One long-term resident described himself as a *fronterizo* (a native of the border). He was born in Ensenada, has lived his life in the border region, and has family on both sides of the border. Residents of San Ysidro, most of whom came from Mexico's central and northern states, especially Baja California, have often led a binational existence for decades and have had ample opportunity to view first-hand the struggles their compatriots suffer in crossing the border to seek a better life.

One group participant in San Ysidro, who had left his home in Veracruz, Mexico, as a young man, told of the toll that this separation from family had taken during the years he traveled throughout California. He now lives and works in San Ysidro while his wife and children live just across the border in Tijuana. Although he admits that this separation does not keep him from seeing his family, he is nevertheless trying to get residency papers for them. He talked about his daily struggle to make ends meet and the sacrifices the family makes to ensure that the children advance in their lives. "God gives me the strength to move forward," he added.

Local residents reflected on the border's power to separate families and compatriots. "San Ysidro and Tijuana are the same town, we are the same people, the same race. It's true that we are united, yet there are thousands of families separated by that border.... When the Berlin Wall fell, people here in the United States shouted with joy. But at the same time they were building that wall [the border fence] ... as if to say, 'You're second-class citizens and we are the bosses.' How sad and depressing, no?"

The narratives from San Ysidro tell of the obstacles to immigrants' incorporation in the United States. Focus group participants spoke about the difficulties their families encounter when trying to immigrate and the complex process they must follow to obtain their U.S. documents.

The Mexican community in San Ysidro faces a broad range of challenges; of special concern to the members of our focus group were teen pregnancy, substance abuse, lack of health insurance, elevated school "dropout" or "push-out" rates, and a lack of jobs and educational opportunities. They expressed frustration at the shortage of good-paying, stable employment options. Local service-sector jobs in the tourism industry, which caters to thousands of cross-border travelers, are fairly plentiful but wages are low, making it difficult for workers in this sector to make ends meet.

Barrio Logan/East San Diego

Barrio Logan is probably the best-known Chicano/Latino neighborhood in San Diego. Here, the Chicano community's political and social struggles are a part of the infrastructure, as depicted in the murals of Barrio Logan's Chicano Park. Although Barrio Logan's history is well established, its future is being contested. Urban development and gentrification in downtown San Diego are shaping Barrio Logan in multiple ways. A representative from the eighth district expressed his concern that Latino residents are disconnected and disengaged from the development process that is poised to transform this neglected area into one of the most lucrative zones for real estate investment.

Recent immigrants find that living in Barrio Logan means living in the shadow of the community's glorified Chicano history and identity. They find it especially hard to adjust to life in this neighborhood because of the economic, political, and social barriers that deny them access to local agencies, institutions, and information. Though they see hope for their children in the United States, their experience has been one of contention and struggle. The area's second-generation Mexicans, meanwhile, struggle with their own resentment over the fact that the new immigrants seemingly choose to remit their income to their hometowns in Mexico rather than invest in local infrastructure. And attempts by local Latino entrepreneurs to get a stake in the rapidly transforming region have met with insurmountable opposition.

As urban development and gentrification restrict Barrio Logan's ability to absorb new immigrants and, in fact, force some immigrants out, the immigrant populations are expanding rapidly in other areas, such as East San Diego, where local residents feel ever more ignored by local government and overlooked by city services.

North County

North County best illustrates the steep gradients of social and economic inequality in San Diego County. Billboards advertising "Homes in the low $500,000's" rise in close proximity to migrant squatter camps hidden in the gullies and hills of this rapidly developing area. The juxtaposition of migrant camps and upscale housing developments has spurred local homeowners to call for the removal of migrants from the area, and immigrants in North County live in fear of "la migra" (the Border Patrol). Our migrant informants in North County said they do not feel sufficiently at ease to *andar libre* (move about freely). One participant spoke of a time in 1987 when migrants were in such fear of *la migra* that they wouldn't go about on the streets. The recent increase in Border Patrol raids in North County has created a similar situation, as noted by the media and human rights organizations in the area.

Enclaves of Mexican immigrants can be found throughout North County. As discussed in Runsten's chapter on *matrículas* in this volume, the distinctive subset of recently arrived Mexican immigrants has shifted the profile of the Mexican community in North County toward a more indigenous characterization. Oaxacan migrant families began to settle here in recent years, and these new immigrant families are integrating into these communities' social fabric. This presence of a large and growing Oaxacan indigenous immigrant community is very visible. Undocumented immigrant parents have citizen children in local schools. Oaxacan hometown associations have mobilized around social and political issues concerning the community. The annual Guelaguetza festival, organized by the Coalition of Indigenous Communities in Oaxaca (COCIO), attracts nearly 5,000 people from throughout Southern California who come to enjoy traditional Oaxacan dishes, music, and so on.

Women immigrants in North County reported that they felt very isolated and often attributed this to not being able to get around by car. One noted that she felt much freer when she learned to use the public bus system to go to and from work. This newfound proficiency, in turn, made her more confident of her ability to make a life for herself in San Diego.

With time and experience, our informants suggest, immigrants are able to adjust to their new lives in this region. The process is eased by family ties and by community systems that originate in Mexico and are carried by migrants as they cross the border. These connections help migrants navigate daily life. Family or community members already in the United States help arriving immigrants find jobs, transportation, housing, and information. One manifestation of these cross-border community ties is a housing pattern in which all residents of an apartment building sometimes come from a single town in Oaxaca.

REVIEWING THE CENSUS DATA

In this section we examine data from the 1990 and 2000 population and housing censuses to determine how the Latino population in San Diego

Table 3.1. Population Changes in San Diego County, 1990–2000

	Hispanic Population			Non-Hispanic Population			Total Population		
	1990	2000	Percent Change	1990	2000	Percent Change	1990	2000	Percent Change
Northern San Diego County									
Escondido	24,984	51,661	107%	83,651	81,867	–2%	108,635	133,528	23%
Oceanside	28,198	48,684	73	100,200	112,221	12	128,398	160,905	25
San Marcos	10,442	20,251	94	28,532	34,909	22	38,974	55,160	42
Vista	17,371	35,119	102	54,501	55,012	1	71,872	90,131	25
Southern San Diego County									
Barrio Logan	20,269	22,221	10	5,440	5,111	–6	25,709	27,332	6
East San Diego	9,183	18,815	105	24,970	20,671	–17	34,153	39,486	16
San Ysidro	18,056	20,657	14	2,776	2,341	–16	20,832	22,998	10
San Diego County	498,578	750,965	51	1,999,438	2,062,868	3	2,498,016	2,813,833	13

Sources: U.S. Census of Population and Housing, 1990 and 2000.

is changing and how the situation differs from one area of the county to another.[3]

San Diego County's Hispanic population is growing much more rapidly than its non-Hispanic population. In the 1990s, the Hispanic population grew 51 percent, exceeding the statewide average of 42.6 percent and accounting for 80 percent of the county's total population growth. The corresponding number for non-Hispanics was only 3 percent (3.8 percent statewide) (see table 3.1). In the specific locales that we examined, the difference was even more pronounced. In North County, for example, Vista's Hispanic population more than doubled while its non-Hispanic population rose only 1 percent; and in Escondido, the Hispanic population more than doubled as well, while the non-Hispanic population *declined* by 2 percent. The Hispanic population of Barrio Logan/East San Diego grew by a modest 10 percent, but in San Ysidro the figure was an impressive 105 percent. What is more, the non-Hispanic populations in both communities dropped during the same period. Thus we find a clear tendency for San Diego's heavily Latino areas to become more Latino at the same time that the non-Hispanic population is abandoning these areas to move to zones of greater housing availability.

One outcome of the rapid population growth is that the Latino population as a share of total population is increasing. County-wide, the Hispanic population increased from 20 percent in 1990 to 27 percent in 2000. In four towns in San Diego's North County, it rose from an average of 23 percent to 35 percent (table 3.2). East San Diego saw a rapid increase—from 27 to 48 percent. And in Barrio Logan and San Ysidro, the Hispanic population increased from already high levels to 81 and 90 percent, respectively. These figures illustrate that the Latino population is largely concentrated in the central and southern areas of San Diego County.

---

3 The reader is cautioned about the inherent risks in using census data to discuss a population that has a large undocumented component and an estimated 7,000 people living in outdoor encampments. For example, it is estimated that the 1990 census missed 60 percent or more of farmworkers. Though the Census Bureau had estimates of the undercounts in 2000, Congress did not allow an adjustment in the census figures to compensate for the undercount.

Table 3.2. Hispanic Population Shares in San Diego County, 1990–2000 (percentages)

Community	1990	2000
Northern San Diego County		
Escondido	23.0%	38.7%
Oceanside	22.0	30.3
San Marcos	26.8	36.7
Vista	24.2	39.0
Total for North County cities	23.3	35.4
Southern San Diego County		
Barrio Logan	78.8	81.3
East San Diego	26.9	47.6
San Ysidro	86.7	89.8
San Diego County total	20.0	26.7

Sources: U.S. Census of Population and Housing, 1990 and 2000.

Another way to consider these regional differences is by the language spoken at home (table 3.3). The county average for households in which Spanish is spoken is 20 percent, but there are wide differences between communities. About 25 percent of North County households speak Spanish at home, but in San Ysidro the figure is 87 percent. The figures on households that speak *only* Spanish are much lower—just 4.3 percent in the county overall, below 10 percent in North County, yet almost 30 percent in Barrio Logan and San Ysidro.

The census data also contain information on the number of housing units in San Diego County, which rose by only 10 percent between 1990 and 2000, at the same time that the county's population increased 13 percent. Because the new housing was not evenly distributed throughout the county, it had differential impacts on residential crowding (table 3.4). The average number of inhabitants per room increased 2 percent in San Diego County overall in the 1990s, but it rose between 3 and 15 percent in the cities of San Diego's North County. The county's central and southern neighborhoods were already much more crowded, and they remain more than twice as crowded as the county average.

Table 3.3. San Diego Communities, by Language Spoken at Home (percentages)

Community	Households Speaking Spanish at Home as Percent of All Households		Households Speaking Only Spanish as Percent of All Households	
	1990	2000	1990	2000
Northern San Diego County				
Escondido	15%	26%	4.2%	8.1%
Oceanside	14	21	3.5	4.4
San Marcos	18	24	5.7	7.0
Vista	17	26	4.1	6.8
Southern San Diego County				
Barrio Logan	73	72	36.3	28.9
East San Diego	22	40	8.7	16.9
San Ysidro	85	87	31.7	28.5
San Diego County	15	20	3.4	4.3

Sources: U.S. Census of Population and Housing, 1990 and 2000.

Table 3.4. Average Number of Persons per Room in San Diego County

Community	1990	2000	Change, 1990–2000
Northern San Diego County			
Escondido	1.13	1.29	14%
Oceanside	1.06	1.11	5%
San Marcos	1.12	1.15	3%
Vista	1.15	1.32	15%
Southern San Diego County			
Barrio Logan[a]	2.99	2.83	–5%
East San Diego	1.66	2.40	45%
San Ysidro	2.05	1.81	–12%
San Diego County	1.12	1.14	2%

Sources: U.S. Census of Population and Housing, 1990 and 2000.
[a] Barrio Logan has a very high number of persons per room in tract 51, probably due to the presence of homeless shelters in the area.

Figure 3.3 maps the residential crowding data by census tract. Apart from military bases, the areas of highest density are congruent with the Latino immigrant population. Housing density is higher among the Latino population in part because rent sharing among many tenants is one strategy for coping with high housing costs. Another explanatory factor is the larger size of Hispanic families: there were 4.1 people per Hispanic household versus 2.4 people per non-Hispanic household in San Diego County in 2000 (table 3.5). The crowding in predominantly Hispanic neighborhoods produces significant impacts in parking avail-ability, noise levels, generation of garbage, and crime statistics, as well as with regard to schools and other services. An Escondido city official noted that on the first day of school a few years ago, 250 more children showed up than were expected. This surprise situation arose because school personnel were basing their expectations on a children-per-housing-unit ratio that no longer held true.[4]

Table 3.5. Number of People per Household, Hispanic and Non-Hispanic, 2000

	Number of Persons per Household	
Community	*Hispanic Households*	*Non-Hispanic Households*
Northern San Diego County		
Escondido	4.8	2.4
Oceanside	4.5	2.3
San Marcos	4.9	2.4
Vista	4.8	2.4
Southern San Diego County		
Barrio Logan[a]	4.4	2.5
East San Diego	4.4	2.9
San Ysidro	4.0	2.5
San Diego County	4.1	2.4

Source: U.S. Census of Population and Housing, 2000.

[a] Barrio Logan has a very high number of persons per household in tract 51, probably due to the presence of homeless shelters in the area.

---

[4] Interview with Jerry Van Leeuwen, City of Escondido, October 28, 2003.

Residential crowding can also be attributed in part to the fact that members of the Hispanic population tend to have less money to devote to housing; their incomes are lower, and many remit significant amounts to their families in their communities of origin, further reducing their expendable funds. Table 3.6 presents median annual household incomes for 1999 for the areas we studied. The median annual income in Hispanic households in portions of North County ($35,000–$39,000) was between 80 and 85 percent of the area's overall median income, even though North County Hispanic incomes exceeded the median for Hispanic households county-wide. Even though the cities in North County are not the wealthiest in San Diego County (their median incomes are below the county average), the county's central and southern neighborhoods are much poorer. Hispanic households in these areas have median incomes ($22,000–$24,000) that are only two-thirds of the median household income for all Hispanics in the county ($35,000) and less than half the overall county median income of $47,000.

Table 3.6. Median Annual Household Incomes in San Diego County, 1999

Community	Median Income, All Households (US$)	Median Income, Hispanic Households (US$)	Hispanic Households' Median Income as Percent of All Households' Median Income
Northern San Diego County			
Escondido	42,567	34,642	81%
Oceanside	46,301	39,449	85
San Marcos	45,908	39,124	85
Vista	45,594	36,599	80
Southern San Diego County			
Barrio Logan	20,858	22,493	108
East San Diego	24,952	23,749	95
San Ysidro	25,729	22,561	88
San Diego County	47,067	34,632	74

Source: U.S. Census of Population and Housing, 2000.
Note: The census misses many recent undocumented immigrants, who likely have lower incomes.

Table 3.7. Median Rents in San Diego County, 2000

Community	All Households		Hispanic Households		Median Hispanic Rent as Percent of Median Rent for All Households
	Median Rent (US$)	Rent as Percent of County Median	Median Rent (US$)	Rent as Percent of County Median	
Northern San Diego County					
Escondido	746	98%	711	106%	95%
Oceanside	818	107	754	113	92
San Marcos	797	105	737	110	92
Vista	788	104	739	111	94
Southern San Diego County					
Barrio Logan	538	71	551	82	102
East San Diego	620	81	586	88	94
San Ysidro	563	74	557	83	99
San Diego County	761	100	668	100	88

Source: U.S. Census of Population and Housing, 2000.

Because Hispanic households are larger, per capita incomes for Hispanics are lower. On average, per capita income among Hispanics in San Diego County was only 52 percent of that for non-Hispanics in 1999. Of course, this is an average and hence is subject to the effect of the very high incomes among some groups of the non-Hispanic population. Figure 3.4 maps 1999 per capita income by census tract. Again, apart from the military bases, the low per capita income tracts conform fairly closely to the maps of the Latino population, with San Ysidro, Barrio Logan, East San Diego, and North County all represented.

Lower household incomes make it much more difficult for Latinos to pay San Diego's high housing costs. Table 3.7 shows median household rents in 2000. North County rents are generally above the county median, while rents in the southern portions of the county are considerably below the median. Hispanics pay between 92 and 95 percent of the median rent in North County, an area of relatively expensive housing.

Some Conclusions from the Census Data

Barrio Logan is the most crowded of the areas we studied. It also has the highest share of linguistically isolated households (only Spanish spoken at home) and the lowest rents and incomes. Interestingly, Hispanics are not the poorest group in Barrio Logan; the neighborhood's African, African American, and homeless populations are poorer.

East San Diego showed the greatest increase in residential crowding (45 percent), which corresponds with relatively low incomes and a rapid rise in the size of the Hispanic population. East San Diego neighborhoods are becoming increasingly Hispanic as non-Hispanic households leave the area.

San Ysidro does indeed seem a part of Tijuana, as the residents claim. It is now about 90 percent Latino, with almost all of these households speaking Spanish at home. Non-Hispanics are moving out. Incomes and rents are low, exceeding only those found in Barrio Logan.

North County cities are considerably wealthier, even though their median incomes are below the county average. Hispanics residing in North County have median incomes that are more than 50 percent higher than those in the county's southern neighborhoods, but rents are higher by about 40 percent. Hispanics account for a much smaller share of the population in North County (35 percent) than in other areas of the county, and they suffer less residential crowding on average than do Hispanics in the southern reaches of San Diego County. However, if we could segregate recent Oaxacan immigrants, this subgroup would display higher residential crowding and much lower incomes.

Finally, despite the difficult situation that recent immigrants encounter in San Diego County, the area's Hispanic population is increasing rapidly, surpassing the rate statewide, and Hispanics constitute a growing share of the county's total population, rising from 20 percent in 1990 to 27 percent in 2000. Projections suggest that Hispanics will account for about a third of the county's total population by the end of this decade.

IMMIGRANT LIFE IN SELECTED SAN DIEGO COMMUNITIES

The Border Patrol is highly visible throughout San Diego. They monitor checkpoints on major freeways and minor roads along the county's northern borders with Orange and Riverside counties, as well as entrances into the county from the east. These checkpoints, which were reportedly established to stop drug traffickers, now constitute a "second border" to U.S. entry for undocumented and pseudo-documented immigrants.[5] Moving northward out of the border region requires navigating or skirting these secondary border checkpoints, an exercise that dissuades undocumented migrants from taking casual trips outside of San Diego County.

Deportation sweeps by the Border Patrol in San Diego communities with high concentrations of Latino families are commonplace, and fear of the *migra* strongly affects work and leisure activities. Some migrant families reported in June 2004 that they were afraid to pick up their children from school because Border Patrol agents were stationed there to detain suspected undocumented immigrants. Fear of the Border Patrol also discourages people from leaving their homes for shopping

---

[5] "Pseudo-documented" refers to immigrants whose application for legal status remains in limbo due to the long wait, sometimes up to fifteen years, for a work visa.

or appointments (Wilson, Reza, and Murillo 2004; Chávez and Renaud 2004; *Los Angeles Times* 2004). Mexican immigrants who live on Indian reservations within San Diego County report that Border Patrol agents sometimes position themselves just beyond the reservation boundaries, waiting for the migrants to leave this protected area. And frequent raids on public busses discourage undocumented immigrants from using public transportation.[6] Thus the region's immigrants navigate an environment that is sometimes violent in its efforts to control undocumented immigration.

Undocumented immigration is so entrenched in San Diego County that it even shapes the lives of the region's youths. In Vista, for example, school-aged Latino children play "Migra" (a kind of "tag") on the school playground, selecting one child as the "Border Patrol agent" while the others pretend to go about their activities as usual. Suddenly someone yells "Migra!" and the chase begins. In a less benign reflection of the impacts of immigration on local youths, in 2000 on the other side of the county, eight young people from the upscale community of Rancho Peñasquitos chased down, assaulted, robbed, and shot five Mexican immigrants living in a nearby migrant camp. Such "sport" has been "played" for years and is one more symptom of the region's virulently anti-immigrant environment.

Our focus groups and interviews concentrated on the challenges new immigrants encounter in the three regions of San Diego County with regard to the key areas of health care, housing, and civic participation. The narratives that emerged do not support the popular perception that immigrants want to take advantage of public welfare systems, as claimed by immigration's opponents. To the contrary, the most common narrative is one of hope—hope that immigrants can move out of poverty and build a better life, especially for their children. Their top priority in the decision to migrate was their children's well-being, for which they are willing to work hard and make sacrifices. These families' resiliency and determination—expressed through their willingness

---

6 Pedro Mojica, a participant at the Ties That Bind conference, noted that immigrants avoid the Escondido-Oceanside express bus because of the frequent Border Patrol raids. Instead, they use the local bus, which adds hours to their journey.

to leave their home country and endure a long and difficult adjustment in the United States—far overshadowed any indication that they view themselves as public charges, welfare recipients, or burdens on the system. Immigrants stressed their desire to *salir adelante*. In all of the San Diego communities studied, this desire to get ahead was the continuing thread woven throughout the immigrants' narratives.

Health Services

The Council of Community Clinics (CCC) is an umbrella organization that provides support to a network of clinics in San Diego and Imperial counties. According to the CCC, San Diego County spends the least of all California counties on health care for uninsured residents. Although it has one of the highest rates of uninsured residents nationwide (27 percent of people below 65 years of age), San Diego County spends only $73 per uninsured resident yearly. In comparison, Alameda County spends $375 per uninsured resident, and Los Angeles County, $281 (CCC Web site, 2004).

Because San Diego has no county-operated hospital or clinical health-care system, the county's uninsured and underserved communities must rely on community health centers for essential public health services, including immunizations, TB screening, HIV/AIDS and STD testing, and so on (CCC Web site, 2004). Private, nonprofit community health centers are dispersed throughout the county. Their operating budgets depend on federal grants and funds, especially Medi-Cal (California's Medicaid program) reimbursements and outside grants. These private clinics often bear the cost of providing public health services for the uninsured; the Council of Community Clinics reports that one-fourth of the care provided at these health care centers is uncompensated, an economic reality that decisively shapes their structure and operation:

> San Diego does not have a county health system. Instead, the County contracts with the private nonprofit community health centers as the sole providers of comprehensive primary health care services to the low-income and uninsured adults, children and families.... San Diego's net-

work of community health centers is one of the largest and most organized nonprofit community clinics systems in the United States. Working together since 1975, the community clinics have the expertise and the leadership to succeed in managed care. San Diego's community health centers have a large Medi-Cal managed care population. Collectively, San Diego clinics provide care to more than 56,000 Medi-Cal managed care lives. This represents almost of a third of the total Medi-Cal population in the county. Medi-Cal accounts for 42% of the total payments to community health centers (CCC Web site, 2004).

Navigating San Diego's complex health system is a challenge for new immigrants. Participants in the focus groups cited cost as the major barrier to health and counseling services. Were it not for various free or low-cost health services, women participants in the focus groups noted, they would have no access to health care when it was needed. Referring to the clinics' sliding-scale payment system, one community resident noted, "For the administrators, $30 is not a lot of money, but for us it is."

Many community residents expressed dissatisfaction with the community clinics, objecting in particular to the long waits, which sometimes mean that workers miss an entire day of work. Mothers, constrained by their children's school schedules, are particularly frustrated by the waits. According to one participant:

> You usually have to wait four hours. Then you get inside and wait for the doctor; you almost fall asleep. They take tests and ask questions. Then someone else asks questions. In the end, they just give you a Tylenol.

Another participant added; "You wait so long that by the time the doctor comes, you aren't in pain anymore!" One woman, who feared she was having a miscarriage, waited for two hours in an emergency room to see a doctor, all the while bleeding vaginally. By the time the doctor was available, the bleeding had stopped. The doctor did a brief examination, told her she was fine, and sent her home. She later received a bill for $1,400 for the visit.[7]

Martínez (2005) found that families were often unaware of the sliding-scale payment option at the local community clinics and opted instead to take day trips to Tijuana to access health and other services, but this option is limited to individuals with documents. Others rely on social networks to bring medicines from Tijuana. And some small stores in North County sell prescription medications to the community, such as injections that are available in Tijuana.

The focus revealed that men's experiences with the community clinics were overwhelmingly negative. They were embarrassed to tell a (usually female) medical assistant the reason for the visit, whether this happened over the phone or face to face. They prefer the more flexible health-care system available in Tijuana, where they found it easier to receive attention, get prescription medications, and see specialists. The Mexican system of private doctors was also preferred for surgeries, because it is seen as easier to navigate than the U.S. system, which requires referrals and insurance approvals.

Language barriers are another concern in the delivery of health services, especially for immigrant women. Doctors who do not speak Spanish and/or do not wait to get an accurate translation of patients' complaints often prescribe ineffective or inappropriate treatments. An English-only doctor had prescribed an inappropriate medication for one focus group participant who complained of chronic headaches. The medication produced a whole set of negative side effects and did nothing to relieve her pain. Some time later, this woman sought care from a Spanish-speaking doctor and learned that, because of communication problems, the previous doctor had prescribed a medication she did not need. The lack of Spanish-language interpreters and physicians can be especially alarming if patients feel they are deliberately being kept uninformed about their health status.

---

[7] A new California law requires all hospitals to reveal for the first time what they charge for services. Though the government and insurers have discounts on these prices, it turns out that walk-ins without insurance are charged exorbitant "rack rates," prices that are set high with an eye to discounting them for insurance. Many immigrants without any knowledge of the system spend years trying to pay such bills (*Wall Street Journal*, December 27, 2004).

Language problems also hinder communication between the immigrant community and clinical staff. In some health-care settings in San Diego County, the staff's Spanish language skills are so limited that they rely on translators from the local telephone company to communicate with patients. Even when clinics have Spanish-speaking front office staff, informants report that these workers are generally unfriendly and treat them like second-class citizens. The immigrants assume this happens because they are poor; they note that clinic staffers act as if these clients should show gratitude for the services they receive. One informant noted, "Often they don't even say good morning or good afternoon."

In North County, where there are large concentrations of new immigrants from indigenous populations in southern Mexico, health and social service agencies are suddenly finding themselves dealing with a population that may not speak Spanish. These agencies are among the first to admit that they have been slow to adapt their services for immigrants, especially farmworkers, to the changing demographics of the Latino population. According to one administrator:

> We are only now beginning to realize that when we used to arrive at a migrant camp and tried to recruit patients, that we might not have been communicating effectively. We didn't know then that most of the camp residents might have spoken an indigenous Mexican language like Mixtec or Trique.

One case in particular illustrates the life-and-death consequences of the barriers to health services for recent immigrants in San Diego County. The death of Lucía's five-year-old son forever altered her view of the health-care system in San Diego's North County. "They let my son die," she stated; "I hate the clinic and I hate the hospital." After being denied an urgent appointment at a local community clinic, she rushed her son, who had chicken pox and was bleeding from his nose and mouth, to the hospital. "They undressed him and gave him Tylenol," and he lay there all night shivering with cold. She could only watch and wait. In the morning the hospital discharged him and said the doctor couldn't see him until the next day. Lucía asked for an interpreter, a doctor, anyone who could communicate with her in Spanish, but to no avail. Her son later died at home; the autopsy results attributed his death to the hospital's failure to provide medication. "How he suffered," Lucía said; "he was in pain for three days, and they didn't give him any medicine!" After the autopsy, she told the doctor, "I gave my son all the love I could; I'm so angry that you let him die!" Lucia attributes the death of her son to poverty, the lack of interpreters, and racism. "Because I had no money, my son got sicker, all because of a lack of money. They say that money corrupts, but at least it gives you options."

Housing

San Diego's housing market is one of the most expensive in the United States. Only a fraction of the region's households can afford to purchase a house, and most immigrants focus on finding affordable apartments to rent. With little chance to buy a home in the United States, immigrants shift their hopes for home ownership to Mexico. Several participants in the San Ysidro focus group own property in Tijuana, even though most are long-term residents in the United States and the majority rent homes from a local housing program. In the Barrio Logan focus group, rent was identified as the residents' biggest expenditure: "First you pay your rent, then you eat."

Most new immigrants concentrate in areas with plentiful rental housing, which local officials view as de facto low-income housing. These areas become immigrant barrios (see figure 3.2 for the census tracts where immigrants cluster), where many individuals share a single unit in order to reduce their housing costs. These crowded living conditions—with many people sharing a single bedroom, bathroom, and kitchen—contribute to the health problems among this population.

Residential crowding impacts quality of life in these neighborhoods. It often means more vehicular traffic, crowding in schools, more intensive use of public facilities and utilities, and deleterious effects on immigrants' physical and mental health. Although many apartment buildings where immigrants live appear well-maintained on the outside, owners allow them to deteriorate on the inside, knowing that undocumented immigrants will not complain to a building inspector. Immigrant tenants also fear retaliation by apartment owners and managers who could enforce the rules against overcrowding if residents complained about their living conditions.

There have been multiple attempts to create affordable housing in various areas within San Diego County, but with meager results, especially when compared to escalating demand. Because of the prevailing view of apartments as low-income housing, there is substantial political resistance to building more such units. Nevertheless, local jurisdictions are trying to build new apartment projects, which, unlike renovations of old apartments, receive financial support from the state and federal governments.[8] Escondido, for example, constructed nearly 500 low-income housing units over the past decade,[9] and Oceanside has a good record in this area as well. But other cities, such as San Marcos, have done little, contributing to the shortage of housing for new immigrants.

In view of the housing shortage, many immigrants opt to settle in informal migrant camps, a pattern with a long history in San Diego County.[10] Camp residents construct makeshift dwellings of wood and cardboard, and insulate them with nylon tarps to protect them from the elements. Most current camp residents (perhaps as many as 95 percent) are indigenous Mexican men who work as agricultural and day laborers. Many are Mixtecos from Oaxaca, and camps often include a number of migrants from the same family or hometown.[11] Our interviews revealed that migrants, who frequently lack any means of transportation, often choose to live in the camps in order to be close to the fields where they work. Others simply do not have enough money to pay rent, underscoring the need to provide housing for poor farmworkers.

Leo Chávez (1992) has provided a detailed look at a migrant camp in Carlsbad, where he found Mixtec men, women, and children living in very unhygienic conditions in the canyons of North County. The local growers with whom he spoke were unconcerned about their

---

[8] Interview with Oceanside City Council member, October 30, 2003.

[9] Interview with Jerry Van Leeuwen, City of Escondido, October 28, 2003.

[10] Eisenstadt and Thorup (1994) document a period of acute popular concern about the migrant camps, when many camps were razed by local enforcement officials.

[11] As noted in the discussion of health services for this population, the demographic shift to a largely indigenous population has also introduced new complications for outreach in the area of housing.

workers' living conditions, even though these posed a serious health risk to the workers. According to the employers: "They choose to live this way. We know of some workers who live in regular housing, but these [other] people are trying to save money to send to families in Mexico so they live this way" (Chávez 1992: 76).

Because migrant camps are now smaller, more scattered, and better hidden than in the past, many local officials and residents believe they have disappeared. It is difficult to estimate with precision the numbers of migrants currently living in San Diego's hidden camps. Eisenstadt and Thorup (1994) calculated that there were some 200 such camps in the early 1990s, with about 30,000 inhabitants. Estimates from the Regional Task Force on the Homeless in 2004 suggested a number between 100 and 150 camps housing some 7,000 inhabitants. Even though the 1994 estimate may have overstated the size of this population, the advance of urbanization in North County since the early 1990s has decreased the amount of open land, suggesting that the number of suitable locations in which to establish a migrant camp is much reduced.

Life in the camps underscores the disparities in income, resources, and health between residents of "America's Finest City" and its thousands of homeless agricultural workers and day laborers. Migrants must contend with the forces of nature, especially when winter rains fall from November to January. However, these residents are subjected to less visible assaults as well. Because today's camp residents are primarily unaccompanied men (unlike the situation in the 1990s, when Chávez found entire nuclear families living in the camps), they suffer the depression that comes with separation from family. Their undocumented status makes them highly vulnerable and decreases the likelihood that they will seek out services and goods from local businesses, depending instead for food and water on the lunch trucks that cater to migrant workers. Fear of the *migra* limits daily life to the workplace and to the paths that connect the camps with the fields and pickup locations for day laborers.

In focus groups conducted in the camps, residents spoke of their disconnectedness with the world outside. One of them called the United States a prison because of the intimidation and exploitation he suffers at work and his constant fear of losing his job—despite the fact that he has documents. The migrants' sense of a lack of freedom was reiterated across the focus groups. "To be trapped, to have no freedom, this makes me sad; my children cannot go outside to play," said one female informant. Many resent the fact that, even though they are better off financially in San Diego, they still have no sense of home and ownership. "Having this money is an illusion. Nothing here is ours, the beautiful clothes, nothing," stated one older man. Life in the camps is also alienating for migrants who miss the support that family provides, further exacerbating their sense of a lack of freedom. According to another camp resident, "We are family people; we have uncles and brothers back home. When we come here, we are alone. We no longer have that unity, and we are not very social with others. Everyone is defensive. I think if we could help each other, like a big family, we would feel free."

The economic imperative, however, overrides the negative aspects of living in migrant camps. According to one camp resident, "Our poverty puts us here; otherwise we would not be here." Another noted, "We are sad because we left our family back home, but now we work in order to send money back home."

Providing farmworker housing is a particularly controversial issue in the coastal community of Carlsbad, one of the largest agricultural zones in San Diego County. Unlike other North County cities, which experienced large increases in their Latino communities between 1990 and 2000, Carlsbad's Latino community contracted by 2 percent as urbanization caused land to be taken out of agriculture. Nevertheless, the city still retains its famous flower and strawberry fields, which require a large seasonal labor supply. This has produced a situation in which gentrified urban neighborhoods exist shoulder to shoulder with migrant camps housing hundreds of farmworkers and day laborers. Each year the city razes the migrant camps for reasons of "public safety." This demolition takes place each February, at the end of the strawberry season but while there are still a large number of farmworkers in the camps. The groups that have come together to oppose the destruction now joke with grim humor that their protests have also become an "annual event," just like harvest season.

Among the groups petitioning the Carlsbad City Council to address the need for farmworker housing are the Ecumenical Migrant Outreach Program, the American Friends Service Committee, and California

Rural Legal Assistance; and they have recently joined forces in these efforts with local leaders of the Oaxacan Indigenous Binational Front (FIOB). Under intense pressure from these farmworker advocates and after hearing testimony from various agency representatives attesting to the urgent need for migrant worker housing, the Carlsbad City Council voted in February 2003 to spend $25,000 to study the possibility of constructing such housing in the city, though the resolution did not pass without opposition. One council member who opposed it noted that he had seen worse living conditions in Mexico, and another objected because he preferred to spend the money on "building the housing rather than studying it."

The study results were reported months later at a city council meeting, at which housing supporters waged a full-scale lobbying campaign. They spoke of the environmental benefits of farmworker housing. In response, the council noted that local agriculture was waning and hence the need for farmworker housing would disappear within ten years. Nevertheless, the city did agree to sign a letter of support for farmworker housing, and the activists deemed that their efforts had produced a positive outcome. Ultimately, however, the group that had applied for funding to construct a farmworker housing project did not receive the monies. Although local activists continue their struggle with the city council to ensure full support for farmworker housing in the future, they are not overly optimistic.

In the meantime, several groups continue their outreach efforts to the men living in the migrant camps. Among them are local clinics, a few nonprofit agencies that provide emergency supplies, and activist church groups that have long had a presence in the camps, including a local Catholic church which offers weekly mass in a camp near Del Mar.

Civic Participation

Given the public hostility toward undocumented immigrants in many parts of San Diego, the constant threat of apprehension by the Border Patrol, and the challenges migrants face in housing and health care, it is not surprising that recent immigrants have a low level of civic participation. Latino political representation is so low in areas of San Diego County that the community of Vista came under a federal voting rights probe, a case that could have been leveled against virtually any community in North County.[12]

Many factors work against civic participation in San Diego more generally. For one, the county encompasses a wide range of very different communities. Roberta Alexander, a local college instructor, noted, "I don't see San Diego as a cohesive city but as a bunch of enclaves, each with its own culture; and those cultures don't necessarily communicate with one another." According to Binh Hue Truong, a Vietnamese refugee, "we have one of the most multicultural populations, and yet it hasn't managed to reach our representation in power." Labor leader Mary Grillo put it as follows: "San Diego is ... more focused on enjoying life than it is on political activism.... There's a total obliviousness to how working people live." And according to Donald Cohen, another labor leader, "San Diego is ... not just conservative, it's like it's on another planet.... America is a relatively apolitical place ... and San Diego is even more so."[13]

This overarching context feeds into the anti-immigrant sentiments in San Diego County. At the conference that gave rise to this volume, Brad Wiscons noted, "political leadership is poor. They are confused about the problems; they claim they want to do things but then they implement contradictory policies." Rocky Chávez, a member of the Oceanside City Council, added that they lacked leadership: "The people lack the expertise and education to talk about migration." He also noted that North County cities do not cooperate much. Indeed, the political leaders we interviewed often had little knowledge of efforts in neighboring cities.

The immigrants in our focus groups expressed frustration with the gulf that separates them from local decision making. San Ysidro residents, for example, felt that they were invisible in local politics and community programs, and that local leaders did not understand or represent their issues. At the same time, focus group participants knew little about local leaders; even when they recognized one by name, they

---

[12] The probe found no wrongdoing, given the fact that many of the region's immigrants are not U.S. citizens, or even in the country legally, and thus are not entitled to local political representation.

[13] Quotations from Mayhew 2003.

distrusted his or her intentions and affirmed that politicians only sought them out at election time. Nor could focus group participants identify organizations that supposedly represent their interests in civic affairs.

There are exceptions, however, such as the mothers in Barrio Logan who became involved in local parent-teacher associations. Their participation highlights the importance of child-related issues as an area where migrants are more likely to get involved. Immigrant parents often feel they lose control over their children in the United States. Parents in our focus groups stated that they feel they lose a part of their child when the child learns English, because that child can now navigate areas that are alien to their parents. Parents also feel that children have too much freedom in the United States. One participant recounted visiting his aunt when he returned to his hometown in Oaxaca. He asked her where her son was working in the United States, and she answered, "He works at the Cholos Company," unaware that *cholo* is the term for a Latino gang member.

Parents also worry that their children are receiving a second-class education in the United States, something that focus group participants in San Ysidro attribute to racism. At the same time, these parents are poorly situated to satisfy the schools' many requirements. Mothers are especially pressured to help their children with homework and to attend school events; and even though they are supportive of school programs such as the drug-awareness activities, they often feel overwhelmed by the schools' demands. Many parents conceded that economic and job pressures prevented them from playing a more involved role in their child's education and school activities.

Nevertheless, their children's education continues to be a primary focus of immigrant parents, who want their children to stay in school and not be forced into the workforce early, as they had been. Women in the focus groups all hoped their children could attend college, acknowledging that to do so, the children would need financial support and immigration documents, two of the many barriers that Mexican immigrant families are struggling to overcome.

Participants were generally encouraged by some local agencies' efforts to identify and organize around issues that are important to immigrants. Family Health Clinic in Barrio Logan, Casa Familiar in San Ysidro, Vista Townsite Community Partners, and community centers in Oceanside and Escondido are among the groups making significant efforts to reach the immigrant community and gain its trust.

COMMUNITY SOLUTIONS

The immigrant community itself is the source of many suggestions and potential solutions for improving the well-being of recent Mexican immigrants in San Diego County. Its members point first to the need for legalization in the United States. As long as this large group of workers and their families remains in an illegal status, it will be very difficult to address the other problems that affect them.

Participants also called for improved relations between local authorities and schools, on the one hand, and the immigrant community, on the other. This, they felt, was key to resolving the multiple issues migrants face in health, housing, and civic participation. Improving the relationship is contingent on agencies refocusing their outreach to the immigrant community. With regard to health and other services, participants asked for easier accessibility and better delivery. Flyers and other such symbolic outreach efforts do little to link community members to needed services. Suggesting how outreach efforts could be improved, one interviewee said it was a matter of "quality, not quantity: quality education, quality health information, quality housing."

To achieve meaningful contact with recent immigrants, agencies must approach them where they live, and not wait for this community to come to them to access their services. One focus group participant expressed pessimism that agencies will ever take the steps needed to break down the barriers between agency and community: "They are never going to come to us.... They will never arrive and say, 'you need this' or 'this will help you.' Never!" This recent immigrant was expressing what so many others have noted—a deep lack of respect for them as human beings. "I have rights," another noted; "even if I don't earn much money, I help bring food to your tables, and because I am a person living in this society, they should listen to me—at least listen."

CONCLUSIONS AND RECOMMENDATIONS

Recent Mexican immigrants in San Diego are marginalized, excluded from housing, health services, and civic activities. This exclusion is a source of anxiety for new immigrants and gives them a sense of disconnectedness. New immigrants respond by activating kinship networks to reduce what they describe as the "sadness" of their situation. Most hold to the hope of "getting ahead" and improving their lives through hard work, educating their children, and moving out of poverty. Many, though not all, are optimistic that local agencies and decision makers will reach out to understand them and improve their lives. This important step will not be possible, however, without first critically examining the way that institutions are working (or not working) with new immigrant communities.

It will be difficult to resolve the problems associated with recent immigrants locally without a change in federal immigration policy. Their undocumented status causes recent immigrants to hide from authorities, effectively denying them access to a wide array of government programs developed to assist low-wage workers. Legalization of this labor force would also make cross-border solutions more feasible. For example, housing shortages would be less acute if these workers could live in Tijuana and commute to work in San Diego County. And these immigrants would prefer to access health services in Tijuana if only their undocumented status did not prevent them from crossing the border. Meanwhile, until service delivery in Tijuana becomes a feasible option, there will have to be better efforts to offer services in San Diego.

There is need for ongoing coordination among agencies and stakeholders, as opposed to the current situation of intermittent collaboration and coordination driven by agencies' funding situations. That is, when specific projects are funded—such as the Migrant Services Project supported in 1991 by the U.S. Department of Health and Human Services, or a similar effort by the California Endowment and another by a low-income housing group—collaboration occurs but it is strictly project-oriented and does not spur a rational division of labor or a shared knowledge of best-practices solutions.

The success of agency programs, as, for example, in health-care delivery, should no longer be measured in terms of the numbers reached but rather in terms of the level of community involvement. Most agencies, especially clinics, could benefit by restructuring their outreach efforts to include going into the community, going to homes in immigrant neighborhoods, and going to the cardboard shacks in migrant camps.

Agencies need a mechanism for accessing information about recent immigrants, including their networks, origins, hometown associations, and cultural norms. Local politicians, service providers, and U.S.-born informants in our study were woefully ignorant of basic facts about the migrant population. Such information could be made available on an ongoing basis by local universities or by the San Diego Association of Governments (SANDAG).

Immigrants need more information, and they need it in a form that is culturally and linguistically appropriate and to which they themselves can have input. Recent immigrants do not know about many available resources, and even when they do gain some access to services, they are often lost in the maze of agency complexity and bureaucracy. Although most immigrants do not use government services, such services are crucial for families with children, who have a compelling need for such information.

Efforts are needed to promote immigrants' civic participation at every level. No immigrant leadership structure has yet emerged, and our focus groups do not believe that other organizations represent their interests. Hometown associations and migrant networks, whose communication channels and resources transcend the border, show great potential for encouraging civic participation among new immigrants in San Diego County.

Resolving the many problems facing recent immigrants will require a long-term commitment by local government and health and social service agencies. There are structural barriers to immigrants' access to services and their participation in their host communities, making it inaccurate to blame immigrants for their low economic and political status and their poor health and educational outcomes. We urge agencies and government bodies to reassess the structures and methods through which they interact with the immigrant community. The key to finding solutions to the complex issues and challenges surrounding the immigrant population is the immigrant community itself. Throughout our study, we were inspired by the power of this community to make the best of a difficult situation and by their persisting desire to *salir adelante*. The immigrant community must be an integral part of any political and social process that has an impact on their lives and well-being.

References

Chávez, Leo. 1992. *Shadowed Lives: Undocumented Immigrants in American Society*. Fort Worth, Tex.: Harcourt Brace Jovanovich.

Chávez, Stephanie, and Jean Paul Renaud. 2004. "Reports Spark Fear in Neighborhoods," *Los Angeles Times*, June 12.

Cornelius, Wayne A. 2005. "Border Enforcement and the Hispanic Community." Presented at the conference "Immigration and U.S. Citizenship in an Era of Homeland Security," Tomás Rivera Policy Institute, Los Angeles, March 31.

Eisenstadt, Todd A., and Cathryn L. Thorup. 1994. *Caring Capacity versus Carrying Capacity: Community Responses to Mexican Immigration in San Diego's North County*. La Jolla: Center for U.S.-Mexican Studies, University of California, San Diego.

Kelly, David. 2004. "A Hospital on Border Going Over the Edge," *Los Angeles Times*, June 20.

Los Angeles Times. 2004. "Sowing Fear among Latinos," editorial, June 23.

Martínez, Konane. 2005. "Health across Borders: Mixtec Transnational Communities and Health Care Systems." PhD dissertation, University of California, Riverside.

Massey, Douglas S., Jorge Durand, and Nolan J. Malone. 2002. *Beyond Smoke and Mirrors: Mexican Immigration in an Era of Economic Integration*. New York: Sage Foundation.

Mayhew, Kelly. 2003. "Life in Vacationland: The 'Other' San Diego." In *Under the Perfect Sun: The San Diego Tourists Never See*, by Mike Davis, Kelly Mayhew, and Jim Miller. New York: New Press.

Wilson, Janet, H.G. Reza, and Sandra Murillo. 2004. "Immigration Arrests not Policy Shift," *Los Angeles Times*, June 11.

Part II

Cross-Border Interactions

4

Mexican Migration Flows in Tijuana–San Diego in a Context of Economic Uncertainty

Rafael Alarcón

Tijuana, Baja California, and San Diego, California, share the busiest international border in the world and play a key role in the global economy. Tijuana is home to important *maquiladoras*[1] like Sony, Samsung, and Panasonic, leading to the city's sobriquet as the "world capital of the television-set industry." And San Diego, whose economy formerly relied on defense-related industries and the presence of the military, has become a key region in the United States for the biotechnology and telecommunications industries.

Together, these cities form a "transfrontier metropolis" in which a growing network of activity systems integrates the populations from both sides of the border through labor, shopping, tourism, education, and family. Similarly, elements of the natural habitat—air, water, flora,

This research was funded by a grant from the International Community Foundation. I appreciate the comments and suggestions from Christopher Woodruff, María Eugenia Anguiano, Luis Escala, Jorge Santibáñez, and Germán Vega on an earlier version of this essay. I am responsible for any errors that might remain. I also thank Francisco Alarcón for assistance in translating this chapter into English, and Francisco Barraza, Carmen Martínez, and Manuel Tapia for research assistance.

[1] Maquiladoras are in-bond assembly plants that assemble goods for export.

and fauna—function without regard for the international border (Herzog 1990: 140).

Immigration has been a key feature of this region. In 2000, this binational metropolis reached more than 4 million residents. San Diego County was home to 2.8 million (70 percent of the regional total); the remaining 1.2 million (30 percent) resided in the municipality of Tijuana. Between 1990 and 2000, Tijuana accounted for most of the region's population growth, contributing nearly half a million people (463,439), while San Diego County added 315,817 new residents. Many of the region's residents are involved in intense transborder activities (see Anguiano, this volume). While most San Diegans have free movement in San Diego and Tijuana, a smaller portion of Tijuana residents have the legal documentation required to take full advantage of the opportunities that this cross-border metropolis offers.

This chapter examines the sociodemographic characteristics of Mexican migratory flows drawn to the Tijuana–San Diego region from other parts of Mexico. It compares two migrant flows between 1993 and 2001, a period of uncertainty caused by economic problems in both nations and by two developments in U.S. immigration policy—the waning impacts of the Immigration Reform and Control Act of 1986 (IRCA) and stepped-up border enforcement beginning in late 1993.

The chapter examines data from the Survey of Migration at Mexico's Northern Border (EMIF) to discern patterns in two flows of Mexican migrants: (1) migrants heading to Tijuana from Mexico's interior, whose main destination is either Tijuana or the United States; and (2) migrants who have spent at least a month in San Diego County and were interviewed in border cities when reentering Mexico. The analysis focuses on migrants' sociodemographic characteristics, social networks, work experience, immigration status, and region of origin in Mexico.

The chapter contains five sections. The first presents the data and methodology used in the analysis. The second provides an overview of the economic transformation of the Tijuana–San Diego region and key U.S. immigration policy initiatives implemented between the early 1990s and 2003. The third uses EMIF data to explore sociodemographic characteristics and region of origin of migrants arriving in Tijuana with the intention of remaining there or continuing on to the United States. The fourth section draws on EMIF data to discern the sociodemographic characteristics, immigration status, work experience, and region of origin of migrants who have lived and worked in San Diego County. The final section discusses some important findings and conclusions.

DATA AND METHODOLOGY

The Survey of Migration at Mexico's Northern Border is an ongoing project of El Colegio de la Frontera Norte and other Mexican government agencies. It began in 1993 as an attempt to estimate and characterize migration flows between Mexico and the United States (in both directions), as well as the flows of migrants coming from the interior and heading to cities in Mexico's northern border area.[2] The EMIF employs techniques used in other disciplines to measure temporary, seasonal, or cyclical movements, drawing an implicit analogy between migratory flows that communicate regions of two countries, on the one hand, and the movement of objects by water currents, on the other. In this sense, border cities with international migratory movements become statistical observatories. Migrant flows that cross the border at a given point and given time must pass through a narrow opening of some sort, like the door in a bus terminal. This fact enables researchers to make an accurate count of migrants at one specific moment, and the application of questionnaires to these migrants can expand our knowledge to include their sociodemographic characteristics.[3]

The EMIF began in March 1993 in twenty-three cities; in the second phase (1994), this number was reduced to the eight cities that had been found in the first year to concentrate 94 percent of the migration flow (Tijuana, Mexicali, Nogales, Ciudad Juárez, Piedras Negras, Nuevo Laredo, Reynosa, and Matamoros) (Santibáñez 1999: 45).[4] By 2001, seven research phases had been completed.

---

[2] This section summarizes the EMIF methodology as described in STPS et al. 2002.

[3] The weighting factors used in the EMIF are calculated for each questionnaire. The calculation is based on the weighting principle of a multi-staged random system that associates a weighting factor with each stage. These stages refer to geographic and time-related dimensions.

[4] The EMIF sample design generates few cases; for the purposes of clarification, numbers in tables corresponding to fewer than thirty observations are set in italics.

In effect, the EMIF is a combination of four surveys that examine: (1) migratory flows from the interior of Mexico to northern border cities; (2) migratory flows from the United States into Mexico; (3) migratory flows from Mexico's northern border cities south into the interior; and (4) migrants deported to Mexico by the U.S. Border Patrol. This chapter draws data from the first two components.

People migrating from the Mexican interior to the border are interviewed in airports, bus terminals, and train stations. These migrants typically are at least 12 years old, were not born in the United States, and are not residents of either the United States or the border city. They are motivated by a number of considerations: employment, business, change of residency, tourism, study, and visits with family or friends—or because they are in transit to the United States. These migrants do not have a set return date.

The second EMIF component—migrants moving from the United States into Mexico who are interviewed in airports, bus terminals, and train stations in Mexican border cities—are also at least 12 years old and were not born in the United States, and they are not residents of the city where the survey is conducted. Their stays of more than a month in the United States are explained by employment, business, change of residency (regardless of the duration of the visit), study, tourism, and visits with family and friends. Santibáñez (1999: 46) notes that the EMIF has a low level of representation of Mexican immigrants residing in the United States. Many of these immigrants do not return to Mexico, and many of those who return do not transit through border cities.

Like all surveys, the EMIF has limitations. The undocumented population is overrepresented because undocumented migrants arrive first to a Mexican city and then cross the border "on foot," making it possible to interview them in transportation hubs in cities on the Mexican side of the border. Documented persons, meanwhile, often travel by plane between a Mexican airport and a U.S. city, putting them outside the EMIF's purview.

ECONOMIC UNCERTAINTY AND U.S. IMMIGRATION POLICY

The economic transformation of Tijuana–San Diego and key U.S. immigration policy initiatives implemented between the early 1990s and

2003 have been crucial in shaping migration flows from Mexico to this region. In the early 1990s, researchers from San Diego State University and El Colegio de la Frontera Norte conducted joint research on this region and found that both cities had experienced rapid population and economic growth in the 1970s and 1980s that led to a deterioration in quality of life, environmental degradation, and virtual stagnation in living standards (Clement and Zepeda Miramontes 1993).

This growth built on San Diego's earlier post–World War II history, when this city was transformed into a major metropolitan area by the combination of a rapidly expanding economy (mostly defense-related) and rapid population growth fed by in-migration from other points in the United States. However, in mid-1993, as the rest of the U.S. economy was emerging from a recession, California's cities were still struggling. "Between mid-1990 and late 1992 over 53,000 jobs (approximately five percent of the labor force) were lost in San Diego County, mainly due to national recession, defense downsizing, financial restructuring, and the adverse state/local business climate" (Clement and Zepeda Miramontes 1993: 93).

In Tijuana, Clement and Zepeda Miramontes found that, although this city had undergone intense economic expansion in the 1970s and 1980s,[5] per capita income had stagnated in the 1980s. Even though maquiladoras, increasing transborder commerce, in-migration, and full employment spurred economic activity, these failed to translate into higher personal incomes. Economic development indicators demonstrated improvements in education and health, but also deterioration in environmental conditions and the availability of public services. Tijuana's main challenge in those years was "to create more jobs, increase the productivity of labor, and retain a higher proportion of the value added in the maquiladora sector" (Clement and Zepeda Miramontes 1993: 93).

Toward the end of the 1990s, James Curry (2000) found a sea change in the manufacturing base of the Tijuana–San Diego region, a change that brought economic recovery accompanied by employment growth. The rise of the technology-based "New Economy" in San Diego fueled

---

[5] Tijuana's economic expansion during the 1980s was at odds with the overall situation in Mexico at the time, which was one of profound economic crisis.

the growth of electronics manufacturing and related research and development activities. Biotechnology and wireless telecommunications became dominant sectors in San Diego. However, although manufacturing is an important component in these industries, most of the manufacturing associated with them was located outside of the San Diego region. Tijuana, meanwhile, was experiencing a manufacturing boom thanks to investments in consumer electronics manufacturing, predominantly by Asian television manufacturers and their suppliers. This investment was stimulated by the passage of the North American Free Trade Agreement (NAFTA) in 1993.

Curry argues that the same global forces are transforming San Diego and Tijuana, but in entirely different ways. San Diego is rapidly becoming an "information age" city, with growth in high technology, research and development, and services, and a concomitant decrease in the importance of manufacturing. In contrast, manufacturing is the key sector in Tijuana, and it has been fueled by foreign firms, mainly Asian, investing in labor-intensive processes.

According to a study by Marcelli, Baru, and Cohen (2000), the City of San Diego and the San Diego Economic Development Corporation targeted nine clusters as "economic drivers" for the San Diego region, and these were to receive public support for growth in the late 1990s. The nine "targeted industrial clusters" were: communications; biomedical; biotech and pharmaceuticals; computer and electronics manufacturing; defense and transportation manufacturing; software and computer services; business services; financial services; and environmental technology.

The rest of the economy was divided into "low-tech non-targeted industrial clusters" and "non-clustered industries." The low-tech non-targeted industrial clusters included visitor industry services, fruits and vegetables, horticulture, medical services, recreational goods manufacturing, and entertainment and amusement. The non-clustered industries comprised all remaining regional economic activity.

The study's findings showed that targeted cluster industries were growing, but the majority of jobs remained in non-targeted and non-clustered industries over 1990–1998. Targeted industry clusters accounted for only 18 percent of the region's workers. The employment patterns revealed a complex picture of the San Diego economy that called into question its definition as an "information age city":

> Employment in targeted and non-targeted industry clusters has increased from 32 to 42 percent of the total labor market between 1990 and 1998, yet the majority of the jobs remain in non-clustered industries.... Overall, from 1990 to 1998 job growth in non-targeted industry clusters, which added 71,079 new jobs, has exceeded job growth in targeted industry clusters, which added 36,794 new jobs. However, non-clustered industries lost 94,045 jobs (Marcelli, Baru, and Cohen 2000: x).

Between at least the mid-1980s and the end of 2000, the maquiladora-based manufacturing industry was one of the engines of regional employment and income growth in Baja California, with growth rates of 10 to 12 percent per year until its peak in October 2000 (Gerber and Carrillo 2002). In fact, between 1997 and 1998, while general manufacturing employment in Mexico grew 1.9 percent, it grew 12.3 percent in the maquiladora sector. Figures on employment and the number of plants reveal that the maquiladora industry in Tijuana grew steadily between 1990 and 2001 (Anguiano, this volume). However, in 2002 this export industry began to experience a slowdown. Maquiladora employment shrank from 1,348,000 in October 2000 to 1,097,700 in October 2002 (Carrillo and Gomis 2003: 320).

A report by the U.S. General Accounting Office (GAO 2003) notes that cyclical and structural factors have contributed to the decline in Mexico's maquiladora employment and production since 2000. The cyclical downturn in the U.S. economy has been a primary factor in the maquiladoras' decline, but increased competition within the U.S. market—particularly from China, Central America, and the Caribbean—is another important factor, as is the peso's real appreciation relative to the dollar. The GAO report also makes mention of the fact that the Mexican government modified the tax regime for the maquiladoras, generating uncertainty among investors. Finally, under provisions of the NAFTA agreement, Mexico has had to phase out some of the benefits previously accorded to the maquiladora sector.

Carrillo and Gomis (2003) use similar arguments when discussing the recent loss in competitive advantage among Mexico's maquiladora industries. With regard to the emergence of China as the maquiladoras' main competitor, these authors note that wages in China (converted to dollars) are less than a fifth of the wages paid in Mexican maquiladoras (50 cents per hour in China versus $2.67 in Mexico). China obviously has a huge labor market; its population is more than twelve times larger than Mexico's (1,295 million versus 100.4 million). And China is the world's leading recipient of foreign direct investment (FDI); China received $216,000 million in FDI between 1997 and 2001, compared to $78,000 million in Mexico (Carrillo and Gomis 2003).

In addition to changing economic conditions, Tijuana–San Diego has also felt the impact of substantial migration flows from Mexico, which are largely shaped by immigration policy. In 1986, the U.S. Congress enacted the Immigration Reform and Control Act (IRCA), which contained three key provisions: an amnesty for some undocumented persons already residing in the United States, sanctions against employers who "knowingly" hire undocumented workers, and increased border enforcement. The amnesty was administered under two programs—a "general amnesty" for undocumented migrants who could prove continuous residence in the United States after January 1, 1982; and the Special Agricultural Worker program (SAW), designed for unauthorized persons who had worked ninety days in agriculture between May 1985 and May 1986. More than 3 million persons legalized under these two programs: 1.7 million "legally authorized workers" (LAWs) who demonstrated long-term residence in the United States, and 1.3 million "special agricultural workers" (SAWs). Of those legalized, 2.3 million were from Mexico (1.3 million LAWs and about 1 million SAWs). Both LAWs and SAWs obtained legal status between the late 1980s and the early 1990s (Massey, Durand, and Malone 2002: 90).

In 1993, the U.S. government stepped up border enforcement to stop undocumented migration from Mexico. This was accomplished through a substantial increase in the budget of the U.S. Immigration and Naturalization Service (INS) and the concentration of border control on the corridors that undocumented migrants had traditionally used (Cornelius 2001; Reyes, Johnson, and Van Swearingen 2002).

According to Cornelius (2001: 661–64), the Border Patrol decided to prevent undocumented entries by deterring would-be migrants rather than by trying to apprehend them at the border or in the interior. This new policy—"prevention through deterrence," put in place by the INS during the Clinton administration—led to strategies such as "Operation Hold the Line" in El Paso in 1993 and "Operation Gatekeeper" in San Diego in 1994, both of which involved the installation of physical barriers and advanced electronic surveillance equipment.

Legalization under IRCA facilitated the settlement of families whose members had become legal residents. But it also encouraged undocumented family members to reunify with a legalized father/husband in the United States (Alarcón and Mines 2002). The intensification in border enforcement accelerated the settlement of undocumented migrants who were already in the United States as they stayed for longer periods in order to decrease the risks of apprehension when trying to reenter the country after a brief return to Mexico. At the same time, fewer border crossings meant less money paid out to the "coyotes" who smuggled people across the border for a (higher and higher) fee. The barriers erected at traditional crossing points have driven migrants into more dangerous areas, where they are subjected to intense heat in the deserts in summer and intense cold in the mountains in winter. Nearly 4,000 people died attempting to cross the border between 1993 and 2003 (Alonso Meneses 2003: 275).

At the end of the day, the broad legalization under IRCA and the installation of repressive border controls together created the conditions for the appearance of two coexisting migrant populations: a consolidated, larger, more stable, and more settled Mexican immigrant population in the United States, and an emerging undocumented and highly vulnerable labor force that faces dire physical risks, even death, in their determination to crossing the border illegally to find work in the United States.

TIJUANA AS A DESTINATION AND U.S. ENTRY POINT

According to data from the EMIF, between March 28, 1993, and July 10, 2001, 8,361 people were interviewed in the Tijuana International airport and at the city's central bus station. All were arriving from the interior of Mexico. Only 9 percent were women. Employing the method of expansion used in the EMIF, we can estimate from this sample that the total number of arrivals to Tijuana from Mexico's interior totaled 3,119,609. If we exclude everyone who did not report a destination or were living in the United States, the number of interviewees drops to 7,965. Out of these, the largest share (68.2 percent) arrived in Tijuana with the "northern border" as their destination. Given that these migrants traveled to Tijuana, it may be assumed that most had this specific city as their final destination.

The fact that over two-thirds stated their intent to remain in Tijuana suggests the strong appeal of this city. The remaining third (31.8 percent) arrived with the explicit intention of "getting to the other side." A high proportion of these migrants had previous migration experience to the United States. Table 4.1 presents the distribution of interviewees' destinations and previous experience in the United States by sex.

Table 4.1. Distribution of Migrants Interviewed in Tijuana by U.S. Migration Experience, Sex, and Destination, 1993–2001

| | Destination | | | |
| | Tijuana | | United States | |
	Men	Women	Men	Women
As proportion of group total	89.6%	10.4%	94.0%	6.0%
Proportion with U.S. migration experience	8.9%	2.1%	66.4%	17.1%
N	4,869	564	2,380	152
N weighted	1,841,157	194,149	894,751	57,684

Source: EMIF, phases 1–7, 1st trimester, 1993–2001.

Table 4.1 reveals that migrants who give Tijuana or the United States as their destination are predominantly men. Yet women account for a larger share among those headed to Tijuana than among those headed to the United States. This suggests that women may perceive higher risks in crossing the border and/or better employment opportunities in Tijuana, primarily in maquiladoras, which hire large numbers of women workers (Alonso Meneses 2003; Carrillo and De la O 2003).

With respect to the role that previous migration experience to the United States plays in the selection of a final destination, the EMIF data are very clear. People who have previous migration experience head to the United States in higher proportions. Two-thirds of males who claim the United States as their final destination reported having been in that country previously. This may signal that many men, with or without legal documents to enter the United States, are involved in circular migration between the United States and their places of origin. For the remaining third of those who claim the United States as their final destination, this would be their first time there.

Only 17 percent of the women headed to the United States had previously migrated there. Most (83 percent) are "first-timers." This may indicate that many of these women are family members (wives, mothers, daughters) hoping to reunite with family members in the United States. A very low proportion of men and women who claim Tijuana as their destination have previous migration experience to the United States: 9 percent for men and 2 percent for women.

An analysis of the sociodemographic characteristics of the men and women interviewed in Tijuana suggests that various factors play a role in the selection of one or the other destination, as presented in table 4.2. Overall, the women are notably older than the men. And when destinations are compared, the men and women who plan to cross into the United States are older than those whose destination is Tijuana. A greater proportion of the men headed to the United States are married or heads of household than is true of those who name Tijuana as their destination. Comparing women in both groups, the highest proportion of heads of household is found among those who want to cross the border. In sum, potential international migrants, in addition to being older, have greater family obligations than do the internal migrants to Tijuana. With respect to ethnicity, about 10 percent of the males in both groups are speakers of an indigenous language; a much lower proportion of women in these groups speak an indigenous language.

In relation to education's role in the selection of an internal versus international destination, EMIF data suggest that higher education levels predispose migrants to choose Tijuana rather than the United States as a destination. This has been observed in other studies (see, for example, Massey et al. 1987). Focusing solely on males, 20 percent of migrants to Tijuana have high school, professional, or postgraduate studies. In comparison, 14 percent of the aspiring international migrants have attained these educational levels.

Table 4.2. Distribution of Migrants Interviewed in Tijuana by Sociodemographic Characteristics and Destination, 1993–2001

Migrants' Sociodemographic Characteristics	Destination			
	Tijuana		United States	
	Men	Women	Men	Women
Median age	26	29	31	35
Married[a]	52.7%	54.9%	67.7%	55.9%
Head of household	56.5%	25.5%	73.4%	37.5%
Speaks an indigenous language[b]	9.7%	3.1%	9.4%	1.3%
Education[b]				
None	5.6%	6.3%	8.5%	9.4%
Elementary school	42.5%	42.3%	53.3%	39.2%
Junior high school	31.9%	31.5%	23.9%	24.3%
High school	12.1%	13.1%	6.8%	13.5%
Professional/postgraduate	7.7%	5.4%	7.3%	13.5%
Not specified	0.2%	1.4%	0.2%	0.2%
Total	100.0%	100.0%	100.0%	100.0%
N	4,869	564	2,380	152
N weighted	1,841,157	194,149	894,751	57,684

Source: EMIF, phases 1–7, 1st trimester, 1993–2001.

[a] Includes married persons and persons in common law unions.

[b] Calculations conducted on a smaller sample: 1,462 male and 222 female migrants to Tijuana, and 501 male and 74 female migrants to the United States.

Note: Numbers in italics represent from 1 to 29 observations.

María Eugenia Anguiano analyzed EMIF data collected in Mexico's northern border cities between March 1993 and March 1994 and found that these cities were becoming more important as destinations than was the United States (Anguiano 2000). More than half (56 percent) of the interviewees (who represented 1,799,261 movements of labor migrants) had a border city as their destination, compared to 44 percent who planned to "get to the other side." Anguiano also found that internal migrants were younger, had fewer family obligations, and had more formal schooling than would-be international migrants.

Another factor in the selection of a destination is geographical origin. The inertia of migration history and the construction of social networks have led to the consolidation of a traditional region of outmigration to the United States. According to Mexico's National Population Council (CONAPO), this region is formed by the following states: Aguascalientes, Colima, Durango, Guanajuato, Jalisco, Michoacán, Nayarit, San Luis Potosí, and Zacatecas (cited in Tuirán 2000: 163). CONAPO identified three other areas as well: the Northern, the Central, and the South-Southeastern regions. The North comprises Baja California, Baja California Sur, Coahuila, Chihuahua, Nuevo León, Sinaloa, Sonora, and Tamaulipas. The Central region is composed of the Federal District, Hidalgo, México State, Morelos, Puebla, Querétaro, and Tlaxcala. And the Southern-Southeastern region includes Campeche, Chiapas, Guerrero, Oaxaca, Quintana Roo, Tabasco, Veracruz, and Yucatán.

Table 4.3 shows the predominance of the traditional sending region as a source of international migrants. It accounts for nearly 60 percent of all migrants who are headed to the United States. Distant seconds are the South-Southeast and Central regions, which together provide 33 percent; the North accounts for the remainder.[6] The regions of residence of migrants who head to Tijuana are much more evenly distributed. Although the traditional sending region still predominates, it contributes only 38 percent, while the other regions have increased their share significantly. The Central and South-Southeastern regions provide nearly half, and the northern region accounts for 13.5 percent.

Research by Carlos Simonelli (2002: 163–64), using data from Mexico's population census to study immigration to Tijuana, found the growing importance of the South-Southeastern and Central regions as sources of immigrants to this city. In 1990 six states were contributing 64.7 percent of the total flow; in order of the number of migrants, they

---

[6] It is important to mention that the EMIF excludes persons heading to the United States if they reside in Mexico's northern border cities. This might explain the low proportion of migrants from the northern region in table 4.3.

are Sinaloa, Jalisco, Federal District, Sonora, Nayarit, and Michoacán. By 2000, 64.4 percent of migrants to Tijuana were coming from (again, in order of importance) Sinaloa, Veracruz, Jalisco, Sonora, Michoacán, the Federal District, and Chiapas. Veracruz and Chiapas had been added, and Nayarit had dropped from the list. It is especially notable that Veracruz, previously not identified as a sending state, now stands in second place. The addition of Chiapas is also significant.

Table 4.3. Distribution of Migrants Interviewed in Tijuana by Region of Residence in Mexico and Destination, 1993–2001

Region of Residence	Destination	
	Tijuana	United States
Traditional	38.0%	59.4%
Northern	13.5%	7.5%
Central	25.9%	16.0%
South-Southeastern	22.2%	17.1%
Total	99.6%	100.0%
N	5,433	2,532
N weighted	2,035,306	952,435

Source: EMIF, phases 1–7, 1st trimester, 1993–2001.

Regarding destination, the Los Angeles metropolitan area has been identified as the leading destination for Mexican immigrants. Using data from the U.S. population census, Ibarra (2003) found that the metropolitan area encompassing Los Angeles, Riverside, and Orange counties had a total population of 16.4 million people in 2000. Of these, 2.3 million were Mexico-born. The EMIF data confirm Los Angeles as the primary California destination for Mexican migrants interviewed in Mexican border cities between 1993 and 2001. Fresno was second, and San Diego, third. Of the persons interviewed during this period, 187 expressed their intention to cross to San Diego (84,174 persons, after weighting). The total number of migrants who intended to cross to the United States was 12,557 (2,564,213, using weighted numbers).[7]

---

[7] The sample used in this calculation includes data from interviews conducted over seven phases of the EMIF (1993–2001).

In sum, even though conventional wisdom portrays Tijuana as a crossing point to the United States, this city attracted more migrants from the interior of Mexico in the 1993–2001 period than were headed north across the border. The data also reveal a selection process that channels migrants to either Tijuana or the United States.

MIGRANTS RETURNING TO MEXICO FROM SAN DIEGO

This section looks at the sociodemographic characteristics of Mexican migrants who, between 1993 and 2001 and after spending more than a month in San Diego, reentered Mexico and were interviewed by EMIF personnel. The flow is divided into two streams depending on whether the migrant self-identified as a resident of the United States or of Mexico. The former group comprises mostly people who have settled in the United States, and the latter are migrants who may be involved in circular migration between San Diego and their homes in Mexico.

According to the EMIF data, 916 interviewees reported having lived in San Diego for at least a month between 1993 and 2001. Using weighted numbers, this equates to a flow of over a quarter-million persons (254,289). U.S. residents made up 61.7 percent of the total flow, and 38.3 percent were residents of Mexico. (It is important to note that the EMIF methodology to measure migration flows does not allow us to estimate the size of the Mexican immigrant population residing in San Diego.)

A comparison of the sociodemographic characteristics of the Mexican and U.S. residents who entered Mexico during the specified period and were interviewed yields some interesting contrasts (see table 4.4). Although both groups contain about the same proportion of males (approximately 82 percent), the U.S. residents are significantly older, have higher levels of education, and are more likely to be household heads and married (including common law unions). This suggests that in San Diego there is an older, better educated, settled population that lives in a family context, alongside a younger, less well educated population that claims Mexico as their country of residence.

The differences between the residents of the United States and Mexico become more salient when we explore the documents that members of both groups used on their most recent entry into the United States (see table 4.5).[8] Almost three-fourths of U.S. residents are citizens of that country (by birth or naturalization) or have an immigrant visa. Only 10 percent use a non-immigrant visa (tourist or student visa, for example) to cross the border. And only 17 percent are identified as undocumented. Corona Vásquez (2000) analyzed EMIF data on Mexican migrants returning to Mexico from the United States (he did not differentiate by country of residence) between March 1993 and March 1994, and found that nearly 50 percent had the necessary documents to cross the border and to work in the United States.

Table 4.4. Mexican Migrants Entering Mexico from San Diego by Sociodemographic Characteristics and Country of Residence, 1993–2001

| | Country of Residence | |
Migrants' Characteristics	Mexico	United States
Percent male	82.1%	81.4%
Median age	30	34
Proportion who are married[a]	59.8%	68.3%
Proportion who are household heads	61.3%	75.9%
Proportion with education beyond junior high school	25.4%	30.7%
N	351	565
N weighted	89,288	165,001

Source: EMIF, phases 1–7, 1993–2001.
[a] Includes married persons and persons in common law unions.

On the other hand, the majority of residents of Mexico (54.4 percent) last entered the United States without using any documents. An additional 25 percent used a non-immigrant visa. This last group obviously includes people with student or tourist visas and who used them for their intended purpose. But it may also include "visa abusers" who used these visas to enter the United States and then worked there without proper work documentation.

---

[8] These most recent trips could have been made at very different times.

Table 4.5. Distribution of Mexican Migrants Coming from San Diego by Immigration Status on Last Trip to the United States and by Country of Residence, 1993–2001

Immigration Status on Last U.S. Entry	Country of Residence	
	Mexico	United States
U.S. citizen	0.8%	9.5%
Immigrant visa	19.1%	63.0%
Non-immigrant visa	25.3%	10.2%
Undocumented	54.4%	17.0%
Unknown	0.4%	0.2%
Total	100.0%	100.0%
N[a]	241	411
N weighted[a]	62,177	125,883

Source: EMIF, phases 1–7, 1993–2001.

[a] This question (8.1) was not introduced in the EMIF questionnaire until phase 3, in July 1996; for this reason the sample is smaller.

Table 4.6 provides evidence of the work experience in San Diego of both groups. The data refer to work performed on the previous trip to San Diego by migrants who were there for at least one month. The first contrast is the high proportion (almost 40 percent) of Mexico residents who reported not having worked in San Diego during their last trip, compared to 17 percent for U.S. residents. Those who identified themselves as Mexico residents and did not work may include persons who were in San Diego for tourism or to visit family and/or friends.

Focusing only on those who worked, residents of Mexico had larger numbers working in agriculture, suggesting that many of them do this type of work in Mexico.[9] Both groups have the same proportion working in construction. However, residents of the United States display higher percentages in manufacturing, wholesale and retail trade, and tourism, among other sectors. U.S. residents also have a higher proportion of workers in all services except domestic work, a job that residents of Mexico perform in proportionately higher numbers.

---

[9] It is important to note that the EMIF excludes inhabitants of the border cities where the survey is being conducted, and thus does not capture commuter workers who might live in Tijuana and work in San Diego agriculture; for more on this group, see Escala Rabadán and Vega Briones, this volume.

Table 4.6. Distribution of Migrants Coming from San Diego by Employment Sector on Last Trip to the United States by Country of Residence, 1993–2001

Employment Sector during Last Trip to United States	Country of Residence	
	Mexico	United States
Agriculture	11.1%	7.6%
Manufacturing	4.9%	9.9%
Construction	11.7%	11.7%
Wholesale/retail	5.1%	11.2%
Transportation, government, FIRE[a]	0.6%	4.1%
Tourism (hotels, restaurants, etc.)	9.4%	14.9%
Domestic services	5.4%	1.9%
Technical and professional services	8.0%	11.2%
Other services	4.3%	9.7%
Not available	0.0%	0.6%
Did not work in the United States	39.6%	17.3%
Total	100.0%	100.0%
N	351	565
N weighted	89,288	165,001

Source: EMIF, phases 1–7, 1993–2001.
[a] FIRE = finance, insurance, and real estate.

In sum, a high proportion of U.S. residents are authorized to work in the United States because they are U.S. citizens or permanent residents of that country. They also have higher educational levels and are employed in sectors that seem to offer better employment opportunities. Residents of Mexico, in contrast, are dispersed across a broader range of employment sectors, which may be the lowest-paying. Some 45 percent work in construction, agriculture, tourism, technical/professional services, and domestic services. This suggests that legal status (which authorizes one to work in the United States) and education channel migrants into different sectors of the labor market.

Table 4.7 shows the region and state of residence of the 351 interviewees who declared themselves to be residents of Mexico. These data demonstrate the importance of the Central and South-Southeastern regions as sources of immigrants to San Diego. Together, these two regions contribute nearly the same share of migrants as do the traditional sending region—around 40 percent—with the Northern region contributing the remainder.

Table 4.7. Distribution of Migrants Reentering Mexico from San Diego by Region and State of Residence in Mexico, 1993–2001[a]

REGIONS	Share Coming to San Diego from Sending Region/State
Traditional	41.3%
Northern	17.9%
Central	23.6%
South-Southeastern	17.1%
Total	100.0%
STATES	
Michoacán	10.0%
Jalisco	8.8%
Guanajuato	8.5%
Guerrero	*7.7%*
México State	*7.1%*
Sinaloa	*7.1%*
Federal District	*6.5%*
Oaxaca	*5.1%*
Morelos	*4.3%*
Nayarit	*4.3%*
Subtotal	69.4%
Other states	30.6%
Total	100.0%
N	351
N weighted	89,289

Source: EMIF, phases 1–7, 1993–2001.
Note: Numbers in italics represent cases based on 1 to 29 observations.
[a] Excludes residents in the United States.

This list of the ten most important states of residency for migrants in San Diego reveals the weight of the traditional sending region, which includes the states of Michoacán, Jalisco, Guanajuato, and, to a lesser extent, Nayarit. However, with the exception of Sinaloa, the remaining states in the list (Guerrero, México State, the Federal District, Oaxaca, and Morelos) all fall within the Central or the South-Southeastern region. This coincides closely with the seven most important states of origin of Mexican immigrants working in Southern California that Cornelius identified in the late 1980s. By order of importance, they are Baja California, Jalisco, Michoacán, the Federal District, Guerrero, Guanajuato, and Oaxaca (Cornelius 1992: 159), confirming the growing participation of immigrant communities that had no established migratory tradition.

FINAL CONSIDERATIONS

This study of Mexican migrants who have been drawn to the Tijuana–San Diego region at a time of economic uncertainty and enhanced border enforcement uncovered some interesting findings. First, border cities, especially Tijuana, are the intended destination of the majority of migrants from Mexico's interior, people who might otherwise enter the United States as undocumented migrants. Thus economic development along the border (including the very significant maquiladora industry) may be diverting labor flows away from the United States.

Mexican migrants, both men and women, who plan to cross the border are older, have more family obligations, and have lower education levels than the migrants who intend to stay in Tijuana. The flow of would-be migrants to the United States continued to be composed mainly of males with previous international migration experience. The high proportion of women who intend to cross the border for the first time suggests that many are trying to reunite with family members in the United States.

Mexican migrants who have lived and worked in San Diego County separate into two groups. One is the older, better educated, settled population that lives in a family context; the other comprises a younger population, with lower education levels, who claim Mexico as their country of residence. Most of the former are authorized to work in the United States and seem to have access to better jobs than those who claim Mexico as their country of residence. The latter are mostly undocumented.

Interestingly, the residents of Mexico come in equal proportions from traditional and new sending regions, confirming that the regional pattern of migration is changing. There is a high proportion of urban migrants coming from new sending regions such as México State and the Federal District, alongside migrant flows from Guerrero, Oaxaca, and Morelos, states that contain many economically depressed areas and have large indigenous populations.

Tijuana contains settled immigrant communities that assist their fellow *paisanos* who want to enter the United States. Kearney and Nagengast (1990: 79) have emphasized Tijuana's role as a launchpad for Mixtecos from Oaxaca who are trying to cross the border. Such networks have been shown to be a crucial resource in the migration process (Massey et al. 1987). Once across the border, the migrants from west-central and southern Mexico are building immigrant communities in San Diego County that maintain a vibrant relationship with sister communities in Tijuana.

References

Alarcón Rafael, and Rick Mines. 2002. "El retorno de 'los solos': migrantes mexicanos en la agricultura de los Estados Unidos." In *Migración internacional e identidades cambiantes*, edited by María Eugenia Anguiano and Miguel Hernández. Mexico: El Colegio de Michoacán/El Colegio de la Frontera Norte.

Alonso Meneses, Guillermo. 2003. "Human Rights and Undocumented Migration along the Mexican-U.S. Border," *UCLA Law Review* 51, no. 1 (October): 267–81.

Anguiano, María Eugenia. 2000. "Migración laboral interna e internacional captada en la frontera norte mexicana: diferencias por sexo y sector de ocupación." In *Migración y fronteras*, edited by Manuel Ángel Castillo, Alfredo Lattes, and Jorge Santibáñez. 2d ed. Mexico: El Colegio de la Frontera Norte/El Colegio de México.

Carrillo, Jorge, and María Eugenia de la O. 2003. "Las dimensiones del trabajo en la industria maquiladora de exportación en México." In *La situación del trabajo en México, 2003*, edited by Enrique de la Garza and Carlos Salas. Mexico City: Plaza y Valdés.

Carrillo, Jorge, and Redi Gomis. 2003. "Los retos de las maquiladoras ante la pérdida de competitividad," *Comercio Exterior* 53, no. 4: 318–27.

Clement, Norris C., and Eduardo Zepeda Miramontes, eds. 1993. *San Diego-Tijuana in Transition: A Regional Analysis*. San Diego, Calif.: Institute for Regional Studies of the Californias, San Diego State University.

Cornelius Wayne A. 1992. "From Sojourners to Settlers: The Changing Profile of Mexican Migration to the United States." In *U.S.-Mexico Relations: Labor*

Market Interdependence, edited by Jorge Bustamante, Raúl Hinojosa, and Clark Reynolds. Stanford, Calif.: Stanford University Press.

———. 2001. "Death at the Border: Efficacy and Unintended Consequences of U.S. Immigration Control Policy," *Population and Development Review* 27, no. 4.

Corona Vásquez, Rodolfo. 2000. "Modificaciones de las características del flujo migratorio laboral de México a Estados Unidos." In *Migración y fronteras*, edited by Manuel Ángel Castillo, Alfredo Lattes, and Jorge Santibáñez. 2d ed. Mexico: El Colegio de la Frontera Norte/El Colegio de México.

Curry, James. 2000. "San Diego/Tijuana Manufacturing in the Information Age." Paper prepared for San Diego Dialogue, May.

GAO (U.S. General Accounting Office). 2003. "Mexico's Maquiladora Decline Affects U.S.-Mexico Border Communities and Trade; Recovery Depends in Part on Mexico's Actions." Report to Congressional Requesters, July.

Gerber, James, and Jorge Carrillo. 2002. "Are Tijuana's and Mexicali's Maquiladora Plants Competitive?" Paper prepared for San Diego Dialogue, July.

Herzog, Lawrence. 1990. *Where North Meets South: Cities, Space and Politics on the U.S.-Mexico Border*. Austin: Center for Mexican Americans Studies, University of Texas at Austin.

Ibarra, Guillermo. 2003. "Migrantes mexicanos en la industria del vestido de Los Angeles," *Migraciones Internacionales* 4, vol. 2, no. 1 (January–June).

Kearney, Michael, and Carol Nagengast. 1990. "Mixtec Ethnicity: Social Identity, Political Consciousness, and Political Activism," *Latin American Research Review* 25: 61–91.

Marcelli, Enrico A., Sundari Baru, and Donald Cohen. 2000. "Planning for Shared Prosperity or Growing Inequality? An In-Depth Look at San Diego's Leading Industry Clusters." San Diego, Calif.: Center on Policy Initiatives, September.

Massey Douglas, Rafael Alarcón, Jorge Durand, and Humberto González. 1987. *Return to Aztlan: The Social Process of International Migration from Western Mexico*. Berkeley: University of California Press.

Massey Douglas, Jorge Durand, and Nolan Malone. 2002. *Beyond Smoke and Mirrors: Mexican Immigration in an Era of Economic Integration*. New York: Russell Sage Foundation.

Reyes, Belinda, Hans Johnson, and Richard Van Swearingen. 2002. "Holding the Line? The Effect of Recent Border Build-Up on Unauthorized Immigration." San Francisco: Public Policy Institute of California, July.

Santibáñez, Jorge. 1999. "Algunos impactos empíricos de las políticas migratorias de Estados Unidos en los flujos migratorios de mexicanos," *Estudios Demográficos y Urbanos* 1, no. 1: 39–74.

Simonelli, Carlos E. 2002. "Cambios recientes en la migración y en la inserción laboral en Tijuana, entre 1990 y 2000," *Papeles de Población 34* (October–December): 59–189.

STPS, CONAPO, INM, and COLEF (Secretaría del Trabajo y Previsión Social, Consejo Nacional de Población, Instituto Nacional de Migración, and El Colegio de la Frontera Norte). 2002. *Encuesta sobre Migración en la Frontera Norte de México, 1999–2000*. Mexico City: STPS.

Tuirán, Rodolfo, ed. 2000. *Migración México–Estados Unidos: presente y futuro*. Mexico City: Consejo Nacional de Población.

5

Cross-Border Interactions: Population and Labor Market in Tijuana

MARÍA EUGENIA ANGUIANO TÉLLEZ

Taking full advantage of all that the Mexico-U.S. border region has to offer, many residents of border cities regularly travel to their sister city in the adjacent country. Despite the wealth of studies on the border region, few analyze the characteristics and dimensions of cross-border interactions among the region's residents. Yet people cross the border on a daily basis as tourists, shoppers, students, and workers, establishing connections among individuals, families, and institutions. They follow norms and rhythms dictated by familial bonds and community connections and by the region's similarities and differences, including its economic inequalities. These activities and experiences regularly unfold within the contiguous area of the two nations that we call the binational border or cross-border region.

I would like to thank Patricia Rosas for translating and editing this chapter. Her clarifications, suggestions, and observations improved it fundamentally. I also want to express my gratitude to Rafael Alarcón, Luis Escala Rabadán, and Germán Vega for their comments on a preliminary version. Any errors or omissions that remain are the author's responsibility.

Table 5.1. Population in Selected U.S. Counties and Mexican Municipalities along the U.S.-Mexico Border, 1990–2000

County/ Municipality/ Regional Total	Total Population		Growth in Absolute Numbers	Average Annual Growth (%)	Proportion of Total Regional Population (%)
	1990	2000	1990-2000	1990-2000	2000
San Diego	2,498,016	2,813,833	315,817	1.2	70
Tijuana	747,381	1,210,820	463,439	6.1	30
Total	3,245,397	4,024,653	779,256	2.4	
Imperial	109,303	142,361	33,058	3.0	16
Mexicali	601,938	764,602	162,664	2.7	84
Total	711,241	906,963	195,722	2.7	
El Paso	591,610	679,622	88,012	1.4	36
Ciudad Juárez	798,499	1,218,817	420,318	5.2	64
Total	1,390,109	1,898,439	508,330	3.6	
Webb	133,239	193,117	59,878	4.5	38
Nuevo Laredo	219,468	310,915	91,447	4.1	62
Total	352,707	504,032	151,325	4.3	
Hidalgo	383,545	569,463	185,918	4.8	58
Reynosa	282,667	420,463	137,796	4.8	42
Total	666,212	989,926	323,714	4.8	
Cameron	260,120	335,227	75,107	2.8	45
Matamoros	303,293	418,141	114,848	3.7	55
Total	563,413	753,368	189,955	3.3	

Sources: Based on data from U.S. Census Bureau Web site, http://www.census.gov/main/www/cen2000html); and INEGI Web site, http://www.inegi.gob.mx.

The sociodemographic and labor profile of Tijuana residents offers a starting point for exploring the socioeconomic structures that catalyze these ongoing interactions between the residents of Tijuana and San Diego. Before examining Tijuana's population structure and labor market in detail, I present a brief discussion of the Tijuana–San Diego conurbation and then examine its cross-border interactions.

THE TIJUANA–SAN DIEGO CONURBATION

In historical terms, the Tijuana–San Diego conurbation is newer than others along the Mexico-U.S. border, yet it is the largest in population and, in the 1990s, experienced the greatest population growth. And if one argues that this megalopolis extends to include Rosarito and Ensenada in Baja California and California's Orange County and Los Angeles County to the north, its population obviously multiplies many times over. In 1990 there were 3.2 million people living in Tijuana and San Diego, a figure that rose rapidly—primarily due to additions to Tijuana's population—to reach over 4 million by decade's end. By 2000, 70 percent of the conurbation's total population (2.8 million) lived in San Diego (table 5.1).

This is not the usual pattern. In city-pair conurbations that extend across the U.S.-Mexico border, the Mexican city is generally markedly larger (although the proportions are relatively balanced in a few cases). One might expect stronger cross-border interactions in city pairs where a large population of Mexican descent lives on the U.S. side (as occurs in Texas cities and towns that neighbor counterpart population centers in the Mexican states of Chihuahua and Tamaulipas). However, the uneven concentration of people in Tijuana–San Diego—and the diversity of activities in which these residents are involved—indicate the probability of a high level of interaction among them.

Economic dynamism has strongly influenced the size of cities and towns on both sides of the Mexico-U.S. border (Alegría 1992). During the 1990s Tijuana experienced the highest average annual economic growth of all counties and municipalities on the Mexico-U.S. border; it was followed by Ciudad Juárez. The maquiladora industry, which made these two cities powerful magnets for migratory labor flows, explains much of this economic dynamism.

The economic asymmetry that exists between Mexico and the United States takes on particular characteristics in the city pairs along the border (Ramírez and Varela 2002). U.S. border cities (with the exception of San Diego) have some of the *highest* poverty rates in the United States, and Mexican border cities have some of their country's *lowest* poverty rates. Although this situation lessens the contrast between populations in paired border cities, this does not mean that the living standards of their populations are in any way comparable. The economic contrasts between nations are conspicuously reaffirmed by the proximity in the San Diego–Tijuana conurbation of one of the richest counties in the United States and a Mexican municipality with a large and poor population. As Norma Ojeda noted, "This city pair is one of the most contrasting and complex border spaces" (Ojeda 2004).

In Tijuana–San Diego, the combination of economic distance (created by markedly unequal socioeconomic structures) and geographic proximity creates opportunities for the populations of the two nations. The comparative advantages of each city's labor and consumer markets—through their differential salaries and prices—multiply the possibilities for employment, acquisition of consumer goods, and use of services on alternate sides of the border. The salary differential attracts workers to San Diego and draws investors and consumers to Tijuana. The variety of goods and services available in the region and the disparity in their price structures lure consumers and users in both directions. Although geographic proximity creates opportunities for residents on both sides of the border, economic differences mean that those opportunities are not equally accessible to everyone living in the area.

Cross-border pedestrian and vehicular traffic is one measure of the binational linkages that exist in the region (see table 5.2). Based on data for 2000, we can estimate an average of six thousand trips from Tijuana to San Diego *per hour*, with obvious consequences for the region's labor force, economy, and environment. Two impacts are of particular note. The first is the pollution produced by vehicles waiting, often for extended periods, to cross the border, and the second is the income flows captured by street vendors and small shops that find their clientele among the people waiting to cross. Philanthropic organizations also benefit financially as their volunteers collect donations from waiting drivers.

Table 5.2. Annual Pedestrian and Vehicular Traffic between Tijuana and San Diego, 1997–2000 (millions of crossers)

	1997	1998	1999	2000
Pedestrians	7.668	7.528	8.242	8.191
Passengers on buses	1.069	1.126	1.166	1.629
Passengers in personal vehicles	37.431	41.363	43.450	41.685
Total	46.196	50.017	52.857	51.505

Source: Based on Nathanson and Lampell 2002: 7.
Note: Includes both Otay and San Ysidro ports of entry.

The volume of cross-border traffic at the San Diego port of entry has led the U.S. government to design a rapid-inspection system to speed up vehicle crossings. The Secure Electronic Network for Travelers' Rapid Inspection (SENTRI) was launched at the Otay Mesa border checkpoint (at the eastern edge of Tijuana) in November 1995 and implemented at the San Ysidro (western) checkpoint in September 2000. By using advanced surveillance technology and interconnected databases, SENTRI enables vehicles registered in the program to pass through border checkpoints more rapidly. However, the program is limited to Tijuana residents who can afford the SENTRI registration fee, who can insure their vehicles at the level required in the United States (including third-party liability coverage), and who have legal documentation to cross the border.

At the end of 2000, the office of the U.S. consul general in Tijuana reported that approximately 4,000 people were using SENTRI: 2,500 U.S. citizens, 1,000 Mexicans, and 500 persons of other nationalities. Most were tourists, businesspeople, mothers, and students. In 2000, SENTRI's annual cost per adult was US$129, with no charge for children under the age of 14; there was a maximum of four occupants per vehicle (Ramírez 2000). After September 11, 2001, as the wait to cross into San Diego lengthened, the number of people registered in the program also increased. At the start of 2004, the U.S. Consulate in Tijuana reported plans to create a SENTRI crossing for pedestrians and add four additional SENTRI lanes for cars at the San Ysidro checkpoint (San 2004). Although the program has been slated to be extended to other high-volume border crossings, two of the three SENTRI locations now in operation serve the Tijuana–San Diego region, underscoring the significance of this area for cross-border interactions. The third checkpoint with SENTRI lanes is one of the three border crossings between Ciudad Juárez and El Paso.

WHO CROSSES THE BORDER AND WHY?

The border region is not just a space offering material resources. It is also a space of social interaction. Olivia Ruiz has defined *transfronterizo* ("transborder") as something that distinguishes a border region from the rest of the two countries and has the potential to unify its residents: "Transborderism occurs in an area that is geographically delineated, and it refers to the activities of people, communities, and institutions of local origin and destination" (Ruiz 1994: 2). Elsewhere, Ruiz defines "transborderism" more generally as an *ongoing interaction* among individuals and institutions belonging to two distinct socioeconomic structures [countries] in the region where their borders join (Ruiz 1992: 143).

A number of factors spur people to travel back and forth across the border, including migratory status, work, family networks, cultural inheritance, and ethnicity. The frequency and nature of the interactions that border residents establish with their neighbors on the other side of the line, which ultimately shape the use of border space, are selectively determined by socioeconomic and demographic factors. Before looking closely at the demographic and socioeconomic features of Tijuana's population and labor market, we need to consider the *reasons* people have for making regular trips across the border. Examining a traveler's place of residence and reasons for crossing may help us sketch out the variety of ways in which the border region's space is used (table 5.3), uses that are the underpinnings of existing cross-border connections.

There are at least three work-related catalysts driving movement across the border. The first and predominant one involves Mexican border residents who are employed, with or without formal authorization, in nearby areas of the United States. The geographic space for the region's "commuter labor market" (or "transmigrant labor market") begins in southern San Diego County and extends as far north as Orange County and even Los Angeles County. Depending on the distance between home and work, these "commuters" can cross into the United States daily, weekly, or at longer intervals. Tito Alegría (2002: 39–40) estimated that Tijuana had 28,656 cross-border commuters in 1996 and 35,943 by 1998 (7.5 and 8 percent, respectively, of Tijuana's working population at the time). Alegría also noted that variations in these flows and their determinants are 1 understood. The commuter labor force joins Mexican workers with a segmented sectoral demand for labor in the United States—including jobs in the formal sector, temporary jobs, and jobs in the informal sector. For example, Mexican women travel from Tijuana to the United States on tourist visas to work as domestics or caregivers for children, the ill, or the elderly; and students in Tijuana find temporary holiday employment in the United States.

A much smaller work-related cross-border flow includes highly qualified workers—business executives, technicians, and other professionals—who live north of the border but work for transnational companies, especially in the maquiladora sector, with subsidiaries in Mexico.

The third work-related flow includes individuals, such as traveling businesspeople or migrants, who reside elsewhere but pass through the Tijuana–San Diego conurbation in transit to other destinations.

Families that have members residing in both countries form another segment of the population that feeds the daily flow across the border. Several studies have analyzed binational and transnational households and families and the use that their members make of the resources the two societies offer (Ruiz 1992; Ojeda 1990, 1995; Ojeda and López 1994; Escala Rabadán and Vega, this volume). In addition to short, periodic visits, family connections often facilitate the decision on the part of Mexican parents to send their child to study in the nearby U.S. city.

Another important segment of the cross-border flow consists of consumers of goods and services who move across the border in both directions. Mexican consumers have access to a diverse range of products in the United States: food, clothing and shoes, household appliances, even automobiles.[1] U.S. residents find lower-cost merchandise

---

[1] Each Thursday, the "Blue Bag" (La Bolsa Azul) is distributed in Tijuana's middle-class residential areas. It is filled with advertising flyers from San Diego County's major shopping centers and stores such as Wal-Mart, K-Mart, Target, Home Depot, Office Depot, and Best Buy.

Table 5.3. Categories of Cross-Border Travelers by Reason for Trip and Place of Residence

Reason for Trip	Residents of Tijuana Traveling to San Diego	Residents of San Diego Traveling to Tijuana
Work	Young adults and adults, men and women, with tourist visas and work permits. In-transit nonresidents of the border	Employees of companies operating with foreign capital
Study	Children and young people	
Family visits	Individuals or families with ancestors or descendants in both countries	
Consumption of goods or services	Shoppers and tourists	
Use of services	Workers and family members eligible for benefits Retirees from the United States	
Supply retail shops	Businesspeople in the formal and informal sectors	Wholesalers of ethnic products
Support for the community	Nongovernmental organizations Volunteers	Nongovernmental organizations Volunteers

and services in Mexico, including drugs and medical care, automobile repair, and real estate. Merchants who sell ethnic products typically obtain their stock from suppliers in the city on the other side of the border. And businesses that purchase used and remaindered merchandise in the United States for resale in Mexico generate employment and income in Mexico and also make a variety of inexpensive goods available to Tijuana residents who, for lack of funds or border-crossing documents, do not otherwise have a direct way to acquire these items (Sierra and Serrano 2002).

Recreation is another catalyst that spurs cross-border trips. Since its founding, Tijuana has been a vacation spot for Californians, who make up the largest portion of visitors to Tijuana. Bringas and Carrillo (1991) estimated that almost 60 percent of these visitors from California are of Mexican descent, suggesting that shared cultural and ethnic heritage may be a key stimulus here. Similarly, California offers multiple recreational options for Baja California residents. These are made even more tempting by special promotions aimed directly at residents of Mexico. For example, Disneyland reduces its admission prices for Baja California residents twice yearly, and the San Diego Zoo offers free admission for the region's schoolchildren every October.

The counterpart of the Mexican cross-border commuter is the retired American who has taken up residence in Tijuana, Rosarito, or Ensenada. These individuals and their families retain access to public services in the United States, which is yet another reason for frequent cross-border travel.

A smaller but important flow involves nongovernmental organizations and other volunteer groups, headquartered in either Mexico or the United States, that operate in the two cities, offering philanthropic assistance to needy people and communities (Kiy and Kada, this volume).

Yet another interaction occurs when Latin Americans residing in San Diego travel to nearby Tijuana to experience a shared ethnicity, language, and sense of belonging rooted in the city's Hispanic culture and identity. Tijuana's ethnic makeup is relatively homogeneous, as is true for most of Mexico (with the exception of its indigenous settlements). San Diego's ethnic composition, which is largely Anglo and Hispanic (table 5.4), has shifted somewhat over the past twenty years as the share of the Anglo population has declined and that of Hispanics has increased. According to the 2000 U.S. census, of the portion of the San Diego population born outside the United States, 53 percent were Latin American; 33 percent, Asian, and 9 percent, European. San Diego was seventh among U.S. cities in 2000 in terms of the size of its Hispanic population (behind New York, Los Angeles, Chicago, Houston, Philadelphia, and Phoenix), with 25.4 percent of its residents identified as Hispanic or of Hispanic origin (U.S. Census Bureau 2000).

Table 5.4. Distribution of San Diego Residents by Ethnicity (percentages)

Ethnic Group	1980	1990	2000
Anglo	74%	66%	64%
Hispanic	15	20	25
African American	5	6	5
Asian and other	6	8	6

Source: Shirk 2002: 42.

TIJUANA'S POPULATION STRUCTURE AND LABOR MARKET

Tijuana's demographic structure and labor market offer a point from which to explore the context and connections that this city's population has established with San Diego.[2] The sociodemographic characteristics of Tijuana residents, the type of jobs the city offers, and the profile of its workers—everything that combines in the city's population and labor context—are factors that stimulate cross-border interactions.

In 2000, almost 2.5 million people lived in Baja California, and almost half of the state's population was concentrated in Tijuana (figure 5.1). In-migration, mostly from Mexico's interior, has added significantly to Baja California's population growth. Of the 1.2 million people living in Tijuana in 2000, 60.3 percent were immigrants, similar to the levels of between 40 and 63 percent found elsewhere in Baja California (figure 5.2). Almost a third (30.4 percent) of Tijuana's population was made up of children under 15 years of age, more than half were between 15 and 64 years of age (57.6 percent), and only 2.8 percent were 65 years of age or older (INEGI 2003).

---

[2] Unless otherwise noted, the information in this section comes from the on-line INEGI databases for Baja California, at http://inegi.gob.mx.

**Figure 5.1. Proportional Distribution of the
Baja California Urban Population, 2000**

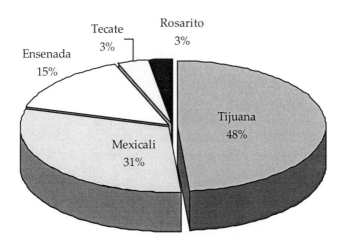

**Figure 5.2. Proportional Distribution of the Baja California
Population by Municipality and Migratory Status, 2000**

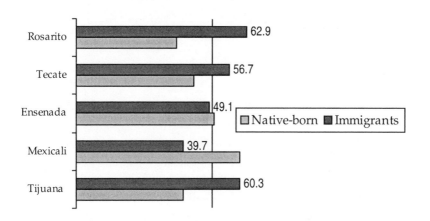

When we examine the Tijuana population by age quintiles, we see a notable bulge in the group between 20 and 40 years of age (both men and women), reflecting the high concentration of people in their most active years of productive work (figure 5.3). This is characteristic of localities with large labor in-migrations. If we examine only the native-born population (figure 5.4), we see that its base is broader, indicating a significant proportion of children and a natural rhythm of population growth.

Figure 5.3. Proportional Distribution of Tijuana's Population by Sex and Age Quintiles, 2000

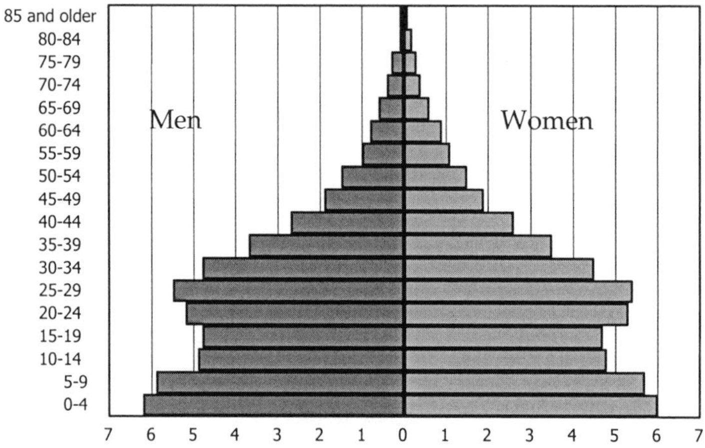

In 2000, the working-age population, defined in Mexico as individuals 12 years of age or older, accounted for almost two-thirds of Tijuana's residents (65.5 percent) (table 5.5). In contrast, the figure for Baja California overall was 55.3 percent, and for Mexico as a whole the working-age population accounted for less than half of total population (49.3 percent). Moreover, almost half of Tijuana's working-age residents were part of the working population, and almost all of them were employed. Almost 60 percent of the jobs are in commerce and services, a third in industry, and 8 percent in construction, with smaller numbers in agriculture, ranching, forestry, and fishing (figure 5.5).

Figure 5.4. Proportional Distribution of Tijuana's Population by Sex and Age Quintiles according to Migratory Status, 2000

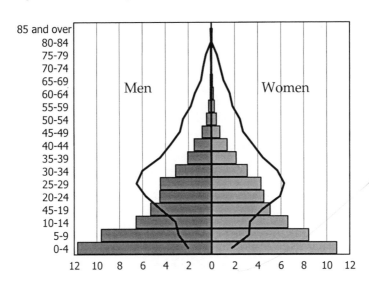

Only a very small portion of the population over age 15 lacks a formal education (figure 5.6). Most residents have completed primary school, and more than half have gone on to junior high, high school, and college, although only 6 percent of the Tijuana population over age 18 has done college-level work. Most of those who completed college have pursued careers in business administration and communications (55 percent) or engineering and technology (24.6 percent). In response to potential local labor demands, most of the more-educated people in Tijuana apply their education in the service sector and industry.

In sum, Tijuana's population is large, has a large immigrant component, is concentrated in the most active stages of work life, and is relatively well-educated. Unemployment levels are low, and most of the working population is employed in the services sector. This profile suggests that Tijuana's workforce includes a strong concentration of workers who could potentially access labor markets north of the border, from San Diego to Los Angeles. However, their qualifications (formal education and work experience), status as migrants, and family and social networks determine precisely which labor market options they can access on both sides of the border. This same group is also a source of frequent visitors who go to San Diego to shop, recreate, or visit relatives.

Table 5.5. Working Population and Employment Rates for Tijuana, 2000

	N	Percentages
Total population	1,210,820	100.0
Population 12 years of age and older	793,112	65.5
Active working population	450,608	56.8
Employed	(446,339)	42.2
Unemployed	(4,269)	0.9
Inactive working population	335,134	
No response	7,370	

Source: Based on data from the sections on economic and labor statistics contained in the National Urban Employment Survey (ENEU), INEGI Web site, http://www.inegi.gob.mx/est/default.asp?c=4753&e02, accessed on February 25, 2004.

Note: The working-age population in Mexican official statistics is defined as including all inhabitants 12 years of age or older.

Although the pull of the U.S. job market is strong, it is offset somewhat by a countervailing attraction from the healthy labor market in Tijuana. Of those employed in manufacturing, commerce, and services in all of Baja California, 58 percent work in Tijuana, reflecting the city's strong employment picture. Tijuana is home to 53 percent of the state's manufacturing plants and more than half of its businesses and services (with the exception of public-sector services) (see table 5.6). Similarly, 62 percent of those employed in manufacturing in Baja California and half of all those employed in commerce and services work in Tijuana.

According to Mexico's 1999 economic census, the leading three industries in Tijuana's manufacturing sector, in terms of their contribution to total production, are automobile and truck assembly, communications and transmission equipment, and communications components. This confirms the primacy of the city's export-oriented assembly

Figure 5.5. Percentage Distribution of the Tijuana Population by Sector, 2000

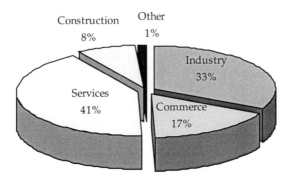

Figure 5.6. Proportional Distribution for the Baja California Population over 15 Years of Age by Educational Level, 2000

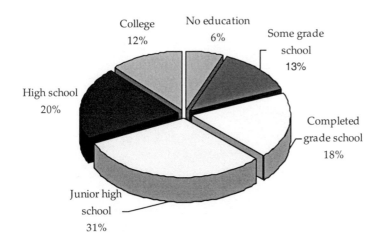

Table 5.6. Number of Businesses and Employees by Economic Sector in Tijuana and Baja California, 1999

	Manufacturing				Commerce				Services			
	Businesses		Employees		Businesses		Employees		Businesses		Employees	
	N	% of State	N	%of State	N	% of State	N	% of State	N	% of State	N	%of State
Tijuana	2,548	52.9	153,530	61.7	13,888	50.7	56,270	52.8	12,476	49.5	62,575	54.6
Baja California	4,813	100.0	248,458	100.0	27,390	100.0	106,441	100.0	25,201	100.0	114,629	100.0

Source: Based on INEGI's 1999 economic censuses, INEGI Web site, http://www.inegi.gob.mx/est/contenidos/espanol/proyectos/censos/ce1999/saic/default.asp?modelo=CMAP&c=932, accessed February 25, 2004.

Table 5.7. Income Distribution for the Employed Population in Tijuana and in Mexico Nationally, 2003

	Level of Income (number of minimum wages)						
	less than 1	1 to 2	2 to 5	5 or more	No Income	No Response	Total
Tijuana	1.5%	7.3%	56.2%	32.5%	2.4%	0.1%	100.0%
Mexico	6.9%	22.5%	46.0%	14.9%	4.1%	5.6%	100.0%

Source: Based on data in the 2004 National Urban Employment Survey (ENEU), INEGI Web site, http://www.inegi.gob.mx/prod_serv/contenidos/espanol/bvinegi/infoinegi/intermedio/ied/eneu1.pdf, accessed February 25, 2004.

plants. In terms of commerce—based on the number of businesses, people employed, and revenue and total payroll—the five leaders are small grocery stores and distributors, gas stations, pharmacies, cosmetics stores, and stores selling folk art. The last three—pharmacies, cosmetics stores, and folk art stores—tend to concentrate in the tourist sections of Tijuana, Rosarito, and Ensenada, where shopkeepers try to lure in American shoppers. Even street venders consider California tourists to be the preferred customers. Clearly, the Tijuana economy is bolstered by the presence of California residents who cross the border to shop, buying an array of goods, including prescription drugs that can be purchased in Mexico cheaply and without a prescription.

Like the commerce sector, the service sector's economic well-being is also bolstered by the flows of tourists arriving from California. Based on the number of establishments, people employed, and revenue contribution, first place goes to restaurants and small eateries (*fondas*), followed by automotive shops and doctors' offices, which, like the pharmacies, offer cheaper prices than those found in California. These locales attract a plentiful clientele of shoppers and retirees from neighboring San Diego, Orange, and Los Angeles counties.

In Tijuana, as in other border towns in northern Mexico, the maquiladora sector has generated employment and investment, along with its own distinctive labor and social dynamic. In 2000, 65 percent of Baja California's 1,218 maquiladoras were located in Tijuana, and they employed 67.5 percent of the people working in this industry. A promotional slogan boasts that Tijuana is "the most visited city in the world." A second, however, identifies Tijuana as "the television-set capital of the world," reflecting the output from local factories operated by Samsung, Sony, Sanyo, Panasonic, and others.

Although Mexico's employment outlook outside of the maquiladora sector was dim at the end of the 1990s (manufacturing employment grew only 1.9 percent from 1997 to 1998), employment growth within the maquila sector was high, at 12.3 percent in the (GEA 1999). In Tijuana, the maquila industry had been on a strong growth path—in terms of both number of plants and number of employees—from 1990 to 2001. Then in 2002–2003, the trend reversed (see figures 5.7 and 5.8), largely as a result of a deceleration in the U.S. economy that began in mid-2000. Another factor was a loss in competitive advantage to other

Figure 5.7. Personnel Employed in Tijuana's Maquiladora Sector, through November 2003

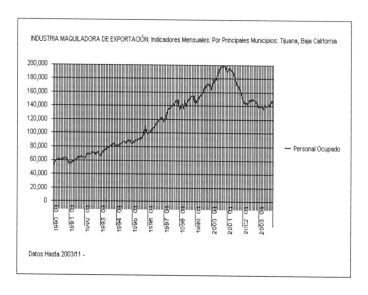

Figure 5.8. Active Firms in Tijuana's Maquiladora Sector, through November 2003

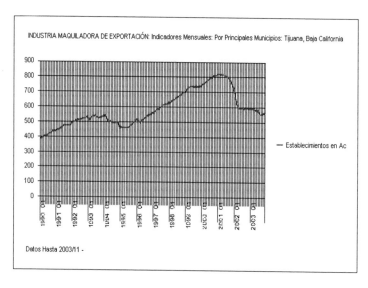

manufacturing countries, such as China, that were also producing for the global marketplace. The slowed growth in Mexico's maquila sector has prompted some companies to abandon Mexico, and others are planning to do so in the near future (Carrillo and Gomis 2003).

Mexico's National Urban Employment Survey (ENEU) reflected the decline. In January 2002, 40 percent of the employed population in Tijuana worked in industry, but by the end of 2003 that figure had sunk to 33 percent. Even so, the city's unemployment rate in 2003 was barely 1.1 percent, compared to 3.25 percent nationwide, which may indicate a reaccommodation of the working population into some of the area's other productive sectors. Indeed, commerce and services increased their shares of total employment from 19.4 percent and 29.8 percent, respectively, in 2001 to 20.5 percent and 33.1 percent in 2003. The ENEU also revealed that, in 2001, 7.4 percent of Tijuana's employed population—approximately 33,000 people—worked in the United States. That figure shrank to 6.8 percent in 2003 (INEGI 2004).

These figures may indicate that Tijuana's working population first moves among the area's productive sectors before considering the alternative of working in the United States. In principle, the decision not to seek work on the northern side of the border may be linked to employment and income factors in Tijuana and to the not insignificant limitations of the neighboring U.S. labor market. The latter include the need to present entry and work permits, as well as the restricted opportunities available to these workers, who because of nationality, ethnicity, language skills, educational level, and work qualifications, are confined to the poorly paid, low-skill jobs generally shunned by U.S. residents (Santibáñez 2000; Alarcón, this volume; Escala Rabadán and Vega, this volume). Additionally, whereas Tijuana's labor market has remained relatively vibrant, San Diego is feeling the effects of the economic slowdown in the U.S. economy, which has had particularly strong impacts in California, making desirable jobs even harder to come by.

Table 5.7 reveals Tijuana's comparative advantage over Mexico as a whole in terms of incomes for the employed population. Whereas almost 30 percent of the employed population nationwide received less than two times the minimum wage, only 8.8 percent of the Tijuana population falls into that category. More than half of the people employed in Tijuana receive between two and five times the minimum wage, placing this city 10 percentage points above the national average. Similarly, for Mexico overall, Tijuana has twice the number of people who receive more than five times the minimum wage.

Given that half of Tijuana's residents are immigrants, that the age distribution of its population peaks at the most productive years, that unemployment is low, and that incomes are higher than in Mexico as a whole, immigrants may see Tijuana as a work *destination* rather than as a transit point to the United States. A common perception is that immigrants are attracted to Tijuana because of its proximity to the United States, where they can potentially access employment opportunities. However, access to that labor market is stymied by the need for entry and work documents and, for some, a lack of preexisting family and social networks that could facilitate their entry into the U.S. workforce. Networks of recent immigrants appear to be located in Tijuana. It is only the more established Tijuana families, those with members residing on both sides of the border, that are well-positioned to take advantage of all that the cross-border region offers, which expands their options for working, shopping, and interacting socially in the two countries (Anguiano Téllez 1998, 2002, Alarcón, this volume).

FINAL THOUGHTS

The size of its population, the intensity of its cross-border flows, and the diversity of its daily interactions make the Tijuana–San Diego conurbation a highly dynamic socioeconomic space on the Mexico-U.S. border. The characteristics of its inhabitants and economic activities are the primary catalysts for those interactions.

In Tijuana we find a population that is heavily immigrant and concentrated in the most active years of economically productive life. The city's income and employment rates are above the national average, and its residents are primarily employed in the commerce and service sectors and the maquiladora industry. At the same time, this population also comprises potential shoppers, visitors, and perhaps workers, who take advantage of the opportunities offered by the proximity of San Diego, other California counties, and the United States in general.

In addition to migrants from the interior of Mexico, Tijuana continues to attract tourists, shoppers, and families from throughout the United States, and especially from California, as well as investors from the United States and Asia Pacific (Lugo and Mungaray 2002). Baja California offers tourists variety, good prices, and quality products and services, which draw them back repeatedly to visit and shop. And national and foreign investors have been drawn to this region by the advantages of its location and its continuously expanding labor market, which, while generating jobs, also creates consumers with sufficient resources to expand the exchange of goods.

Both domestic and world events—such as the devaluation of the peso and the terrorist attacks of September 11, 2001—have influenced the daily dynamics of the Tijuana–San Diego conurbation. Despite this international region's economic inequalities and marked contrasts—or perhaps because of them—residents of the Tijuana–San Diego region have established cooperative networks and multiple strategies that enable them to continue constructing a transborder space of intense interaction.

References

Alegría, Tito. 1992. *Desarrollo urbano en la frontera México–Estados Unidos.* Mexico City: Conaculta.

———. 2002. "Demand and Supply of Mexican Cross-Border Workers," *Journal of Borderlands Studies* 17, no. 1: 37–55.

Anguiano Téllez, María Eugenia. 1998. "Migración a la frontera norte de México y su relación con el mercado de trabajo regional," *Papeles de Población* 4, no. 17: 63–69.

———. 2002. "Migración y mercado laboral en la frontera norte de México," *Cooperación Internacional* 5, no. 8: 111–20.

Bringas, Nora L., and Jorge Carrillo, eds. 1991. *Grupos de visitantes y actividades turísticas en Tijuana.* Tijuana: El Colegio de la Frontera Norte.

Carrillo, Jorge, and Redi Gomis. 2003. "Los retos de las maquiladoras ante la pérdida de competitividad," *Comercio Exterior* 53, no. 4: 318–27.

GEA (Grupo de Economistas y Asociados). 1999. "Perspectivas del empleo y los salarios en 1999," *Este País*, April, pp. 12–13.

INEGI (Instituto Nacional de Estadística, Geografía e Informática). 2003. *Baja California: perfil sociodemográfico.* Mexico City: INEGI.

———. 2004. *Encuesta Nacional de Empleo Urbano.* Available at http://www.inegi.gob.mx/prod_serv/contenidos/espanol/bvinegi/infoinegi/intermedio/ied/eneu1.pdf.

Lugo, Sonia, and Alejandro Mungaray. 2002. "La competitividad regional de Baja California," *Comercio Exterior* 52, no. 8: 660–66.

Nathanson, Charles E., and Julio Lampell. 2002. "Identifying Low Risk Crossers in Order to Enhance Security at Ports of Entry into the United States." San Diego Dialogue *Forum Fronterizo* Briefing Paper, January. Available at http://www.sandiegodialogue.org/pdfs/poe_dc_jan02.pdf; accessed on February 25, 2004.

Ojeda, Norma. 1990. "Los hogares transfronterizos en Tijuana: un análisis propositivo." Paper presented at the annual meeting of the Association of Borderland Scholars, Tijuana, February 21–24. Mimeo.

———. 1995. "Familias transfronterizas y trayectorias de migración y trabajo." In *Mujeres, migración y maquila en la frontera norte*, edited by Soledad González et al. Mexico City: El Colegio de México/El Colegio de la Frontera Norte.

———. 2004. "Cruzar la frontera para abortar en silencio y soledad," *Frontera Norte* 31, no. 16: 131–51.

Ojeda, Norma, and Silvia López. 1994. *Familias transfronterizas en Tijuana: dos estudios complementarios.* Colección Cuadernos, no. 6. Tijuana: El Colegio de la Frontera Norte.

Ramírez, Cecilia. 2000. "Fracasa la línea de cruce rápido," *Frontera*. Available at http://www.frontera.info/buscar/traernotanew.asp?NumNota=75387.

Ramírez, Ramón, and Rogelio Varela. 2002. "Asimetría económica entre Baja California y California," *Comercio Exterior* 52, no. 8: 667–71.

Ruiz, Olivia. 1992. "Visitas y convivencias de los norteamericanos de ascendencia mexicana en Baja California." In *Historia y Cultura* (conference proceedings). Ciudad Juárez: El Colegio de la Frontera Norte/Universidad Autónoma de Ciudad Juárez.

———. 1994. "La relación transfronteriza." Paper presented to the Seminario COLEF III, Tijuana, October 20–22. Mimeo.

San, Luis Adolfo. 2004. "Alistan Línea Sentri para peatones," *Diario Frontera*, February 11. Available at http://www.frontera.info/buscar/traernotanew.asp?NumNota=232814.

Santibáñez, Jorge. 2000. "Los tijuanenses que trabajan en San Diego," *Diario Frontera*, September 8. Available at http://www.frontera.info/buscar/traernotanew.asp?NumNota=64713.

Shirk, David, ed. 2002. *Guía sobre California y la región de San Diego para funcionarios públicos mexicanos*. La Jolla: Center for U.S.-Mexican Studies, University of California, San Diego/Universidad Autónoma de Baja California. Available at http://www.sandiegodialogue.org/pdfs/mex_briefing.pdf.

Sierra, Olga, and Sandra Serrano. 2002. "Patrones y hábitos de consumo en Baja California," *Comercio Exterior* 52, no. 8: 701–708.

6

Living and Working as Cross-Border Commuters in the Tijuana–San Diego Region

LUIS ESCALA RABADÁN AND GERMÁN VEGA BRIONES

The Mexico-U.S. border has been the target of intense inquiry among different social actors in both the United States and Mexico. As several observers have noted, much of the discussion portrays this region in one of two ways. The first is a perspective that emphasizes the striking differences between these nations' social, economic, and political systems. In recent years, this view has been particularly influential in U.S. media and political circles, underlining the gaps between these societies. The second perspective privileges the social and economic relations between the region's two nations, based not only on a shared history and culture but also on increasing transborder linkages.

We thank Richard Kiy and the International Community Foundation for funding this research, and Chris Woodruff for his invitation to present our results at the Center for U.S.-Mexican Studies. Thanks also go to our research assistants, Carmen Martínez and Manuel Tapia, for their valuable help; Francisco Barraza and Eduardo González for statistical assistance; and Óscar Sosa for support during the interview phase of the research. We are grateful as well to our colleagues and friends María Eugenia Anguiano and Rafael Alarcón, of El Colegio de la Frontera Norte, for their helpful comments on an earlier draft of this essay.

The latter perspective, with its emphasis on interdependence, has also pointed to the significant differences *within* the border region. Of all the distinct binational areas along this border, San Diego and Tijuana together constitute the most populous and economically relevant. Indeed, the most distinctive feature of the San Diego–Tijuana region is the variety—and intensity—of the many flows that run across this segment of the border. The escalating population growth and urbanization of both cities have turned them into a single large metropolitan area divided by the international border, making this line one of the busiest in the world in terms of the volume of cross-border traffic. In turn, trade and economic development have served to stimulate transborder linkages. In fact, much of Tijuana's economic development is intertwined, not with the rest of Mexico, but with California, especially San Diego. This can be explained by geographic proximity, as well as the significant economic asymmetry between San Diego and Tijuana.[1]

One outcome of the enduring relationship between these cities has been the growth and consolidation of transborder social interactions.[2] There is a significant flow from Tijuana to San Diego comprised of individuals who cross the border on a regular basis for specific purposes: work, study, family visits, tourism, and shopping. And there is a similar flow from San Diego to Tijuana for tourism, shopping, family visits, and affordable medical, dental, and pharmacy services—as well as for work in the case of *maquiladora* managers and people providing community support through volunteer efforts and nongovernmental organizations (see Power and Byrd 1998; Anguiano, this volume).

These various flows have attracted the attention of scholars, policymakers, political representatives, and organizers on both sides of the

---

[1] There is a wide-ranging academic literature on the U.S.-Mexico border in general, and on the Tijuana–San Diego border in particular. Among the works that we found particularly useful are: Bustamante 1981; Martínez 1994; Rey et al. 1998; Spener and Roberts 1998; Vila 2000; Taylor 2001; and Alegría 2002.

[2] We use the term "social interactions" to emphasize the pervasive flows across the border. In this usage, we are inspired by Jorge Bustamante's (1981) seminal work on this topic.

border.[3] Of special and recurring interest have been "commuters" or "transmigrants," defined as individuals who reside on the Mexican side of the border and work nearby in Southern California.[4] Tijuana's proximity to San Diego has facilitated the growth of this group, which has become a significant component of the regional labor market. The "commuter" population has experienced significant growth in absolute terms, increasing from 28,000 individuals in 1996 to 33,000 in 2001. And it has continued to be quite stable as a share of Tijuana's labor force (7.5 percent in 1996 and 6.8 percent in 2003) (Alegría 2002; Coubès 2003; Anguiano, this volume). Although these percentages may not seem particularly large, commuter workers' importance to the local economy is considerable for two primary reasons: they receive higher wages on average than the remainder of Tijuana workers, and their consumption has an important impact on the wholesale/retail trade and service sectors in both cities. In fact, although they constitute less than 10 percent of Tijuana's working population, commuters account for approximately 20 percent of total wages received by all residents of Tijuana (Alegría 2002). By spending their U.S. incomes on goods and services on both sides of the border, they generate multiplier effects throughout the regional economy (see, among others, San Diego Dialogue 1994; Alegría 2000a; BorderValues 2002). These workers generate further benefits through the taxes they pay in the United States, even though they do not take full advantage of the public services for which they are

---

[3] Some long-standing issues under examination with regard to the U.S.-Mexico border are urban space (see, for example, Alegría 1992; Herzog 1990a); tourism (Bringas and Carrillo 1991; Bringas 2003); transborder family relationships (Ruiz 1998); family and health (Ojeda 1999); identity issues (Ruiz 1996; Vila 2000). A recent edited volume (Brooks and Fox 2002) includes several chapters on transborder social movement networking between Mexico and the United States, written by both scholars and activists and addressing issues such as environment, labor and human rights, social justice, indigenous populations, and immigrants' political rights.

[4] Scholars have been examining this specific population for at least two decades. See, for example, the works of Beatriz Acuña (1983, 1986) and Guillermo Arámburo (1987). During the 1990s, other scholars such as Herzog (1990b) and Alegría (1992) expanded the scope of academic inquiry on this group in light of the increasing importance of and attention to the U.S.-Mexico border.

eligible there. They also pay local taxes in Mexico through their consumption of goods and services and through ownership of real estate (Alegría 2000a).

In this chapter, we review some salient features and dynamics of the social interaction represented by Tijuana's commuter workers. Our approach is twofold: we use census data to identify some key sociodemographic features of this dynamic, and we examine workers' perceptions regarding their daily routines and their strategies to cope with their cross-border lives. Although several scholars have studied various aspects of commuter workers using either their own research instruments (surveys, interviews) or Mexico's official databases, there are data sets that remain relatively unexplored, thus opening new research avenues on the significance and size of this group. This chapter draws on two main sources for information on Tijuana's commuter workers. The first is the 10 percent sample of Mexico's 2000 population census (Muestra del Diez por Ciento del XII Censo General de Población y Vivienda). This 10 percent sample contains two variables that, in combination, may reveal the presence of cross-border workers: place of residence and place of work.[5]

Census data, like all data, are limited in terms of their ability to capture prevailing population dynamics. Therefore, we selected seven individuals with whom we carried out in-depth interviews over a three-month period in 2003, and these case studies are our second source of information on Tijuana commuters. The case studies provide a qualitative perspective on this type of border interaction and hence complement the census data. They also provide depth and texture by incorporating cultural patterns and interpretations of these workers' back-and-forth condition. Our aims in including this qualitative component were to provide depth to our quantitative data and to uncover the ways in which Tijuana commuter workers view and deal with their daily cross-border life. These cases do not represent a random sample of Tijuana's cross-border workers; nevertheless, we took care to select them in such a way that they faithfully reflected some core features of

---

[5] For the purposes of this work, "Tijuana" or "the Tijuana region" denote data from the municipalities of both Tijuana and Rosarito.

the group. We included social and geographic diversity by selecting commuters who resided in different areas of Tijuana—ranging from middle-class neighborhoods like Playas de Tijuana to poorer areas like Mesa de Otay—on the assumption that differences in residential area might denote varying income levels and, possibly, different points of view regarding the strategy of residing and working on opposite sides of the border. We found that our interviews with commuters allowed us to better address the broad questions of who these cross-border workers are and how they construct their dynamics.

SOCIODEMOGRAPHIC FEATURES OF TIJUANA'S CROSS-BORDER WORKERS

In this section, we present some findings regarding the sociodemographic features of this specific subgroup of the Tijuana population. Table 6.1 presents our calculations of the numbers and percentages of people who live and work in the Tijuana region vis-à-vis those who live in Tijuana but work in California. From the approximately half-million individuals that compose Tijuana's working population, almost 6 percent are cross-border workers. This finding is important because it generally confirms previous estimates of the size of this population. For example, Alegría (2000b) calculated its size at 28,656 in 1998, or 7.5 percent of Tijuana's workforce, based on data from Mexico's National Urban Employment Survey (ENEU). The disparity between Alegría's and our estimates can be attributed to the different data sources used. ENEU's estimates are based only on Tijuana, whereas our analysis includes both Tijuana and Rosarito. We included Rosarito, which is just south of Tijuana, because it is the place of residence for many cross-border workers.[6]

---

[6] Herzog's study of Tijuana commuters (1990b), based on a 1983survey, found that 13 percent lived in Colonia Libertad. In light of the growth of the region's population and neighborhoods over the last two decades, we think this clustering is unlikely to have persisted. Our interviewees knew many commuters who lived in other areas in Tijuana and Rosarito, suggesting a more scattered distribution throughout the region. As Inocencio A commented, "at my job there are many guys that go back and forth; five or six live in Tijuana, one in Rosarito, one in Colonia Libertad, one in El Soler, and two in La Mesa."

Table 6.1. Tijuana's Estimated Working Population by Work Location

	Total Working Population	Work Location	
		Tijuana	United States
Census sample	26,005	24,492	1,513
Weighted N	478,742	451,356	27,386
Percent		94.2%	5.7%

Source: Authors' calculations based on INEGI 2000.

We were somewhat puzzled by the seemingly small size of Tijuana's transmigrant population given its importance as an example of the extent and density of social interactions within the Tijuana–San Diego region. We will develop this theme at various points in our discussion of our interview results.

Figure 6.1 presents the gender distribution of individuals who live and work in Tijuana. According to the census sample, 16,214 Tijuana workers (66.2 percent of the total number of individuals who live and work in that city) are men; 8,278 (33.7 percent) are women. Of the transmigrants, 1,161 are men (76.7 percent), and 352 (23.2 percent) are women.

Figure 6.1. Proportional Distribution by Gender of Individuals Who Live and Work in Tijuana Population

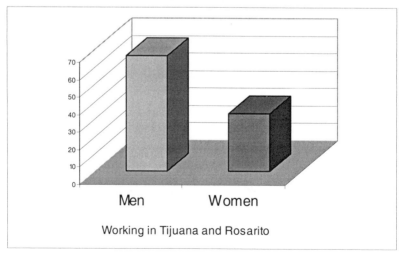

Source: INEGI 2000.

Translating these figures into weighted numbers yields 300,703 men and 150,653 women, or 94.2 percent of Tijuana's working population that lives and works in that city, with the remaining 5.7 percent—21,051 men and 6,335 women—being commuter workers.

Table 6.2 illustrates a particularly interesting feature in our commuter population: birthplace. Most are not natives of Tijuana or even Baja California, but were born in other states of Mexico.

Table 6.2. Tijuana's Working Population by Workplace, Gender, and Birthplace (percentages)

| | Work Location | | | |
| | Tijuana | | United States | |
Birthplace	Men	Women	Men	Women
Baja California	27.8%	29.6%	34.3%	36.0%
Other Mexican state	71.5	69.8	53.7	47.1
United States	0.4	0.4	11.5	16.1
Other	0.3	0.2	0.5	0.7
Total	100.0%	100.0%	100.0%	100.0%

Source: INEGI 2000.

This birthplace distribution confirms Tijuana's importance as a magnet for immigrants who come from elsewhere in Mexico to work in the city's industrial sector (particularly in maquiladoras) and as a staging point for others planning to continue on to the United States in search of work, many of whom ultimately settle in Tijuana and take jobs there (Alarcón, this volume).

More unexpected is the difference that emerges with respect to country of origin. There is a higher proportion of people born in a country other than Mexico among the individuals commuting to work in the United States than among the general working population of Tijuana. Most of these non-Mexico-born workers were born in the United States. Our interviews gave further evidence on this point, reflecting a long-standing practice among some Tijuana women to cross the border to San Diego County or elsewhere in California to give birth[7] and then return to Tijuana to raise their children, who may later become commuter workers. For example, Miroslaba M decided to give birth to her two sons at a private hospital in San Diego. Even though these medical services were relatively expensive, she considered it worth the cost because her sons would have both U.S. and Mexican citizenship. Both children live in Tijuana with Miroslaba and their step-father, where Miroslaba says she feels more comfortable raising a fam-ily (author interviews).

As many authors have noted (see Herzog 1990b; San Diego Dia-logue 1994; Ruiz 1998, among others), border-crossing activities are embedded within complex patterns of cross-border social relationships (of kinship and friendship, for example) that exist because of geo-graphic proximity, and these extend to being born "on the other side." In this sense, commuter workers form an important layer of this bor-derlands social system. The transmigrants we interviewed attributed their decision to live on one side of the border and work on the other to their prolonged experience moving back and forth between Tijuana and San Diego, usually in response to cross-national family and friend-ship ties. Transmigrants born in the United States have the additional boon of double citizenship, which means that they do not need special documents to cross the border or to work in the United States, a situa-tion that undoubtedly paves the way for these workers to adopt this transborder path.[8]

---

[7] Many women living on the Mexican side of the border go to U.S. hospitals to give birth, thus making it possible for their children to have U.S. citizenship. Of course, the quality of services is also a strong incentive to give birth in these hospitals. For further discussion, see, among others, Roberts 1999; Vega Briones 1999.

[8] We are not implying that all Tijuana commuters have U.S. citizenship, but all of the seven workers we interviewed have at minimum a document (a tourist or "laser visa"; the latter replaced the border crossing card in 1999) that per-mits them to cross the border daily, making it feasible to hold a job "on the other side."

Inocencio A,[9] now 31 years old, was born in Tijuana and lived there until he was 5, when his family moved to Chula Vista, in southern San Diego County. He remained there until age 26, then married a woman from Tijuana's Colonia Libertad whom he met at a Tijuana dance spot that both he and his future wife went to weekly, underscoring the back-and-forth dynamics of people in the border region. Once married, they decided to settle and raise their family in Tijuana, where they have lived since 1999. Inocencio A's uncles live in California and Texas, and he has siblings, married to either people from Tijuana or "*emigrados*," on both sides of the border. He began to work in Chula Vista as a teenager and has held several jobs there, eventually working in the auto supplies industry. He is currently an assistant manager at a large auto-parts' supplier in National City. The family prefers living in Tijuana's Mesa de Otay neighborhood, not only because it is more affordable than southern San Diego but also because it is close to the Otay border gate, where Inocencio A crosses daily on his commute to work. As Inocencio commented, "I've gone back and forth all my life, for family reasons, for entertainment, for shopping, all my life; on weekdays I cross to work, on the weekends we cross to visit my parents in southern San Diego, pretty close to the border."

Another of our interviewees is Enrique H, a 43-year-old man born and raised in Santa Ana, California. He has been working in construc-

---

[9] The profiles of the workers we interviewed are as follows: Inocencio A, a 31-year-old male, was born in Tijuana, has a high school diploma, and works in an autoparts store in Chula Vista, in southern San Diego. Antonio P, a male, 52 years old, was born in Rosarito, has a BA degree in literature, and works as a high school teacher in National City in southern San Diego. Guadalupe O, a 55-year-old female, was born in Tijuana, has an associate's degree, and works as a bank employee in downtown San Diego. Enrique H, a 43-year-old male, was born in Santa Ana, California, has a high school diploma, and works as a construction worker in the San Diego area. Agustín C is 56 years old, was born in Tijuana, completed junior high school, and works as a school janitor in Imperial Beach in southern San Diego. Liliana E, a 25-year-old woman, was born in Orange, California, has a high school diploma, and works as a store employee in San Ysidro in southern San Diego. Miroslaba M is 33 years old, female, was born in San Luis Potosí, Mexico, has a high school diploma, and works cleaning houses in San Diego and Tijuana.

tion in California since 1980, a trade he learned from his father and uncles, who came from Jalisco to settle in Orange County. He met his wife, a native of Mexico City, during a trip to central Mexico. They have lived in Tijuana since 2000, and Enrique commutes every day to different construction sites in the San Diego area. His parents, uncles, and some siblings still live in Santa Ana, and he visits them occasionally.

Both Inocencio and Enrique were drawn to jobs in the United States because of the higher wages available to them there. One strong indication of the wage differential within Tijuana's working population is home ownership. Although available data do not address the issue of the quality of the dwellings, it is likely that cross-border workers' access to higher wages may explain why approximately three-fourths of them own their own home (table 6.3).

Table 6.3. Distribution of Tijuana's Working Population by Workplace and Home Ownership (percentages)

	Work Location	
	Tijuana	United States
Owner	67.6%	76.1%
Non-owner	32.3	23.9
Total	100.0%	100.0%

Source: INEGI 2000.

These figures suggest a pattern for most Tijuana commuters: their access to a higher income makes it feasible for them to buy a home in Tijuana, thus reinforcing their strategy of working in one nation while living in the neighboring one, a pattern that is given added appeal by the skyrocketing prices in the Southern California housing market.

The commuter workers we interviewed returned repeatedly to the importance of housing in their transborder dynamics. The spiraling cost of real estate in Southern California led them to give particular emphasis to the affordable housing available in Tijuana. As Enrique H noted, "the advantage I find in living in Tijuana is that it's not as expensive as on the other side; for me it's really cheap because we make good money [in San Diego]. If you want to rent a place in San Diego, how much is it? You end up paying at least $1,500, even $2,000 a month." Liliana E added, "I like to live in Tijuana because you can make more money [in San Diego] and pay less rent, the food is more affordable and so are the house expenses; that's the big plus, while over there the rent is really huge."

Table 6.4 presents the main occupations of commuter workers that we identified in our research. Although the census sample uses a broader array of work options, we group them into four major categories for present purposes. The "employee or worker" category reveals the high proportion of wageworkers among Tijuana's commuters, especially when compared with the "business owner" category. These data also reveal a small but important proportion of "self-employment," which is considerably higher among those who work in Tijuana. This speaks to the predictably stronger presence of informal work on the southern side of the border.

Table 6.4. Distribution of Tijuana's Working Population by Workplace and Occupation (percentages)

| | Work Location | | | |
| | Tijuana | | United States | |
	Men	Women	Men	Women
Employee or worker	73.1%	79.3%	85.7%	87.9%
Laborer or peasant	1.6	0.2	1.2	0.4
Business owner	6.0	3.7	4.4	2.0
Self-employed	17.0	13.3	7.3	8.6
Unpaid worker in family business or on the land	0.5	1.4	0	0.6
Not indicated	1.9	2.1	1.5	0.5
Total	100.0%	100.0%	100.0%	100.0%

Source: Based on data in INEGI 2000.

These figures were at least partially supported by our interviewees. All identified themselves as "employees or workers," and they all had steady, regular employment. For example, Agustín C has worked as a janitor for ten years at a school in Imperial Beach. Guadalupe O has been commuting to work as a bank employee for ten years; her job for the last five has been in downtown San Diego. Liliana E, despite being very young, has been commuting to work as a store clerk for six years and has been at her current job for three years. Taking the census sample data on occupations one step further, we can identify some categories that are of particular importance in terms of Tijuana's commuters. Tables 6.5 and 6.6 show the ten main occupations among Tijuana's commuters, both men and women. Probably the most revealing aspect is their concentration in two categories: "housekeeping" (17.7 percent of women) and "construction" (8.9 percent of men).

Table 6.5. Distribution of Tijuana's Male Commuters by Occupation (absolute numbers and percentages)

Type of Work	N	Percent
Construction	1,739	8.9%
Retail personnel	917	4.7
Janitors in offices, schools, hospitals, etc.	868	4.4
Gardeners at businesses, residential complexes, etc.	816	4.2
Workers in food manufacturing	727	3.7
Drivers of trucks, pickups, and freight vehicles	684	3.5
Mechanics, maintenance/repair workers	676	3.4
Painters	515	2.6
Carpenters, cabinet makers, etc.	494	2.5
Gardeners at private homes	480	2.4
Other	11,715	59.7%

Source: Based on INEGI 2000.

Perhaps the most notable feature of the occupations of Tijuana residents working in the United States is that they are low-skilled. If we combine the numbers for men and women, the top five occupations among Tijuana commuters are: construction (1,770 cases, or 6.4 percent of this population), retail personnel (1,613, or 5.9 percent), gardeners (1,321, or 4.7 percent, if we add the two gardener categories), housekeeping (1,261, or 4.6 percent), and janitors (1,045, or 3.8 percent). These five occupations, which are usually viewed as requiring limited professional skill, correspond to 25.4 percent of these workers, or one out of four commuters. While these men and women perform a range of jobs that do demand some professional skills and training (as drivers, mechanics, secretaries, and carpenters), it was only among women commuters that we found some indication of skilled occupations (as accountants and financial assistants, and as managers, administrators, and supervisors).

Table 6.6. Distribution of Tijuana's Female Commuters by Occupation (absolute numbers and percentages)

Type of Work	N	Percent
Housekeeping	1,126	17.7%
Retail personnel	696	10.9
Caregivers to children, the ill, and the elderly	442	6.9
Cashiers and collectors	325	5.1
Secretaries	301	4.7
Janitors in offices, schools, hospitals, etc.	177	2.8
Accountants and financial assistants	154	2.4
Workers in food manufacturing	150	2.3
Merchants	128	2.0
Department managers, administrators, supervisors	118	1.9
Other	2,757	43.3%

Source: INEGI 2000.

The information gleaned from our interviews was consistent with this pattern. As noted with regard to data presented previously, our interviewees all had steady trajectories as employees in fields that reflect the types of occupations presented in tables 6.5 and 6.6. There is strong labor demand across an array of low-skilled jobs in San Diego County that increases the chances that Tijuana's cross-border workers will be able to enter this labor market, as has occurred among women working as domestics and men employed in construction. For example, Miroslaba M has been cleaning houses in the San Diego area four days a week for seven years, earning between $50 and $70 per house. On the other days of the week she does the same work in the Tijuana-Rosarito area, where she charges $30 per house. In another case, Enrique H, who has a ten-year trajectory in California construction, commented that this industry's increasing demand for workers in low-skilled positions has made it an appealing option for individuals who, like him, live in Tijuana. Moreover, the transformation in this industry's hiring practices as it has moved toward more subcontracting has made it easier to be hired and paid without many questions asked. As Enrique H. noted:

> I belong to a network of about two hundred people in San Diego, and some people are in charge. If you're done working with someone, you just ask them and they tell you "call this other guy, he's looking for workers," and usually it works out fine. But everyone I know [from Tijuana who works there] works for cash. Nobody works for a check because then you have to work by the hour, and then you have to make sure you do it let's say in eight hours per day, day after day. And with us it's different; it takes you two or three hours and they pay you for the day. I like it better like that because I make more money and they don't deduct anything for taxes. That way I just have to report a minimum income by the end of the year when I do my taxes.[10]

Table 6.7 presents our main findings regarding educational levels among Tijuana workers, both commuters and those employed in Tijuana. Following the same criteria applied in the preceding tables, we have collapsed the census sample groupings into a smaller number of categories. The largest group is those among Tijuana's working popu-

---

[10] Enrique H's narrative of his work trajectory is consistent with the transformations in this industry in California. For an insightful assessment of recent changes in hiring practices in the construction industry in Southern California, see Milkman and Wong 2000.

lation who have completed high school or college, but the proportion is even higher among commuters. This is consistent with previous findings about Mexican cross-border workers that point out the relatively high level of formal education among them, especially in light of their relatively low-skilled occupations within the U.S. labor market.[11] Moreover, female commuters, despite being the smallest group considered, have the highest educational attainment. We may speculate, in light of the important proportion of them born in Baja California, whether this achievement is related to their extended access to resources and networks (including educational options) on both sides of the border.

Table 6.7. Distribution Tijuana's Working Population by Workplace, Gender, and Educational Attainment (percentages)

	Work Location			
	Tijuana		United States	
Education	Men	Women	Men	Women
None	4.6%	3.9%	4.0%	4.4%
Some elementary school	13.3	10.3	12.3	5.8
Completed elementary school	18.1	16.5	16.0	15.8
Junior high school (*secundaria*)	31.1	30.0	27.6	26.6
High school (*preparatoria*) and bachelor's degree	32.8	39.4	40.1	47.5
Total	100.0%	100.0%	100.0%	100.0%

Source: INEGI 2000.

---

[11] Zenteno and Rodríguez's (1996) work on Mexican transmigrant workers in Mexico's border cities pointed to the higher levels of formal education among commuters compared with the rest of the working population, based on ENEU data for 1993. They concluded that neither gender nor status as household head were strong predictors of becoming a cross-border worker. Age and education, especially a high school degree, were better indicators. In addition, the context of the Tijuana–San Diego region, where the urban labor market in San Diego exerts a strong demand on Tijuana—compared to other twin-city regions along the border—makes this even more likely.

These results are consistent with our interviewees' profile. Only one had ended formal schooling at junior high school; the others had a high school diploma or higher. The fact that the employment information shows Tijuana's commuters holding primarily low-skill jobs (construction work among men, housekeeping among women) might suggest that these workers are overqualified for their work positions, though none of our interviewees pointed to this consideration as a major concern.

Perhaps the most noteworthy feature with respect to their educational background was precisely their transborder trajectories. Guadalupe O, for example, attended elementary school in Tijuana, and junior high and high school in San Ysidro, where she received an associate's degree in business administration. Afterward she went to work in Tijuana. Liliana E attended preschool and elementary school in Tijuana, and then junior high and high school in Chula Vista. Both of these women had to move back and forth across the border on a daily basis to attend school "on the other side." According to Liliana E:

> This meant I had to go to bed at 8 or 9 at night, to wake up at 4 in the morning in order to be at the line to cross by 5:30. I used to ride with a friend of my mom, and then I got back home with her. She had like a small school bus, and afterwards in high school I came back with friends and all the people who went back to Tijuana in the afternoon.

Our informants confirmed that this strategic practice has been going on among Tijuana residents for years, even generations. This behavior is not based on an assumption that schools are better in California simply because they are U.S. schools. Rather, language training is the main reason that families send their children to school on the other side.

The foregoing tables presented information on some relevant features of commuter workers. An additional area of interest to us is their use of services. Social visits, consumption and entertainment, and the use of health and education services are also important features in the prevailing interactions among border populations. Perhaps the most striking case is the utilization of health services, where we find dramatic differences between workers in Tijuana and the population of cross-border workers (table 6.8).

Table 6.8. Distribution of Tijuana's Working Population by Workplace and Use of Health Services (percentages)

| Health Service Utilized | Work Location | | | |
| | Tijuana | | United States | |
	Men	Women	Men	Women
Mexican Social Security (IMSS) clinics	46.3%	54.4%	8.2%	15.2%
Other public health services[a]	7.5	8.6	2.7	3.0
Private doctor's office, hospital, clinic	41.1	33.4	75.8	70.2
Other private health services	1.2	1.5	1.3	1.2
No services used	3.9	2.1	12.0	10.4
Total	100.0%	100.0%	100.0%	100.0%

Source: INEGI 2000.

[a] IMSS and ISSSTE (the Social Security Institute for State Employees) are the two main providers of health services funded by the Mexican government. These services are complemented by others provided by Mexico's national oil company (PEMEX), the army and navy, and clinics operated by the Health Ministry or IMSS Solidaridad.

The starkest contrast in terms of health services utilization is the strong use of public health services on the Mexican side of the border. Those who work in Tijuana rely heavily on public services, whether it is the Mexican Social Security Institute (IMSS) or other public health services available in this city. The high level of IMSS users is consistent with a large working population in a city with substantial industrial activity.

Tijuana's commuters, in contrast, make much less use of public health services, but instead rely predominantly on private doctors, hospitals, and clinics. We found this somewhat puzzling. It is understandable that Tijuana's commuters opt not to use public health options in Mexico in light of their social status. But as mentioned above, these workers pay income taxes (both federal and state) in the United States, which may allow them to access some health care services on that side of the border. In this instance, the information we gathered through our interviews helped resolve this potential paradox. Five of our seven interviewees had health insurance coverage in the United States, which in principle expands their options.[12] Inocencio A summed up his binational approach to health care as follows:

> I go to the doctor on both sides. We have insurance through my job, and two of my kids were born over there [in San Diego]. I have a doctor and benefits, but we try to have a doctor [on both sides] in case of an emergency, just in case you have to wake up at midnight because the kids feel sick. If that happens, we take them to the doctor here in Tijuana. Now, if the doctor says "hospital," then we cross the border and get them to the hospital over there. It's because that's covered by my insurance and it's fine like that.

One important factor that border area residents consider when utilizing health care services is convenience, and if they can have access to health care on both sides, that will be their preferred option. They also emphasize the marked differences between health care in Tijuana and San Diego. A major difference is cost. As Inocencio A commented, "if you have to go to the doctor, I'd rather go here in Tijuana, not to the other side, because my [U.S.] insurance company charges me a lot!" Antonio P elaborated this point further:

> All my students at the high school [where I work] in National City come to Tijuana when they need medical attention.... These kids live over there, and National City is

---

12 Two of our interviewees had no health coverage in the United States. One had an arrangement with a private doctor in San Diego, paying $200 a month in weekly installments in order to obtain medical services when needed.

one of the poorest cities in the United States. It's obvious then that the parents are going to take them to doctors in Tijuana, because in Tijuana when you go to the doctor's office, it's going to cost you between $3 and $20, and most of the time that includes prescriptions, whereas in San Diego it costs up to $100, sometimes more, even for things as simple as the flu, and they don't give you the medicines.

Most of the differences in health care provision on opposite sides of the border do not relate to cost, however. The main distinction regards the quality of the services provided, as the following comments from our interviewees illustrate:

> The fact is that doctors over there [in the United States] ask for a lot of medical tests and end up giving you only Tylenol, or they refer you to a specialist and then to another one, whereas here in Tijuana they take care of you quickly. That's why I'd rather see a private doctor here (Liliana E).

> Regarding health services, I'd rather take care of that here [in Tijuana]. I don't even like them over there. It's too fastidious, the [health] system over there is too cold (Agustín C).

> Unfortunately, over there [in the United States] doctors do not listen to you. It's not that they're not capable, but sometimes they're like irritated.... You know, sometimes you show up and they order a test and this and that. And the [medical] attentions I've received here in Tijuana have been really good (Guadalupe O).

> I have insurance in the United States, but forget about it! I only use it when it's really necessary ... to get treatment. Jeez, it's a never-ending death! I think doctors need to be more aware of it, of the [medical] system they've got. Specialized medicine has no sensitivity. I say it's sort of dehumanized; they don't give any attention to what they

say to you, to how they say it, none of that.... That's the main problem with the medical system over there (Antonio P).

These comments suggest that our interviewees' perceptions of services like health care are significantly influenced by cultural patterns. While the economic divergence between Tijuana and San Diego (or the United States more generally) is a factor, their positive or negative assessments of alternative health care options were based primarily on non-economic reasons. These ranged from instrumental ("we try to have a doctor [on both sides]") to skeptical ("the fact is that doctors over there ask for a lot of medical tests and end up giving you only Tylenol") or openly unfavorable ("[U.S. doctors] don't give any attention to what they say to you, to how they say it").[13] These perceptions reveal a very selective, strategic approach to the services available on either side of the border, providing further evidence for the attentiveness and selectivity cross-border workers apply when taking advantage of their access to an expanded market of goods and services.

TIJUANA'S CROSS-BORDER WORKERS: GENERAL PERCEPTIONS AND CULTURAL PATTERNS

Our inquiry into the dynamics of Tijuana's cross-border workers to California would not be complete without a more detailed, qualitative consideration of this group. The extended interviews we conducted enabled us to flesh out some of these workers' general perceptions regarding their back-and-forth lives between two cities, two states, and two nations.

One recurring assessment that we uncovered in the interviews was the very positive view that these workers hold regarding living in the U.S.-Mexico border region in general, and in the Tijuana–San Diego area in particular. All of the workers we interviewed were well attuned to both the advantages and the disadvantages of their cross-border

---

[13] These observations recall Pérez Abreu and Ojeda's (1999) discussion of the "quality" and "warmth" that women observed with respect to such services in Tijuana.

lives, but the overall favorable perception is paramount, and it pervades their attitudes toward most aspects of their condition as cross-border workers. Two statements by Agustín C illustrate the general viewpoint that informs commuter workers' opinions on every aspect of social life at the border:

> Well, that's the good thing about living at the border, the choices you've got for buying things. You have more options and quality in the United States.... We learn to live in this limbo in the middle of these two things. You have to live the best you can in this area because it's so special. You go south from Sonora, and the way people think is completely different, the way they are and everything. Go north of California, and everyone thinks different. That's why the border region is very, very special, and well, it must be because I was born here, I grew up here, and this area is very good. We have all these chances that many people don't have. We can't complain, we're very special people.

> I guess we get the best we can from both countries. For us Mexicans in Tijuana, "the other side" means work, cheaper and better gas for your car, good wages, affordable food and stuff, while for the Americans Mexico means cheaper health services, tourism, the chance to relax, and more affordable living costs. There are opportunities on each side of the border.

Agustín's second statement above highlights the fact that the positive aspects of life on the border are viewed as benefiting all of the people who live in this region, not just those on the Mexican side.

In addition to this overall positive evaluation of life in the border region, the workers we interviewed noted specific advantages that enhanced their transborder condition. One key advantage is their access to two different consumer markets, which helps them cover their daily needs. According to Enrique H:

> For the grocery shopping, my wife buys whatever she
> needs for the house here [in Tijuana], and I bring the big
> packages from over there [San Diego], stuff like toilet tis-
> sue, soap, shampoo. I buy it at Wal-Mart, close to my job.
> It's cheaper, and these are huge packages. Here in Tijuana
> we go to the Comercial Mexicana.

Inocencio A noted that he and his family are also cross-border shoppers:

> We do our shopping on both sides, over there [in San
> Diego] we buy mostly at Wal-Mart, and here [in Tijuana]
> we buy some stuff at Price Club, some at Gigante, like
> beef, fruits and vegetables, cleaning supplies, bread, some
> stuff for the bathroom. All the other stuff I buy over there
> [San Diego].

Perhaps the most salient feature of this pattern of accessing consumer markets on both sides of the border is its highly strategic approach. Far from demonstrating a blind loyalty to goods and services
in either nation (and belying the widespread belief among Mexicans
that everything produced in the United States is better and anything
made in Mexico is inferior), these workers take full advantage of their
access to an expanded supply of consumer choices as well as to Southern California's relatively higher wages.

This strategic attitude is revealed in key areas such as housing,
where particular emphasis is placed on the affordability of the housing
available in Tijuana. Cross-border workers' strategic perceptions also
apply in their utilization of services. Although some of the people we
interviewed mentioned that they take advantage of educational opportunities on both sides of the border, most cross-border choices in the
area of services utilization concerned health services. The strategic
choice that Tijuana's commuter workers have made to live in Tijuana
and work in California is apparently reinforced by considerations that
are less tangible than wage differentials, affordable housing, and expanded health care options. The following comments are representative in this regard:

Maybe it's that personal feeling of freedom. The system in the United States is very cold, kind of closed. Everything is so systematized, very repetitive … and then you start losing this freedom. I mean, you start losing your identity. Here in Tijuana we still have the advantage of that freedom (Agustín C).

I like the freedom you have when you live in Tijuana. In the United States there's freedom, but it's somewhat different here. Over there you play your radio loud with your friends, you're having a drink at home in your own yard, and someone shows up and tells you, "turn it down!" But that doesn't happen in Tijuana. You can be up until 4 or 5 in the morning, and nobody tells you a thing (Inocencio A).

Life over there [in the United States] is so boring. I like the way you live in Tijuana much more. I like the buses passing, the rocks in the street. I don't know, I'm very used to the way things are here. I don't like it over there. I guess I get fed up; I just don't like to live over there. And besides, if you don't have a car you can't go anywhere. It's sort of a hassle! (Liliana E).

For these cross-border workers, the notion of "freedom" clearly conveys a sense of the cultural difference that makes living in Tijuana more attractive. Indeed, Tijuana is depicted as a warm, tolerant, and easygoing place, thus validating their choice to live there. Conversely, the United States in general—and implicitly "laid-back" Southern California, particularly San Diego—is perceived as cold, dull, and inhospitable. These contrasting perceptions provide further confirmation of the value of working on one side and living on the other, as our interviewees noted:

I don't like living over there. I think life over there puts too much emphasis on routine; it's monotonous. I like the country [the United States], the cities. I like to go shopping, have lunch or dinner, look at places, but then afterwards you go back home. I remember once I visited my mom's nephew in Los Angeles for a week, and the first day was fine, and so was the second. But by the third day I just wanted to go back. It was like 5, 6 in the afternoon and everyone was inside their homes, everything in silence. So I like to go back and forth daily; but to settle and live over there, no way! (Inocencio A).

To me there's no such thing as "patriotism." I think that patriotism does not exist; I don't believe in the idea of "nation." Nation is whatever gives you the chance to live well, that's my motherland. What's her name? Well, who knows? As long as it gives you the chance to move on, to get a decent, honest job, and you don't need to say "yeah, let's die for the U.S.," right?... I guess I have that advantage, of working in the United States and living here [in Tijuana]. I don't have a problem with that (Agustín C).

Last but not least, the commuter workers we interviewed pointed out the downside of the trade-off: the border crossing itself. When asked about the disadvantages of being a cross-border worker, they emphasized the daily annoyance of the long queue to cross the border. But they also recounted the ways they have learned to cope with it. A standard procedure they use to deal with "the line" is to arrive at the border gate very early. For example, Enrique H is at the line at 4 a.m., Monday to Saturday, which enables him to cross in 15 minutes on average. Once he is on the U.S. side, he drives east to the construction site he works at and naps for an hour. This strategy works well for him:

You just lie down in your car; it's not that bad. And you cross the border pretty quick. That way your car won't overheat [while waiting in the line to cross], and best of all, you aren't mad and tired after being in line.

Overall, the workers we talked with have simply learned to cope with the wait. This implies an acceptance of the daily border crossing as part of their lives. According to Agustín C:

You end up learning how to deal with it, with the way the lines of cars move, but most of all with that inner sensation that you get, that anxiety you experience when you realize it's getting late. That's why you have to learn to be patient. For example, I have learned to read, to write, to listen to music while I'm in line.

CONCLUSIONS

We noted early in this chapter that a current perspective on the Mexico-U.S. border emphasizes the contrasts between these nations, a perspective that has been pervasive in U.S. politics and media, a vision that portrays this border as a clear-cut line neatly separating and differentiating these neighboring nations and their societies. Tijuana's cross-border workers hold an opposing perspective. This sector of Tijuana's working population embodies the intertwining social relations and interdependence across adjacent regions on either side of the border. We focused on Tijuana's commuters—their sociodemographic features and general perceptions—in order to shed light on the extent and importance of the cross-border dynamics in the Tijuana–San Diego region that link these cities—and, ultimately, their states and nations.

Southern California, particularly San Diego, exerts a strong attraction on the Mexican working population, stronger than is found in any other sister-city pair along the Mexico-U.S. border. The wage differential goes far toward explaining the presence and vitality of cross-border workers in this region, despite this group's relatively small size when compared with the working population as a whole. Examining this group of workers through a combination of census data and in-depth interviews enabled us to better assess main characteristics of transborder workers and the dynamics they have developed.

We find that these workers fill a particular niche in the San Diego labor market. The vast majority work in low-skilled occupations despite their relatively high education levels. By performing these jobs while living in Tijuana, they exert a decisive impact on the regional economy through the taxes they contribute, the goods they buy, and the services they utilize on both sides of the border.

Tijuana's commuters do more than merely reflect wage differentials across the border. We view them as a privileged window onto the complex web of social and cultural relations across this border and the decisions and strategies its inhabitants devise in order to carry out their frontier lives. Prevailing cross-border linkages in this region, which are based on networks of family and friendship, give way to complex patterns of border-crossing activities, communications, and interactions. Tijuana commuters are but one of the resulting configurations, one that conveys an important picture of the transborder way of life.

References

Acuña, Beatriz. 1983. "Migración y fuerza de trabajo en la frontera norte de México," *Estudios Fronterizos* 2 (September–December).

———. 1986. "Transmigración legal en la frontera México–Estados Unidos," *Cuadernos de Ciencias Sociales*, Serie [Universidad Autónoma de Baja California] 3, no. 1.

Alegría, Tito. 1992. *Desarrollo urbano en la frontera México-Estados Unidos*. Mexico City: CONACULTA.

———. 2000a. "Transmigrants, the NAFTA, and a Proposal to Protect Air Quality on the Border." In *Shared Space. Rethinking the U.S.-Mexico Border Environment*, edited by Lawrence Herzog. La Jolla: Center for U.S.-Mexican Studies, University of California, San Diego.

———. 2000b. "Juntos pero no revueltos: ciudades en la frontera México-Estados Unidos," *Revista Mexicana de Sociología* 62, no. 2 (April–June): 89–107.

———. 2002. "Demand and Supply of Mexican Cross-Border Workers," *Journal of Borderlands Studies* 17, no. 1 (Spring): 37–55.

Arámburo, Guillermo. 1987. "Commuters en la frontera México-Estados Unidos," *Estudios Fronterizos* 5, nos. 12–13.

BorderValues. 2002. "Border Values: San Diego–Tijuana." Preliminary report. San Diego.

Bringas, Nora. 2003. "Algunos aspectos sobre el turismo en la frontera norte de México." In *Por las fronteras del norte: una aproximación cultural a la frontera norte de México*, edited by José Manuel Valenzuela. México City: Consejo Nacional para la Cultura y las Artes/El Colegio de la Frontera Norte.

Bringas, Nora, and Jorge Carrillo, eds. 1991. *Grupos de visitantes y actividades turísticas en Tijuana*. Tijuana: El Colegio de la Frontera Norte.

Brooks, David, and Jonathan Fox, eds. 2002. *Cross-Border Dialogues. U.S.-Mexico Social Movement Networking*. La Jolla: Center for U.S.-Mexican Studies, University of California, San Diego.

Bustamante, Jorge. 1981. "La interacción social en la frontera México–Estados Unidos: un marco conceptual para la investigación." In *La frontera del norte: integración y desarrollo*, edited by Roque González Salazar. Mexico City: El Colegio de México.

Coubès, Marie-Laure. 2003. "Evolución del empleo fronterizo en los noventa: efectos del TLCAN y de la devaluación sobre la estructura ocupacional," *Frontera Norte* 15, no. 30 (July–December).

Herzog, Lawrence A. 1990a. *Where North Meets South: Cities, Space and Politics on the U.S.-Mexico Border*. Austin: Center for Mexican American Studies, University of Texas at Austin.

———. 1990b. "Border Commuter Workers and Transfrontier Metropolitan Structure along the U.S.-Mexico Border," *Journal of Borderlands Studies* 5, no. 2 (Fall).

INEGI (Instituto Nacional de Estadística, Geografía e Informática). 2000. *Muestra del Diez por Ciento del XII Censo General de Población y Vivienda*. Mexico City: INEGI.

Martínez, Oscar. 1994. *Border People: Life and Society in the U.S.-Mexico Borderlands*. Tucson: University of Arizona Press.

Milkman, Ruth, and Kent Wong. 2000. "Organizing the Wicked City: The 1992 Southern California Drywall Strike." In *Organizing Immigrants. The Challenge for Unions in Contemporary California*, edited by Ruth Milkman. Ithaca, New York: School of Industrial and Labor Relations, Cornell University Press.

Ojeda, Norma, ed. 1999. *Género, familia y conceptualización de la salud reproductiva en México*. Tijuana: El Colegio de la Frontera Norte.

Pérez Abreu, Rafael A., and Norma Ojeda. 1999. "Percepción femenina de la calidad y calidez de los servicios en salud reproductive: una aproximación estadística." In *Género, familia y conceptualización de la salud reproductiva en México*, edited by Norma Ojeda. 1999. Tijuana: El Colegio de la Frontera Norte.

Power J. Gerard, and Theresa Byrd, eds. 1998. *U.S.-Mexico Border Health. Issues for Regional and Migrant Populations*. London: Sage.

Rey, Serge, Paul Ganster, Gustavo del Castillo, Juan Álvarez, Ken Shellhammer, Norris Clement, and Alan Sweedler. 1998. "The San Diego–Tijuana Region." In *Integrating Cities and Regions: North America Faces Globalization*, edited by James Wilkie and Clint Smith. Guadalajara: UCLA Program on Mexico/Centro Internacional Lucas Alamán para el Crecimiento Económico.

Roberts, Bryan. 1999. "Households Structures and Trends along the U.S.-Mexico Border." In *Preliminary Findings and Report in the Workshop: Family and Household Dynamics.* El Paso: University of Texas at El Paso/DIF Ciudad Juárez.

Ruiz, Olivia. 1996. "El ir y venir: la relación transfronteriza." In *Reflexiones sobre la identidad de los pueblos,* edited by Ramón Eduardo Ruiz and Olivia Ruiz. Tijuana: El Colegio de la Frontera Norte.

——. 1998. "Visiting the Mother Country: Border-Crossing as a Cultural Practice." In *The U.S.-Mexico Border: Transcending Divisions, Contesting Identities* , edited by David Spener and Kathleen Staudt. Boulder, Colo.: Lynne Rienner.

San Diego Dialogue. 1994. *Who Crosses the Border: A View of the San Diego/Tijuana Metropolitan Region.* San Diego, California: San Diego Dialogue.

Spener, David, and Bryan R. Roberts. 1998. "Small Business, Social Capital, and Economic Integration on the Texas-Mexico Border." In *The U.S.-Mexico Border: Transcending Divisions, Contesting Identities,* edited by David Spener and Kathleen Staudt. Boulder, Colo.: Lynne Rienner.

Taylor, Lawrence D. 2001. "Approaches to Building Cooperative Linkages in Human Resources Development in the San Diego–Tijuana and Vancouver-Seattle Binational Corridor Regions," *Journal of Borderlands Studies* 16, no. 2 (Fall): 41–69.

Vega Briones, Germán. 1999. "Changes in Gender and Family Roles in the Mexican Border: The Ciudad Juárez Case." PhD dissertation, University of Texas at Austin.

Vila, Pablo. 2000. *Crossing Borders, Reinforcing Borders: Social Categories, Metaphors, and Narrative Identities on the U.S.-Mexico Frontier.* Austin: University of Texas Press.

Zenteno, René, and Héctor Rodríguez. 1996. "La población transmigrante en las ciudades fronterizas mexicanas." Research report for the project "Labor Markets and Small and Medium Enterprises in the Mexico–United States Transborder Region." Tijuana: El Colegio de la Frontera Norte.

7

Building a Case for Cross-Border Service Provision for Transnational Mexican Migrants in San Diego

RICHARD KIY AND NAOKO KADA

The San Diego–Tijuana border has been described as a fascinating interface between "haves" and "have-nots," a place where "a third world environment [is] slammed up" against one of the most affluent metropolitan regions in the world (*Haus der Kulturen der Welt*, September 2002). Though the contrast *between* San Diego and Tijuana is undoubtedly vivid, another, no less stark contrast exists *within* each of these two communities. San Diego County houses some of the most exclusive communities in North America, but also migrant camps with no clean water. While San Diego County is the most prosperous county along the U.S.-Mexico border, the poverty level in some of its communities near the border has been rising in recent years, due in part to an influx of people from Mexico's migrant-sending regions. Tijuana, too, is a very prosperous city, one of the most prosperous in Mexico, but its cost of living is also high. This fact, coupled with growing in-migration, has meant that over half of the city's new residents live in squatter communities that lack basic infrastructure.

In both San Diego and Tijuana, government agencies face the growing fiscal challenge of providing sufficient and effective services, especially in the areas of education and health, to their growing migrant populations. As their populations increase, fueled in large part by migration from the interior of Mexico and beyond, public resources to provide services to this growing population have not kept pace in either city. As the unfunded mandates have multiplied at the state and local levels of government in both San Diego and Tijuana, so too has the demand for the nonprofit sector to play a role in filling at least some of these service gaps. Increasingly, the region's migrant-serving nonprofit organizations are playing crucial roles in providing essential social services to migrants in the San Diego–Tijuana region.

This chapter first describes the shared challenges that San Diego and Tijuana face in responding to the service needs of their underprivileged and underserved communities, and it makes the case for greater cross-border collaboration among nonprofit organizations from both sides of the international border. The chapter then offers an overview of the role of the nonprofit sector in responding to the needs of the region's underprivileged and underserved residents, especially recent migrants from Mexico's interior. Using case studies of nongovernmental organizations (NGOs) that have engaged in cross-border collaboration, the chapter demonstrates that such collaboration across the U.S.-Mexico border is beneficial to both the organizations themselves and to the clients they serve. Drawing upon surveys conducted by the International Community Foundation (ICF) of migrant-serving organizations in San Diego County, the chapter also points to obstacles that have impeded cross-border collaboration between NGOs in the binational region, and it offers suggestions for overcoming these obstacles. Finally, the chapter advocates thinking beyond the immediate border region and connecting NGOs, government agencies, and private foundations in San Diego with the migrant-sending communities across Mexico that are home to the families and extended families of the border region's migrants.

SAN DIEGO–TIJUANA: A REGION OF CONTRASTS

San Diego's economy is highly diversified, with rapidly growing high-tech sectors such as biomedical research and wireless communications. Yet over 18 percent of the local San Diego economy is still composed of sectors that rely heavily on a migrant workforce (legal and undocumented, and primarily from Mexico); these sectors include tourism and hospitality (11 percent), agriculture (1 percent), and construction (6 percent).[1]

The San Diego economy's reliance on migrant labor has produced some stark contrasts between poverty and prosperity. Rancho Santa Fe, in San Diego's North County, ranks as the most affluent community in the United States; yet its nearby canyons are home to some 10,000 to 15,000 migrant workers living in encampments that lack running water, sewerage, or electricity (see Bade, this volume). Because of San Diego's high living costs, countless other migrants and their families live in overcrowded housing, with two or more families in a single apartment. Due to these disparities, some parts of San Diego County have rising indices of urban poverty. According to a recent report from the Brookings Institution, San Diego ranks 6th nationwide among metropolitan areas experiencing marked increases in poverty in their respective regions; a total of ten San Diego census tracts saw marked increases in poverty between 1990 and 2000 (Jargowky 2003). A review of *matrícula consular* data for San Diego County reveals a positive correlation between those areas experiencing increases in poverty and those with high concentrations of Mexican migrant workers (see Runsten, this volume).

Across the border in neighboring Tijuana, a similar contrast is visible between haves and have-nots. Well-appointed houses line the coast, but half of all newly arriving migrants—some 40,000 a year—live in unserviced squatter communities, commonly known as *colonias populares*. The colonias have little or no clean water, and water-borne infectious disease and other health risks are prevalent. Tijuana's urban poverty and its growing number of colonias[2] signal that the pressures of human migration are binational, and the need to proactively address migrant needs is shared by the United States and Mexico. Moreover, many members of San Diego's Latino population, which is growing in

---

[1] San Diego Economic Development Corporation, March 2003 employment figures for San Diego County.

[2] Their total combined area is increasing by an estimated 2.25 hectares a day (Ganster 1999).

absolute terms and also as a proportion of the county's population, have kinship and cultural ties that bridge the international border. For these Latinos, particularly recent immigrants, cross-border service provision could make culturally competent services available, often at a more affordable price than in San Diego.

SAN DIEGO'S CHANGING DEMOGRAPHICS

San Diego's population, paralleling the statewide and nationwide trend, is becoming more Latino each year. In 1990, according to the U.S. census, 20.4 percent of the county's 2.5 million residents were of Hispanic origin.[3] In 2000, 26.7 percent of the county's 2.8 million residents were of Hispanic origin, and the vast majority (84 percent) were of Mexican descent.[4] By 2025, the U.S. Census Bureau estimates that, at over 43 percent of California's population, Hispanics will be the largest ethnic group in the state (Campbell 1996). Demographic change in San Diego County will come somewhat more slowly, but U.S. census projections suggest that one in three San Diego residents will be Hispanic by 2020, and Hispanics will become the largest group in the county by 2036.[5]

U.S. census data also show that San Diego County's Hispanic population is highly concentrated in areas close to the border, within the City of San Diego, and in the cities and unincorporated communities of San Diego's North County: Vista, Valley Center, Carlsbad, San Marcos, and Oceanside. In 2000, 69 percent of Hispanics in the county lived in just ten communities within these subregions. Today, 26 percent (more than a fourth) of Hispanic residents reside in "South County," the areas south of downtown San Diego that extend to the border with Tijuana (see table 7.1). Another notable feature of this population is that, except

---

[3] Data from the U.S. Census Bureau, at http://quickfacts.census.gov/qfd/states/06/060731k.html, last accessed 2/20/04.

[4] U.S. Census Bureau, at http://quickfacts.census.gov/qfd/states/06/060731k.html, and Hispanic Marketing Council, at http://www.sandiegoadclub.com/hispanic.html (both last accessed 2/20/04).

[5] Hispanic Marketing Council, citing State of California Department of Finance population projection in 1998 and SANDAG population projections of 2000. Available at http://www.sandiegoadclub.com/hispanic.html (last accessed 2/20/04).

for those residing in Chula Vista, 20 percent or more of the Hispanic population in these subareas do not speak or read English well.

Disturbingly, the median household incomes of some of the communities listed in table 7.1 are much lower than the county average, and their incidence of poverty is rising. In Logan Heights and San Ysidro, in San Diego's South Bay, almost 50 percent of families with children under age 18 fall below the poverty line.[6] Despite San Diego's affluence, the pockets of urban and rural poverty across the county are growing. Many county communities where poverty increased by at least 1 percent between 1990 and 2000 are in areas where the Mexican migrant population has been growing and where the Hispanic population share is higher than the county average (see Runsten, this volume).

Given the characteristics of some San Diego communities—Hispanics accounting for a third and sometimes almost two-thirds of the population, rising poverty, and a significant percentage of residents unable to communicate effectively in English—it is clear that those NGOs that have traditionally provided social services in these communities must adapt to serve their large and growing Hispanic population more effectively. The task is complicated further when NGOs attempt to address the needs of more recent migrants, many of whom are transnational residents with ties to towns and villages throughout Mexico and, in some cases, speak only an indigenous language.

TRANSBORDER RESIDENTS, TRANSNATIONAL MIGRANTS: TWO DIFFERENT WORLDS

The economic impacts of the growing numbers of Mexican migrants have been felt in both domestic consumer spending and in the remittances they send to their communities of origin. According to the U.S. Department of Treasury, estimated remittances to Mexico were expected to exceed US$13 billion in 2003.[7] Collectively, Mexican migrants in the United States are having a profound economic impact on sending communities south of the border, helping to create employment and providing disposable income in otherwise impoverished regions of

---

[6] U.S. Census 2000; SANDAG Data warehouse.

[7] U.S. Treasury Department, Office of Public Affairs, October 1, 2003.

Table 7.1. San Diego County's Hispanic Population by Community

Rank	Area	Total Population	Hispanic Population	Percent Hispanic	Percent Hispanic with Little or No English
1	South Bay (excluding Chula Vista, National City, Sweetwater)	124,020	73,885	59.6%	20%
2	Mid City-San Diego	168,125	62,538	37.2	25
3	Chula Vista	108,907	62,238	57.1	16
4	Southeastern San Diego	156,124	61,809	39.6	21
5	Central San Diego (including Barrio Logan)	155,827	58,223	37.4	20
6	Escondido	146,288	53,681	36.7	28
7	Oceanside	151,545	48,268	31.9	22
8	Vista	95,714	36,374	38.0	27
9	National City	53,859	32,171	59.7	21
10	Sweetwater	74,542	27,210	36.5%	25%

Source: U.S. 2000 Census; SANDAG Data Warehouse.

Mexico. According to the Banco de México, remittances by Mexican migrants living in the United States outpaced income from tourism and from foreign direct investment in 2001 (*Boston Globe* 2003). In 2001, Mexico's National Population Council (CONAPO) estimated that as many as 1.3 million households—more than one in ten families—depended on remittances, primarily from migrants in the United States, as their main source of income. This point is underscored by the fact that over 9 million Mexico-born residents—or close to 8.4 percent of all living Mexicans—are currently in the United States.[8]

Although they are often grouped together simply as "Mexicans," it is important to differentiate "transborder residents" and "transnational residents" in the San Diego–Tijuana binational region. Transborder residents are individuals with valid documents that allow them to freely and legally cross the border for work, study, or pleasure. A large share of transborder residents have family and friends on both sides of the border. For them, the availability of cross-border work and study opportunities and services is a fact of life and one of the unique advantages of life in a border zone. Unlike their transborder resident counterparts, transnational residents lack legal documentation to freely cross the border. The vast majority are from Mexico's impoverished interior. Most are isolated from families and friends, although some bring their families with them and some live with other migrants from their home village or region. Transborder residents and transnational residents certainly face some shared challenges, but transnational residents have other unique and pressing needs, needs that have largely gone unrecognized or underserved.

Both transborder residents and transnational residents in San Diego–Tijuana seek the special opportunities present in this binational region. Many come for the region's high wages (especially in San Diego, but also in Tijuana relative to the country's interior). Others cross the border to study or for services or shopping in San Diego. Yet

---

[8] U.S. Census 2000 data indicate that there are 9,177,437 Mexico-born residents in the United States. According to the 2000 Mexican census, Mexico's population is 100,399,761. Not counting Mexicans in third countries, the total combined population of Mexico-born individuals in the United States and Mexico would be 109,399,761.

not all enjoy the strategic economic benefits of life on the border. According to a recent survey, over one-third of Tijuana residents have never been to San Diego,[9] primarily because they lack border crossing cards or valid visas. A growing number of Mexican transnational residents who have crossed illegally into San Diego now avoid crossing back into Mexico because of the high financial cost and risk associated with reentering the United States under the heightened security measures in effect since the implementation of "Operation Gatekeeper" and the terrorism incidents of September 11, 2001.

For an estimated 183,500 undocumented transnational Mexican residents now living in San Diego County—accounting for 63 percent of the Mexico-born population in the county[10] and 6.5 percent of the county's total population (Office of Policy Planning and Evaluation 2003)—the border remains impermeable and unforgiving. Unlike their transborder counterparts, San Diego' transnational migrants, more often than not, have needs that are difficult to meet—because they lack information on available services, because they do not know their rights as migrants, because they fear that use of services could lead to deportation, and/or because they are physically constrained from crossing the border to seek more cost-effective and culturally competent service options. As a result, the number of transnational residents living on the margins grows, and more and more are joining the ranks of the working poor, living in overcrowded housing or migrant camps, surviving without medical or dental insurance, and suffering increased isolation from their communities of origin.

TRANSBORDER AND TRANSNATIONAL RESIDENTS OF THE BORDER REGION: ISSUES AND NEEDS

All migrants face the challenges of adjusting to life in their adopted land. Most encounter communication problems; this is especially true

---

[9] Cross Border Business Associates survey of San Diego–Tijuana residents, December 2003 (commissioned by the ICF). For survey methodology, see www.icfdn.org.

[10] The foreign-born population of San Diego totals 658,437, or 23.4 percent of the county's population. Foreign-born Mexicans total 289,059, according to U.S. Census 2000 data.

for indigenous migrants, many of whom speak only their native language and have no Spanish, much less English. Mexican migrants are highly diverse; for example, migrants from the states of Oaxaca, Guerrero, Jalisco, Michoacán, and Baja California make up over half of San Diego County's Mexican migrant population.[11] In other words, Mexican migrants in San Diego come from many different cultures. Each of the five Mexican states that send large numbers of migrants to San Diego County contains many different indigenous migrant-sending communities, which makes the migrant population even more diverse. Migrants from rural areas, especially from indigenous communities that have maintained their cultural and social heritage, pose special challenges to public and nonprofit service providers because these agencies are likely to be unfamiliar with the cultures and social norms of these indigenous communities.

In addition to language barriers and cultural adjustments, many migrants suffer the hardship of separation from family and friends. Many migrant workers leave their family in Mexico, disrupting family life for both the workers and their families. Some fortunate migrants encounter other migrants from their home community, with whom they are able to form a "transnational community." Through this community, migrants can maintain social, cultural, economic, and political ties with their communities of origin, and draw support through the pooling of resources and through mutual assistance.[12] However, not all migrants are able to benefit from established transnational communities. In addition, even when they can form part of a transnational community, transnational migrants still face many challenges in their daily lives that their transborder counterparts do not. These include a high cost of living compared to the migrants' earning power, occupational and environmental health risks, cultural adjustment problems and discrimination, lack of legal protections, contract violations and illegal recruitment by some employers, debt bondage and confiscation

---

[11] Calculation based on *matrícula consular* numbers, including for both documented and undocumented migrants.

[12] For a thorough discussion of transnational communities, see, for example, Georges and Georges 1990; Portes 1997.

of passports by human smugglers and employers, insecurity of land tenure and/or risk of eviction, and deportation.

First, because of their undocumented status, transnational migrants tend to be employed in lower-paying sectors or in jobs without benefits, or both. For example, a survey conducted by Bonnie Bade (see Bade, this volume) revealed that 49 percent of migrant farmworkers in Vista, California, are undocumented. Even working at minimum wage or below, these workers are able to earn far more than they could in their rural home villages, whose agricultural crops cannot compete with imports under the North American Free Trade Agreement (NAFTA). Yet because of the high cost of living in the United States, these relatively better wages cannot cover reasonable housing costs or health care, especially when one considers that a primary goal of the migrant workers is to send a share of their wages back to their families in Mexico.

Second, transnational migrants do not have easy access to the culturally competent and affordable health care, social services, or education available in Tijuana, in sharp contrast to their transborder resident counterparts. Because of increased security measures in place at the border, an ever-smaller segment of transnational migrants appear willing to risk crossing back to Mexico for fear of being unable to return to work in San Diego. Nor are they likely to actively seek public services in San Diego, either because they are afraid to reveal their undocumented status or because the services are (or are perceived to be) unavailable or unaffordable to the would-be user.

Third, a number of transnational migrants are likely to have entered the United States via human-trafficking organizations—and are often abused by the traffickers. Some traffickers have abandoned truckloads of migrants, leaving them no way to escape from the containers that concealed them. Migrants often pay exorbitant fees to their *coyotes* (human traffickers), leaving them so deeply indebted that they cannot afford adequate housing, let alone medical care.[13] Many migrants have

---

[13] For example, ten migrant workers in Carlsbad told a reporter that together they owed $10,000 to the trafficker that helped them cross into the United States without work permits (Gaona 2004a).

little option but to live in camps that lack such basic necessities as running water, or to crowd into apartments where they barely have enough space to lie down. Poor living conditions and lack of medical care make this population highly vulnerable to health problems, especially infectious diseases. Young children and older workers in these transnational migrant communities are particularly at risk. And although young adult workers in these groups may not suffer serious health problems, they can be transmitters of infectious diseases from their workplaces in the fields or in services to the more vulnerable younger and older populations.

Fourth, transnational migrants fear discovery of their undocumented status; to avoid the risk of deportation, they avoid contact with public agencies and involvement in politics or labor unions. They are not likely to seek to improve their working and living conditions through negotiation with their employers, through unions, or through public or nonprofit agencies. When undocumented immigrants are discovered and deported,[14] they often have difficulty reintegrating into their home communities because of their migration experiences, including, for better or worse, some Americanization of their tastes and values and the fact that, despite its challenges, life on the other side can in some ways be better than life at home.[15]

In sum, Mexican migrants, especially transnational migrants, have many pressing needs. Left unattended, these needs can have a significant impact on the larger society, especially in the areas of health and education. Migrants' needs are not being, or cannot be, addressed by government entities alone, for reasons explored in the following section. In order to provide effective services to the Mexican migrant population in San Diego, then, the nonprofit sector must play a more active role.

---

[14] Migrants are sometimes deported after dark, even when the deportees include women and minors. See "Mexicali Group Takes Issue of Unsafe Deportation of Minors to the OAS," Frontera Norte Sur, online news services, August 1, 2003.

[15] Interview with Jaime Boloñes, executive director of Fundación Comunitario de Oaxaca (FCO), October 2003.

THE ROLE OF THE NONPROFIT SECTOR IN MIGRANT SERVICES IN THE BORDER REGION

As discussed above, Mexican migrants have distinct needs depending on their legal status and the region and culture from which they originate. Because of its proximity to Tijuana, San Diego County is uniquely positioned to address the region's migrant issues by making optimal use of the broad range of professionals south of the border who have practical experience in addressing migrants' needs. Many of San Diego's transborder residents are already procuring cross-border services in health and education from nonprofits and other private institutions in Tijuana, but such service provision options are easily available only to those who can legally cross the border.

Given recent cuts in governmental funding to health and human services across California, San Diego's transnational migrants are finding migrant service agencies (governmental and nonprofit) short on staff and resources to adequately address their growing needs. In recent years, the state has even decided to divert some of the funding hitherto reserved for local governments (Larson 2003). California's proposed budget for 2004–2005 cuts more than $2.7 billion from health and human services, and $880 million of this cut is from the Medi-Cal health program for the poor. Health and Human Services and Education are the two areas scheduled for the deepest cuts: the K–14 education budget will shrink by $2 billion and higher education by $730 million. The allocation for Business, Transportation and Housing will be cut by $1 billion and Youth and Adult Correction by $440 million (California Health and Human Services Agency 2004: 5). These cuts will have the sharpest impact on the working poor, who are much less likely than more affluent California residents to find alternative avenues for services, except for those provided by the nonprofit sector. At a time when the nonprofit sector itself faces a funding challenge due to the economic downturn in the United States and in California in particular, this same sector faces a growing demand as those who previously received services from public agencies will turn increasingly to the nonprofit sector for assistance.

Given the current uncertainty with respect to funding, a growing number of nonprofit leaders, particularly those who work with the migrant community, are expressing uncertainty about the future. According to an Aspen Institute study of the impact of state fiscal crisis on nonprofit organizations across the United States, a likely prognosis for the nonprofit sector is "death by a thousand cuts" (Bowman 2003: 1). According to the Aspen Institute, the crisis facing such nonprofits is exacerbated by the fact that government contracts and grants account for 31 percent of the income of community-serving nonprofits across the United States. The nonprofits' true dependence on government funds is reportedly much higher, however, because they often report income from governmental sources as fee-based income (Bowman 2003: 3).

The crisis facing community-serving and social service–based nonprofits is most pronounced among those serving the migrant community. Here the nonprofits are often hampered by their inability to effectively advocate for the people they serve because of their clients' migratory status.

In those cases where migratory status is not an issue, many migrants do not receive services due to their lack of knowledge about available services or simply out of fear of visiting an agency that may be perceived to be associated with the government. Compounding matters, many migrants coming to San Diego in search of work have limited educational levels or few skills that meet workplace requirements in the region. Without workplace retraining, these migrants have limited possibilities for earning higher incomes in the future, and as their number grows, more of them are likely to have difficulty finding jobs. Thus the combination of scarce resources and growing migrant needs is creating more unfunded mandates for local and state agencies in San Diego, as well as for nonprofit organizations committed to serving the needs of this growing segment of the population.

WHY CROSS-BORDER COLLABORATION IN THE NONPROFIT SECTOR?

Given that Mexican transnational migrants in the United States maintain regular ties with their communities of origin, there is a compelling case for the cross-border provision of services (education, health, and human services), particularly in a border community such as San Diego, where a growing number of migrant-specific issues and needs have transboundary impacts and consequences. Migrant youths on both sides of the border often have to change schools because of their parents' high job-related mobility, which can lead to lower levels of educational attainment among this group. Preventable and curable diseases such as tuberculosis have become a serious problem in the border region because of patients, many of them migrants, failing to complete their treatment course, or simply not treating the disease, knowingly or unknowingly. In short, the binational nature of these issues requires binational solutions, and nonprofit agencies (and public agencies) need to be aware of the benefits of binational collaboration.

A key advantage of collaboration is that migrant-serving organizations share knowledge in order to better serve their migrant clients. As profiled below, some of Baja California's NGOs have extensive knowledge and experience in servicing the growing Mexican migrant community, given that 43 percent of would-be cross-border migrants arriving in Tijuana ultimately stay in Tijuana. San Diego's service-providing NGOs can benefit greatly from closer collaboration with these NGOs, and some are already doing so. But such collaborations are still few and far between. One example of cross-border collaboration, albeit not between NGOs, is the "border pedagogy" initiative between California State University San Marcos and the Universidad Iberoamericana, where K–12 educators from both sides of the border get together to discuss how best to educate the region's youth, and migrant youth in particular. Thanks to this initiative, border educators are increasingly finding that they share the same children and the same problems, and can thus benefit from learning from each other's experience.

A second reason to collaborate is that some issues simply cannot be addressed by local nonprofits alone, and some clients need support that San Diego–based nonprofits are little prepared to provide. This is particularly the case when trying to address the needs of both migrants and their sending communities, which calls for enhanced collaboration between San Diego's nonprofits and the growing number of migrant-serving organizations. Today, there are over 1,500 Mexican hometown associations across the United States, including some in San Diego County. There are also umbrella organizations that represent and/or serve migrants from the same region of origin.

In San Diego's North County, for example, the *oaxaqueño* community is represented by a budding grassroots organization called the Coalition of Indigenous Communities of Oaxaca (COCIO), which numbers over two hundred members with representation from Oceanside, Carlsbad, San Marcos, and Vista. Thanks to its broad-based network of *oaxaqueños* in San Diego, COCIO has already raised $8,000, in partnership with the International Community Foundation and Oaxaca-based Centotl, A.C., to fund an agriculturally based productive employment project in the village of El Trapiche in Oaxaca's Central Valley. COCIO also has been instrumental in raising money for local events celebrating the birthday of Oaxacan-born President Benito Juárez (March 21), the Guelaguetza (mid-August), and the Day of the Dead (November 2). A similar binationally oriented *oaxaqueño* organization—the Oaxacan Indigenous Binational Front (FIOB)—has offices in Tijuana and Fresno, California, and work under way in Escondido.[16]

Collectively, COCIO and FIOB provide San Diego nonprofit organizations and government agencies with unique knowledge and experience in reaching out to the Mixtec community of San Diego's North County. These organizations' members have the needed indigenous language capabilities and are in frequent communication with their communities of origin and, in the case of FIOB, the Mixtec community immediately across the border in eastern Tijuana, Rosarito, and San Quintín. Both groups, however, remain underfunded and understaffed. COCIO still relies solely on volunteers, and there is a pressing need to strengthen the leadership and organizational skills of its key officers. Now in the process of applying for its 501(c)3 status, COCIO hopes that over time it can play a more proactive role in meeting its community's wide-ranging needs, including outreach in parental education and occupational health issues. There is also a desire among many COCIO members to expand the level of assistance to their communities of origin in Oaxaca.

Third, and related to the second point above, many San Diego–area nonprofits are ill-equipped to provide effective services to migrants, especially indigenous migrants, due to a lack of cultural understanding of the Mexican and migrant populations. A number of Mexico-based

---

[16] For information on FIOB, see www.laneta.apc.org/fiob/.

nonprofit agencies have the essential knowledge, skills, and cultural competence that could enable San Diego NGOs to address the unique needs of Mexico's transnational migrant community. Mexican NGOs can also provide value-added services in a cost-effective manner and leverage community-based networks in migrant-sending regions. Some excellent examples already exist of binational partnerships that help provide culturally sensitive and effective services to Mexican migrants in the San Diego–Tijuana area (analyzed in detail below).

Illustrating the challenges involved in providing culturally competent services to migrants, a survey conducted by ICF in early 2004 among migrant-serving NGOs in San Diego found that, for some NGOs, up to half of their service population spoke neither Spanish nor English well (they spoke an indigenous language such as Otomí, Mixteco, or Chontal). Although all the NGOs that responded to the survey said that they had staff, volunteers, or interpreters who speak Spanish fluently, only one had staff, volunteers, or certified interpreters who could speak an indigenous language of Mexico. Also, in some organizations, the percentage of Spanish-speaking staff or volunteers was much lower than the percentage of Spanish-speaking clients. Many organizations responded that they did not know the language skills of their volunteers.

While it seems that there would be obvious interest in greater collaboration with Mexican nonprofit organizations to address these language skill gaps, this same survey also found that there is very little activity on the part of San Diego migrant-serving NGOs to actively collaborate with Mexican NGOs. Some of the most common reasons for not considering cross-border collaboration were the wait time at the border, distance, and lack of funding. Other obstacles that NGOs mentioned were contract restrictions and legal issues, lack of organizational capacity to carry out binational collaboration, inability to find partners in Mexico, language barriers, and safety concerns.

Over all, the results of the ICF survey were not very encouraging. Only twelve out of over thirty organizations returned their survey, indicating that binational collaboration is not a priority or a strong interest for the vast majority of migrant-serving NGOs in San Diego. Of the twelve NGOs that responded, only three had ongoing binational partnerships with Mexican NGOs, professionals, or government enti-

ties. Of the nine NGOs that currently have no ongoing binational partnerships, five said they have no plans for such collaboration, one did
not specify whether it was interested in binational partnerships, one
said it was open to collaboration but it has not been necessary, and
only two said they are interested in collaborating with Mexican NGOs
(see table 7.2).

Table 7.2. Survey of San Diego's Migrant-serving NGOs, 2004

Question: Do you have an ongoing partnership with Mexican NGOs, professionals, or government entities?	"Yes" Responses
Yes, we have an ongoing partnership with Mexican NGOs/professionals/government	3
No, but we are interested	2
No, because it has been unnecessary, but we are open to collaboration	1
No, and we have no plans for binational partnership	**5**
N/A	1
Total (questionnaires sent to over 30 NGOs)	12

Source: ICF survey of San Diego migrant-serving NGOs, February/March 2004.

The survey results demonstrate that San Diego NGOs have yet to
realize the potential of cross-border collaboration. In addition to the
reasons the NGOs offered for not pursuing cross-border collaboration,
their lack of appreciation for cross-border partnerships also stems from
the fact that little is known about existing cross-border partnerships
and the benefits they have conferred. Still, in cases where there is binational collaboration, nonprofits based in San Diego and Tijuana have
been able to expand and improve their service to migrant populations
on both sides of the international border.

MAKING THE CASE FOR CROSS-BORDER SERVICE PROVISION

As mentioned above, some Baja California nonprofits are already providing cross-border services to the growing number of San Diego's
transborder residents who seek affordable health care. A case in point

is the Hospital Infantil de las Californias, which receives patients, including children, from as far north as Oceanside.[17] Other transborder residents and some returning transnational migrants have used (the more affordable) drug-rehabilitation clinics in Tijuana and Tecate, including the Centro de Recuperación y Rehabilitación para Enfermos de Alcoholismo y Drogadicción, A.C. (CRREAD).

Baja California nonprofits also provide services to Mexican migrants who are either en route to the United States or returning to Mexico because of loss of employment, sickness, or deportation. These organizations include the Instituto de Derechos Humanos de Indigentes y Migrantes, A.C.–Albergue San Vicente; Albergue Juvenil del Desierto, A.C.; and Casa del Migrante de Nuestra Señora de Guadalupe en Tecate, A.C. As the post–9/11 emphasis on national security "collides with a long tradition of protecting the juvenile," an increasing number of unaccompanied minors are facing deportation for violation of immigration rules (Bernstein 2004). In this context, migrant-serving organizations such as those cited above, as well as Casa YMCA de Menores Migrantes in Tijuana which provides shelter and counseling for deported migrant youth, play an increasingly crucial role in protecting minors deported from the United States.

Some of the largest unmet social service needs are to be found among San Diego's migrant workers and their families who are unable to cross into Tijuana. Although the physical border presents an obvious barrier, this does not mean that cross-border service provision is impossible. On the contrary, through effective partnering, binational collaboration, and better use of technology (telemedicine, distance learning, Internet chat, and video-teleconferencing), San Diego–area migrant-serving organizations are able to expand and improve service delivery to their communities without requiring their clients/patients to cross the international line. Because San Diego and Tijuana have one of the most extensive cross-border fiber optic networks on the border, they are ideally positioned to benefit from such initiatives.

---

[17] The hospital does not currently keep a record of the percentage of patients coming from Southern California.

CROSS-BORDER SERVICE PROVISION CASE STUDIES

Nowhere is the need for binational collaboration on migrant-related issues greater than in the areas of health and education. Though more binational collaboration is needed, some impressive steps are being taken by San Diego and Tijuana–area nonprofits in tuberculosis prevention, sexually transmitted diseases, family planning, and parental education.

Tuberculosis

San Diego County is believed to have the highest incidence of tuberculosis (TB) in the border region,[18] and Baja California has the highest TB rates in all of Mexico. This is due in part to the regional prevalence of drug-resistant TB (Besser et al. 2001; Secretaría de Salud 2002: 55). The transitory nature of the region's migrant population is a contributing factor in the spread of TB; some migrants diagnosed with TB in San Diego begin the course of treatment there but return to Mexico before they complete it. Patients who fail to complete treatment are likely to develop a drug-resistant strain of TB. The binational nature of the TB challenge has been acknowledged on both sides of the border, and binational solutions have been implemented. To reduce the incidence of drug-resistant TB, public health workers and health professionals on both sides of the border have begun networking to ensure that patients complete their treatment regardless of whether they are in the United States or Mexico (Romero 2002).

San Diego–based Project Concern International (PCI) has been a leader in this area with its Border Health Initiative, an ambitious TB prevention program that promotes binational collaboration and health education outreach in partnership with a Tijuana affiliate, Patronato de Medicina Social Comunitaria, A.C. (PMSC). Together, PCI and PMSC have worked across the San Diego–Tijuana region, Imperial County, and Mexicali to build the capacity of health care providers working in TB and to promote binational coordination for TB treatment. They have also jointly supported training in tuberculosis for community-based

---

[18] San Diego County is one of the twelve highest TB incidence areas in the United States.

promotores, with a focus on early detection/treatment and outreach skills. Through funding from the San Diego Health and Human Services Agency's CURE-TB program, PCI maintains a referral and case-tracking system that provides a 1-800 telephone number to connect TB patients and services across Mexico and the United States. The San Ysidro Health Center and North County Health Services, along with the County of San Diego, have also actively promoted TB prevention and education among the region's migrant community.

HIV/AIDS

San Diego County ranks third highest in California in the number of HIV cases.[19] Between January 1995 and September 1997, the number of reported AIDS cases among Hispanics in San Diego rose 7 percent. San Diego is an area of high drug consumption, which increases the risk of transmission through shared needles. Of the 11,069 AIDS cases reported in San Diego County as of December 31, 2001, 20 percent were Hispanics, and 81.5 percent of the Hispanics were of Mexican origin. The typical person in San Diego living with AIDS is a white male between the ages of thirty and forty-nine. The second most numerous group is Hispanics, and a growing number of those at risk are migrant laborers. By comparison, Tijuana ranks third nationally in the number of reported HIV cases. Between 1984 and 1997, 1,428 AIDS cases were reported in Baja California; 59 percent were in Tijuana, where the infrastructure for HIV/AIDS prevention and treatment services is very limited. There are only two clinics and a handful of private labs that offer HIV screening in Tijuana; their services are too expensive for the average person, so most patients go untreated and/or unreported.

Among the nonprofits actively providing HIV/AIDS–related cross-border services are, again, PCI and PMSC. They have developed binational advocacy campaigns and provided capacity building to Baja California–area nonprofits involved in HIV/AIDS care and education

---

[19] The source for information in this paragraph is the Project Concern Border Health Initiative, HIV/AIDS programmatic initiatives, 2004.

in San Diego–Tijuana and the Imperial County–Mexicali region.[20] In collaboration with the California Department of Health Services, PCI has also undertaken research to study HIV prevalence among young Latin American MSM (men who have sex with other men) in San Diego–Tijuana. Through its annual HIV/STD conference "The Border That Unites Us," PCI has been working to expand knowledge and increase awareness of HIV, AIDS, and STDs (sexually transmitted diseases) among health providers and community members in San Diego–Tijuana. Their efforts have also included binational outreach to youth in San Diego–Tijuana.[21]

The San Ysidro Health Center (SYHC) has also been involved in binational collaborative work. This center—started in 1968 through a partnership between residents of San Diego's South Bay, the University of California, San Diego (UCSD) School of Medicine, and Mexican partner organizations—provides HIV/AIDS care through a program called CASA (Coordinated Assistance Services and Advocacy). According to SYHC, it is the only provider of HIV/AIDS services in San Diego's South Bay. Over six hundred people access CASA services every month, and an average of six to seven of these people are new HIV-positive patients. CASA offers culturally competent medical and social support services for people infected or affected by HIV/AIDS. Its core services include medical care, case management, treatment adherence counseling, access to medication through the AIDS Drug Assistance Program, and on-site translation. Support services such as transportation assistance, outreach, legal and benefits counseling, and mental health counseling are also offered.

In recognition of SYHC's efforts, it was chosen in 2000 to serve as lead community agency for the federally funded Southern California Border HIV/AIDS Project. This project is one of only five recipients of a Special Projects of National Significance (SPNS) grant for border

---

[20] These include Gente Positiva, Christies Place, BICEPS, and Programa Amigo, a Mexicali-based clinic that provides a full range of HIV/AIDS services to patients from both sides of the border.

[21] Project Concern Border Health Initiative, HIV/AIDS programmatic initiatives, 2004.

health demonstration projects.[22] The primary purpose of the Southern California Border HIV/AIDS Project is to improve HIV/AIDS outreach, access to testing and primary care services, and cross-border linkages for people who live or work in the U.S.-Mexico border region of San Diego and Imperial counties. It is a truly collaborative project; its core participants are SYHC (as lead community agency), UCSD's Center for Community Health/Division of Community Pediatrics (which conducts program evaluation), and community health centers (CHC) in the Southern California border region. The project will also develop a binational referral program so that patients moving from one side of the border to the other will continue to receive care. Four CHCs serve as service delivery hubs to conduct outreach and coordinate systems of care: Clínicas de Salud del Pueblo serves as the CHC hub for Imperial County; SYHC serves the South Bay; Family Health Centers serves central San Diego; and Vista Community Clinic serves North County.

SYHC's work through the Southern California Border HIV/AIDS Project is leading to the development of a comprehensive resource guide that will provide information about health and other HIV-related resources along the border in both the United States and Mexico. The guide will enable HIV-positive men and women to find the services for which they are eligible in Tijuana, Mexicali, San Diego, or Imperial County. A social marketing campaign is also being developed to encourage people to be tested for HIV.

The Binational AIDS Advocacy Project (BAAP) is truly binational in nature. It founded its Tijuana office in 1997 and its San Diego office in 2000.[23] Starting with 50 clients in Tijuana in 1997, by 2000 it was serving over 1,500 clients in Tijuana and 600 or more in San Diego. BAAP undertakes prevention and education campaigns and provides assistance to HIV/AIDS–infected persons and their families. Its services include professional and peer advocacy, referrals for treatment, and support group meetings in San Diego and Tijuana. It maintains a Web-

---

[22] SPNS is administered by the U.S. Department of Health and Human Services' Health Resources and Services Administration. It has funded thirteen HIV/AIDS–related initiatives, including the US/Mexico Border Health Initiative.

[23] See the Binational AIDS Advocacy Project Web site at www.baap.org.

searchable database of HIV/AIDS services in each Mexican state, and it provides information on health services and benefits available through federal and local governments in both San Diego and Tijuana.

Reproductive Health

Another area demonstrating significant binational collaboration is reproductive health and family planning. Remarkable progress has been made through an innovative binational partnership between Tijuana-based Fronteras Unidas Pro Salud, MexFam (the Mexican affiliate of Oxfam), and Planned Parenthood of San Diego and Riverside counties.

Fronteras Unidas Pro Salud was established to improve and expand family planning services in Mexico. It provides basic medical service and education to low-income residents of Baja California. It offers low-cost family planning services, prenatal care, and cervical and breast cancer screening. It also trains community and juvenile health workers, called *promotores* (the vast majority of whom are women, or *promotoras*).

The Promotores Program trains volunteers, who receive forty hours of family planning and reproductive health education. These volunteer healthworkers share family planning information and distribute low-cost contraception in their neighborhoods and communities. They also refer patients to local clinics for more extensive care, and they accompany them to the clinics to provide childcare, help with forms, and give moral support. *Promotoras* and *promotores* receive continuing education classes throughout their involvement with the program, including CPR and first aid training, and instruction on menopause, chronic and degenerative diseases, alcoholism, and nutrition.

In the past two years, 75 *promotores* have assisted some 30,000 people. This highly successful program, which produces a high number of contacts at a low cost, has proven to be a very effective method of outreach and education with this population. It has been replicated, through Planned Parenthood, for use with migrant farmworker populations in San Diego's North County and eastern Riverside County. Planned Parenthood uses educational materials that Pro Salud distributed to its Mexican clients, which resonate culturally with Mexican migrants in California and hence are more effective.

Like PCI, PMSC, and SYHC, Pro Salud has also been working to create awareness among migrants at risk of HIV/AIDS, particularly migrant workers staying at the Casa del Migrante in Tijuana on their way to the United States or on their return to Mexico. Since 1999, 11,158 young migrant men have received education and information relating to HIV/AIDS, and thousands of condoms have been distributed.[24]

Environmental Health and Justice

The Environmental Health Coalition (EHC) is one of the oldest community advocacy groups dedicated to environmental health and justice. Founded in 1980, it focuses on environmental health and justice issues in San Diego and Tijuana communities, "providing technical and organizing assistance to populations adversely affected by toxic chemicals."[25] Its effective community organizing and advocacy has produced many victories, including the designation of 2,200 acres of coastal wetlands as the South San Diego Bay National Wildlife Refuge; a ban on the use of methyl bromide in areas adjacent to poor Latino communities in San Diego (the first such policy enacted against this toxic pesticide in the United States); and the awarding of the nation's first "Emerging Brownfield" grant from the U.S. Environmental Protection Agency (EPA) to the City of San Diego to relocate polluting industries out of residential communities of color.[26]

Since its inception, EHC has engaged in cross-border collaboration with Tijuana residents through its Border Environmental Justice Campaign. In particular, it has supported residents of Colonia Chilpancingo, which abuts the abandoned Metales y Derivados lead smelter.[27] The smelter, owned by a U.S. corporation, moved to Tijuana in 1982; it was closed in 1994 for failing to comply with Mexican environmental laws and regulations. Yet its abandoned site still contains at

---

[24] Fronteras Unidas Pro Salud, 2003.

[25] "Campaign Overview," from the Environmental Health Coalition Web site, http://www.environmentalhealth.org/overview.html.

[26] "About EHC," at http://www.environmentalhealth.org/about.html.

[27] *Toxinformer* 21:3 (July 2002), statement by Colectivo Chilpancingo, at http://www.environmentalhealth.org/ToxieJuly2002Eng.htm (last accessed 11/30/03).

least 6,000 tons of hazardous waste (Cantlupe and Wilkie 2004), posing serious health risks to colonia residents. EHC has been working with community organizations in Tijuana, pressing first for closure of the smelter and now for its cleanup.

This collaboration reached a high level with the establishment of the Colectivo Chilpancingo Pro Justicia Ambiental, which formed in 2000 and opened its office in the colonia in June 2002. The Colectivo advocates for environmental justice and for restoring a healthy environment, with its current focus on the cleanup of the Metales y Derivados site.

EHC provides information on health, environmental, and environmental justice issues to the Colectivo, plays an advisory and support role for its actions and protests, and invites the media and other groups to participate in these activities. And EHC provided training for *promotoras* who worked in Chilpancingo in 2002.[28]

Recent changes within the Mexican federal government have delayed progress on the Metales y Derivados cleanup. Meanwhile, a new binational technical committee—comprising Mexican federal, state, and municipal government officials and U.S. EPA representatives—has been tasked with finding a viable solution to contamination at this site. In February 2004, the EPA announced that the United States and Mexico plan to remove at least fifty 55-gallon drums filled with lead wastes beginning in summer 2004 (Cantlupe and Wilkie 2004). Although this is a welcome first step, thus far the cleanup plan has developed without community input. The Colectivo has not been included in the meetings, but it continues to reiterate its right to join this cross-border effort with Mexican and U.S. federal officials (*Toxinformer* 22:4 [October 2003]: 10).

Education

Beyond transboundary health issues, measured progress has been made to employ cross-border services provision in the area of parent

---

[28] The EHC's unique leadership development and environmental health and justice training for Latinas is called SALTA (Salud Ambiental, Latinas Tomando Acción, or Environmental Health, Latinas Taking Action). See *Toxinformer* 22:1 (January 2003): 6.

education. One successful example is a partnership between Excellence and Justice in Education (EJE), a grassroots organization based in El Cajon, California, that serves Latinos, and Tijuana-based Escuela para la Familia. EJE was founded in 1991 to bring together parents, students, and community members committed to improving students' academic achievement as well as communication between Latino parents and the schools. Since its inception, EJE has sought to involve parents in the school system, to improve services for all students, and to create positive impacts upon society. Toward these ends, it has organized educational programs for Latino parents; Escuela para la Familia has been recruited to provide similar courses in El Cajon and Lemon Grove, California.

At the governmental level, San Diego County's Migrant Education program is collaborating with Mexico's Education Ministry (SEP) in the innovative Plaza Comunitaria program. This program seeks to help migrant families raise their level of education, with a focus on literacy; reinforce attitudes and values among students that encourage strong family, community, and work relationships and stimulate pride in their culture of origin; and strengthen migrant parents' Spanish language ability so that Spanish can serve as the foundation for learning English.[29] In an effort to extend Plaza Comunitaria to other communities, the County of San Diego and the Mexican Consulate in San Diego are working to engage the support of local philanthropists, family foundations, and corporate donors for this binational education initiative. They are proposing a satellite-based distance learning program to be administered by local nonprofit groups, San Diego County, and the Instituto Tecnológico y de Estudios Superiores de Monterrey (ITESM).[30] Apart from the benefits it offers through parental and adult education, Plaza Comunitaria provides a vivid example of the type of expanded binational coordination that will be needed—among government agencies (local, state, and federal) from both countries, in partnership with

---

[29] See the Web page of the San Diego County Office of Migrant Education, at www.migrantweb.org.

[30] Interview with Ed López, San Diego City Schools Board of Education, January 2004.

private funders—to address the growing needs of our shared transnational communities.

Another binational education initiative is Project California, which provides K–12 and adult educational enrichment in Spanish. This joint initiative between the Mexican government and the San Diego County Office of Education will contribute significantly to the academic achievement of K–12 students by bringing them high-quality digital content in Spanish, aligned to California academic content standards, and developed by Mexican government education agencies. The benefit to California is that the program will enable learners of English in California to master math and science concepts through high-quality supplementary content in Spanish at the same time that they are gaining the English language competence that will ultimately enable them to compete academically in California.

The second component of Project California involves expanding Plaza Comunitaria using the same digital content, provided by the Mexican government agency CONEVyT. Content is delivered via a portal in Mexico City and brought to California through a mirror site administered by the San Diego County Office of Education. Spanish speakers aged 15 years and older can enroll in courses to further their vocational or higher education or to pursue other educational opportunities in California. These Adult Spanish Literacy Services will be available to Spanish-speaking families residing in areas of high-density Hispanic population in California.

This collaborative effort between the San Diego County Office of Education and two Mexican government agencies—the National Institute for Adult Education (INEA) and the National Council for Workforce Education and Lifelong Learning (CONEVyT)—is supported by the Corporation for Education Network Initiatives in California (CENIC), Mexico's Education Ministry (SEP) and Foreign Ministry (SRE), and the Institute for Mexicans Abroad (IME). In California, project affiliates include the Mexican consulates in San Diego and Sacramento and the Sacramento County Office of Education (SCOE). The project was inaugurated in July 2003 via a live videoconference with Mexican President Vicente Fox, U.S. Secretary of Education Kerry Mazzoni, and officials from San Diego and Sacramento. The San Diego County Office of Education plans to expand Project California's outreach to communities in San Diego's East County and North County in collaboration with nonprofit organizations. ICF is assisting the Office of Education by providing links to NGOs such as EJE.

Prisoner Reentry

In California alone, there are currently over 20,500 Mexican undocumented inmates in state prisons, or about 12.6 percent of the entire prison population (SDCCD 2003: 1). At the California City Correctional Center (CCCC), located a hundred miles east of Los Angeles, 95 percent of the inmates are undocumented immigrants from Mexico, and over 60 percent come from just five Mexican states: Michoacán, 18.8 percent; Sinaloa, 13.9 percent; Jalisco, 11.8 percent; Tabasco, 9.9 percent; and Baja California, 9.8 percent (SDCCD 2003: 2). According to tests administered at CCCC, these inmates have, on average, the equivalent of a third-grade education and show serious literacy deficits (SDCCD 2003: 5). Upon release, they are deported to Mexico; the majority (70 percent) are sent to Tijuana without any prisoner reentry support. The result is that these former inmates ultimately find their way back across the border and into a life of crime, which lands them back in prison. According to the California Department of Corrections (CDC), about 20 percent of its undocumented parolees released to the U.S. Immigration and Naturalization Service (INS) for deportation returned to California (SDCCD 2003: 1). Hence the need for proactive binational solutions to the question of prisoner reentry, an issue that should be of growing concern to the United States and Mexico alike.

STRIVE/Second Chance, a San Diego–based group that is a leader in prisoner reentry initiatives, is doing much to help the growing number of Latino ex-offenders reintegrate to the regional workforce. This is a unique space for a collaborative binational partnership, yet there are currently no programs to assist deported Mexican ex-offenders in their country of origin. The California City Correctional Center has taken a first step with its continuing education program for Mexican and Spanish-speaking inmates which gives participants the opportunity to complete their secondary education and receive occupational training that could lead to employment upon their release. Through an initial seed grant, the San Diego Community College District, in partnership with

ICF, began exploring opportunities for collaboration with the nonprofit sector and trade associations in Mexico (in particular, the American Chamber of Commerce in Mexico, or AMCHAM), with a focus on identifying possible job opportunities with U.S. companies in Guadalajara for former CCCC inmates from Jalisco. Unfortunately, this initiative was never fully implemented due to insufficient funding.[31]

IMPLICATIONS OF MIGRATION BEYOND THE BORDER REGION

Although the transboundary issues facing the San Diego–Tijuana metroplex are unique, the demographic and sociological changes in this region are not unlike those occurring in metropolitan areas throughout North America. The pressures of human migration are not limited to San Diego, as underscored by migrant surveys conducted by El Colegio de la Frontera Norte (COLEF). Among migrants arriving to Tijuana between 1993 and 2001 and intending to cross into the United States, a mere 1.6 percent gave San Diego as their final destination. Over 22.5 percent indicated that they were headed to other destinations in California, and over 76.1 percent planned to go to other U.S. states (see the chapters by Alarcón and Anguiano, this volume).

COLEF's research findings are supported by the fact that there are now over 20.6 million people of Mexican descent in the United States. Of this population, nearly 9.2 million were born in Mexico (Malone et al. 2003). Again according to census data, about 4.7 million are undocumented, representing 55 percent of the total undocumented population in the United States. Given the growing number of Mexico-born people—legal and undocumented—throughout the United States, the need for cross-border services will expand over time to communities across the United States. Their challenges will be even more daunting than those in border communities, because these heartland communities do not have ready access to the value-added skill sets of Mexican nonprofit professionals, including culturally and linguistically competent care, that are available in border communities like San Diego–Tijuana.

---

[31] For more information on this pilot program, and the obstacles to its full implementation, see SDCCD 2003.

Today there are an estimated 183,500 undocumented Mexicans residing in San Diego, people who would not remain in San Diego County if they did not have gainful employment. The codependence between undocumented Mexican workers and the regional economy and employers is self-evident. Yet San Diego County's high living costs, shortage of affordable housing, increased incidence of poverty, and proposed cuts in social services by state agencies are causing many transnational migrants now living in the region to look elsewhere for a better life. Research conducted by the University of Southern California confirms that California's share of new immigrant arrivals dropped sharply between 1990 and 2000 compared to other regions of the country—such as Texas, Georgia, and North Carolina—that offer would-be migrants employment opportunities coupled with more affordable housing and lower living costs (Blood 2004). In fact, the Carlsbad Hiring Center, run by the nonprofit job-training and job-placement organization SER/Jobs for Progress, has in recent years been assisting San Diego–area Mexican migrants search for jobs across the country, placing applicants with out-of-state employers in twenty-seven states (Gaona 2004b).

What is happening at the Carlsbad Hiring Center is not an isolated trend. According to the Pew Hispanic Center, Latino immigrants are among the most mobile and versatile segment of the U.S. labor force. The number of employed Latinos rose by 659,641 to 17.7 million between the fourth quarter of 2002 and the fourth quarter of 2003 compared to the non-Latino labor force, which has over 121 million workers but had fewer than 371,066 newly employed workers during that time. These job gains are largely attributable to Latino workers' willingness to take low-wage jobs and to relocate anywhere in the country, as well as to the existence of family networks that serve as sources of employment information. According to Pew researcher and study co-author Rakesh Kochhar, "the one thing that characterizes immigrants is that they're go-getters and they're here to work. To them it's not critical whether they do it in California or New England" (Sánchez 2002).

Yet not all of San Diego's Mexican migrant labor force is mobile. For a variety of reasons, including employment situation, schools, and so on, a sizable number of transnational Mexican migrants and their families are opting to stay in San Diego County, even though the area's high cost of living has contributed to a growing incidence of poverty among this undocumented population. By contrast, transborder residents, who can legally cross the border, have enjoyed an improved standard of living by combining a U.S. paycheck with Tijuana's more affordable housing and culturally competent education and health care options (see Escala Rabadán and Vega Briones, this volume).

According to some San Diego County–area transnational migrant residents, there is a perception among San Diegans that Baja Californian transborder workers (who lack legal work authorization) take their jobs and in some cases depress entry-level wages because they can afford to work for less. As one undocumented San Diego resident put it, "the cost of keeping a job and supporting a family in San Diego is painfully high. For those living in Tijuana, the only cost for a job here is the price of a trolley ticket or gas and a few hours of delay at the border."[32] In effect, the border is increasingly blurring distinctions between poverty and relative prosperity predicated, in part, on visa or migratory status.

LEARNING FROM SAN DIEGO

The San Diego–Tijuana border also teaches us that, just as U.S. nonprofits would be well served to seek the support of Mexican nonprofits to address growing transnational needs in the United States, the ebb and flow of transnational migration across the border dictates a broader look at addressing the shared transboundary impacts that are the consequence of human migration.

The issue of prisoner reentry is a case in point. As mentioned above, the majority of former Mexico-origin inmates are deported back across the border with no prisoner reentry support, an issue that should be of growing concern in both countries. Some important initiatives have been launched to address this issue in San Diego–Tijuana, as described previously. Yet initiatives of this type are sorely needed in Mexico as well, particularly to help Mexican ex-offenders reintegrate to their country of origin after deportation. This need is urgent, given that immigration officials are considering increasing the number of deportees

---

[32] Interview with an anonymous resident, October 2003.

sent directly back to their home communities (Walker 2004). A pilot program to deport illegal crossers to places further from the international border—to places unfamiliar to the crossers so that supposedly they would be discouraged from making repeated attempts to cross the border illegally—was implemented in 2003 (Gilot 2003). While immigration officials argue that this pilot program was successful in reducing the number of repeat crossers in dangerous desert locations (possibly contributing to a reduction in the number of deaths among these crossers), the Department of Homeland Security is only beginning to explore facilitating the reentry of these individuals to their communities of origin. In the absence of such services, the impact of deportation is likely to be very negative, both for the deportees and for the communities that receive them.

The impact of human migration is also felt in the migrants' final destinations, which are becoming quite diverse. Canada is now feeling the impacts, both positive and negative, of transnational migrants. Although the number of Canada's transnational migrants (who are not legally permitted to work) is very small (some 200,000, compared to 8 million in the United States) and accounts for a small share of immigrants (estimated at 8 percent), Canada nevertheless faces the challenge of addressing these transnational migrants' rights and responsibilities (especially tax payments) and meeting their service needs (Jiménez 2003).

The San Diego–Tijuana region's experience with key issues regarding the opportunities and challenges of cross-border migrant service provision places it in a position to offer some valuable lessons for communities elsewhere in North America, from Canada to Mexico.

- *Mexico's transnational migrants in the United States face many unique challenges,* both in their adopted land and with regard to their family members who remain in their communities of origin. It is crucial that governmental and nonprofit service providers work together to provide more culturally competent care, always taking into consideration these unique needs.

- *Greater binational collaboration is needed among nonprofits.* Several San Diego nonprofits are collaborating with their Tijuana counterparts and demonstrating that cross-border service provision partnerships can and do work. However, many more such collaborations are needed, not just in San Diego–Tijuana but across North America, on common issues of concern, particularly issues of education and health for Mexican transnational communities.

Opportunities are emerging for U.S. service providers to partner or align with nonprofits based on the border or in other Mexican states to provide skilled professionals with experience in addressing specific migrant needs. Curiously, few Mexican nonprofit professionals are taking advantage of the opportunities afforded them under NAFTA to obtain professional services or TN visas to procure services in the United States.[33] The ICF is currently heightening collaboration among community foundations in migrant-sending regions of Mexico. The first such collaboration, with the Community Foundation of Oaxaca (FCO), seeks to identify Oaxacan NGOs capable of providing value-added services to Oaxacan communities in San Diego and Tijuana, to expand opportunities for philanthropy and grant-making to Oaxaca, and to promote productive employment opportunities in migrant-sending communities in Oaxaca by facilitating economic development and trade of local goods in Southern California.

- *There is a need to tap the vast potential of Mexico's hometown associations and other migrant support organizations.* As ICF's experience with COCIO demonstrates, migrant support organizations provide nonprofit agencies with a unique skill set and community-based knowledge crucial to efforts to address the needs of Mexico's ethnically diverse migrant labor force. With over 1,500 hometown as-

---

[33] The TN visa for professionals is available only to citizens of Mexico and Canada. A citizen of a NAFTA country may work in a professional occupation in another NAFTA country provided that (1) the profession is on the NAFTA list, (2) the alien possesses the specific criteria for that profession, (3) the prospective position requires someone in that professional capacity, and (4) the alien is going to work for a U.S. employer. The spouse and unmarried, minor children of the principal alien are entitled to the derivative status, but they are unable to accept employment in the United States. Aliens entering under this classification are considered non-immigrants.

sociations across the United States, opportunities exist for more effectively reaching the growing numbers of transnational migrants nationwide. Most Mexican hometown associations and support groups are in their infancy, and most need funding for organizational capacity building and leadership development to be effective.

- *Transnational communities require greater inter-jurisdictional cooperation.* It is essential that municipal agencies throughout San Diego County and across the country share lessons learned and best practices on the unique needs of transnational migrants in their jurisdictions. In the case of Mixtec and other Oaxacan migrants, there is a compelling need for the educators and social service and health professionals serving communities of San Diego's North County (Oceanside, Vista, San Marcos, Carlsbad) to work together closely on common challenges they face when addressing migrant worker issues and needs.

   Given that the impacts of human migration do not respect international borders, U.S. and Mexican municipal officials have much to learn from each other about how to address the unique needs and challenges of Mexico's migrant workers and their families. Here binational sister-city relationships can prove fruitful. Oceanside, California, for example, has a sister-city relationship with Ensenada. Although little has been done thus far to cement this institutional relationship, Oceanside has much to learn from the work of Ensenada-based nonprofits and local agencies that deal with the needs of migrant workers in the San Quintín Valley in Baja California.

   A unique opportunity also exists to expand trade, tourism, and cultural exchanges with the communities that send migrants to the San Diego–Tijuana region. After all, given that 11 percent of San Diego's migrant population comes from Oaxaca, there is a fair argument to be made that the region has more in common with this migrant-sending Mexican state than with Shannon, Ireland, with which San Diego is currently pursuing a sister-city relationship. Enhanced ties with migrant-sending regions have an added benefit beyond the obvious goodwill to be gained; they would also help local social service agencies better appreciate the unique needs of area migrant workers and their families.

- *Investment in migrant education and health care needs is critical.* To redress economic and social inequalities in San Diego and beyond, investments must be made in improving the quality of education and health care options for migrant populations. A growing number of migrant workers and their families in San Diego originate from rural communities with extreme poverty, particularly in the states of Oaxaca, Chiapas, Guerrero, Michoacán, and Jalisco. The low educational attainment levels of most arriving migrant workers, coupled with the challenges of urban adaptation, exacerbate other challenges, particularly in the areas of health and their children's education.

  In San Diego, a growing number of mostly migrant schoolchildren and youths are being left behind educationally. In both San Diego and Tijuana, high school dropout rates are higher among migrant youth than their nonmigrant peers. Unless public schools receive additional resources with which to meet the needs of this unique student population, the region's competitiveness is likely to suffer.

  A range of health care issues affect this transnational community, which is largely uninsured and is highly susceptible to otherwise preventable or treatable diseases, including tuberculosis, hepatitis, sexually transmitted diseases, obesity, and diabetes. The migrant families in San Diego and Tijuana also experience problems of mental illness, stress, and domestic violence as a result of family separation and unhealthy living conditions.

  Opportunities exist for groups based in San Diego and Baja California to collaborate with nonprofits in migrant-sending regions through expanded "cross-border casework" to address the needs of transnational migrants. Geneva-based International Social Services (ISS) provides a successful model of cross-border casework through its efforts to link its agencies in mainland China with Chinese migrant–serving organizations in Vancouver and New York.[34]

---

[34] Chinese Immigrant Service Network International (CISANI) conference, Honolulu, October 2003.

ISS has proven the value of this approach in the areas of asylum, child abduction, unaccompanied young migrants, child/youth deportation, and "pre-entry" education for migrants traveling overseas (*ISS Newsletter* 3, March 2002).

In Vancouver, the United Chinese Community Enrichment Services Society (SUCCESS) and the Hong Kong/Guangzhou branch of ISS are collaborating to address migrant needs on an intracountry basis. This partnership coordinates co-funding for casework in migrant-sending regions of China and provides education for migrants before their entry to Canada, along with information on immigrant rights and the risks of human smuggling, cultural training (to help migrants adjust to urban living), and survival English language training. According to Ken Tung, Executive Director of SUCCESS, ISS's pre-entry training in English, computer literacy, and cross-cultural issues gives would-be Chinese migrants a significant advantage when they arrive in Canada. Tung also notes that ISS's support for cross-border casework has been instrumental in improving SUCCESS's ability to serve its client base in the greater Vancouver area. According to Tung, "it's a real win-win for all involved." [35]

CONCLUSION: FUTURE CHALLENGES AND OPPORTUNITIES

A key lesson from San Diego is that investment in the region's transborder residents and transnational migrant communities is crucial. The children of this fast-growing population form an important part of the region's future.

The growing number of unfunded education and health mandates at the state and local levels will compel San Diego–area nonprofit agencies to make some tough choices in coming years regarding staffing levels and the services provided to the general public. Absent increased funding from the federal government or private foundations, many of San Diego migrants' needs will go unmet. Yet every crisis brings opportunities.

---

[35] Interview with SUCCESS staff members, October 2003.

Opportunities exist for greater involvement in binational public-private collaborations such as Plaza Comunitaria, Project California, and the innovative prisoner reentry initiatives of the California City Correctional Center. There is also an expanding role for Mexican philanthropic institutions and corporations in addressing transboundary needs of Mexican migrants abroad, and for good reason. The growing Mexican consumer market in the United States for Mexican consumer brands like Maseca, Cemex, Gigante, Jumex, Bimbo, Citibank/Banamex, and Telmex calls for greater corporate social responsibility among Mexico's leading businesses with operations in the United States. A good starting point would be to support leadership development and organizational capacity building in the growing number of Mexican hometown associations and other migrant support organizations.

The convergence of improved information technology, broadband communications, and NAFTA's trade-in-services provisions presents enterprising Mexican nonprofits with additional opportunities to dramatically expand service delivery to transnational migrants across the heartland of the United States and Canada. Through expanded binational or even trinational collaborations extending far beyond the immediate border, nonprofits in North America can provide services to benefit transnational migrants as they spread across North America and begin building new lives in adopted homes in Alaska, North Carolina, Georgia, and Ontario.

References

Bernstein, Nina. 2004. "Children Alone and Scared, Fighting Deportation," *New York Times*, March 28.

Besser, Richard E., Bilge Pakiz, Joann M. Schulte, Sonia Alvarado, Elizabeth R. Zell, Thomas A. Kenyon, and Ida M. Onorato. 2001. "Risk Factors for Positive Mantoux Tuberculin Skin Tests in Children in San Diego, California: Evidence for Boosting and Possible Foodborne Transmission," *Pediatrics* 108, no. 2, available at http://medicine.ucsd.edu/peds/Pediatric%20Links/Links/General%20Pediatrics%20Outpatient/Risk%20Factors%20for%20Positive%20PPD%20in%20SD%20Pediatrics%20August%202001.htm (last accessed 2/25/2004).

Blood, Michael. 2004. "California No Longer Luring Lion's Share of Immigrants," *San Diego Union Tribune*, February 18.

Boston Globe. 2003. "Immigrants, US Dollars Paying Off in Homeland," September 9.

Bowman, Woods. 2003. "Fiscal Crisis in the States: Its Impact on Non Profit Organizations and the People They Serve." Washington, D.C.: The Aspen Institute, November.

California Health and Human Services Agency. 2004. "2004–2005 Budget Proposal Summary. January 2004," in pdf format at http://www.chhs.ca/gov/ (last accessed 3/23/04).

Campbell, Paul R. 1996. "Population Projections for States by Age, Sex, Race, and Hispanic Origin: 1995 to 2025." U.S. Bureau of the Census, Population Division, PPL-47, http://www.census.gov/population/www/projections/ppl47.html (last accessed 2/20/04).

Cantlupe, Joe, and Dana Wilkie. 2004. "Cleanup Slated at Toxic Plant," *San Diego Union Tribune,* February 16.

Ganster, Paul. 1999. "Tijuana, Basic Facts," at http://www-rohan.sdsu.edu/~irsc/tjreport/tj1.html.

Gaona, Elena. 2004a. "Workers Leaving Camps: City Worried Dwellings Would Cause Pollution," *San Diego Union Tribune,* February 14.

———. 2004b. "Long Distance Commute: Carlsbad Hiring Center Helps Immigrants Find Jobs across U.S.," *San Diego Union Tribune,* February 22.

Georges, Eugenia, and Elaine Georges. 1990. *The Making of a Transnational Community: Migration, Development and Cultural Change in the Dominican Republic.* New York: Columbia University Press.

Gilot, Louie. 2003. "Repatriation Program Ends," *El Paso Times,* October 1.

Jargowsky, Paul A. 2003. "Stunning Progress, Hidden Problems: The Dramatic Decline of Concentrated Poverty in the 1990s." Brookings Institution Center on Urban and Metropolitan Policy, Living Cities Census Series, at http://www.brookings.edu/es/urban/publications/jargowskypoverty.htm (last accessed 2/25/04).

Jiménez, Marina. 2003. "200,000 Illegal Immigrants Toiling in Canada's Underground Economy," *Globe and Mail,* November 15.

Larson, Stephen. 2003. "California Cities Face Tough Economic Times Ahead," *San Diego Daily Transcript,* February 11.

Malone, Nolan, et al. 2003. "The Foreign Born Population: Census 2000." Washington, D.C.: U.S. Census Bureau, December.

Office of Policy and Planning, U.S. Immigration and Naturalization Service. 2003. "Estimates of the Unauthorized Immigrant Population Residing in the United States: 1990 to 2000." Washington, D.C., January 31. In pdf format at http://uscis.gov/graphics/shared/aboutus/statistics/Ill_Report_1211.pdf.

Portes, Alejandro. 1997. "Globalization from Below: The Rise of Transnational Communities." University of Oxford Transnational Communities Programme Working Paper No. WPTC-98-01. In PDF format at http://www. transcomm.ox.ac.uk/working%wopapers/portes/pdf.

Romero, Fernando. 2002. "Making Connection between Immigration and Tuberculosis," *Border Reflections* 34 (February/March), http://www. pciborderregion.com/newsletter/1600_EN/1600_3_EN.htm (last accessed 2/20/04).

Sánchez, Leonel. 2002. "Go-anywhere Latino Immigrants Fare Very Well in Landing Jobs," *San Diego Union Tribune*, February 24.

SDCCD (San Diego Community College District). 2003. Report to the Rockefeller Foundation on the California/Mexico Correctional Workforce Partnership Pilot Program.

Secretaría de Salud. 2002. *Salud México 2001*, at http://www.ssa.gov.mx.

Walker, S. Lynne. 2004. "U.S., Mexico to Shape Repatriation Plan: Illegal Crossers Would Be Returned to Villages," *Sign On San Diego*, February 21.

Acronyms

AMCHAM	American Chamber of Commerce in Mexico
CAWHS	California Agricultural Worker Health Survey
CCCC	California City Correctional Center
CDC	California Department of Corrections
CENIC	Corporation for Education Network Initiatives in California
CHC	community health center
COCIO	Coalición de Comunidades Indígenas de Oaxaca / Coalition of Indigenous Communities of Oaxaca
CONAPO	Consejo Nacional de Población / National Population Council
CONEVyT	Consejo Nacional de Educación para la Vida y el Trabajo / National Council for Workforce Education and Lifelong Learning
EHC	Environmental Health Coalition
EJE	Excellence and Justice in Education
EMIF	Encuesta sobre Migración en la Frontera Norte de México / Northern Mexico Migration Survey
ENEU	Encuesta Nacional de Empleo Urbano / National Urban Employment Survey
EPA	U.S. Environmental Protection Agency
FCO	Fundación Comunitaria de Oaxaca / Community Foundation of Oaxaca
FDI	foreign direct investment
FIOB	Frente Indígena Oaxaqueña Binacional / Oaxacan Indigenous Binational Front
ICF	International Community Foundation

IME	Instituto de los Mexicanos en el Exterior / Institute for Mexicans Abroad
IMSS	Instituto Mexicano del Seguro Social / Mexican Social Security Institute
INEA	Instituto Nacional para la Educación de los Adultos / National Institute for Adult Education
INEGI	Instituto Nacional de Estadística, Geografía e Informática / National Institute of Statistics, Geography, and Informatics
INS	U.S. Immigration and Naturalization Service
IRCA	Immigration Reform and Control Act of 1986
ISS	International Social Services
ISSSTE	Instituto de Seguridad Social y Servicios para los Trabajadores del Estado / Social Security Institute for State Employees
ITESM	Instituto Tecnológico y de Estudios Superiores de Monterrey / Monterrey Institute of Technology and Advanced Studies
LAW	legally authorized worker
NGO	nongovernmental organization
PCI	Project Concern International
PMSC	Patronato de Medicina Social Comunitaria, A.C. / Foundation for Community Medicine
SAW	Special Agricultural Worker program
SCOE	Sacramento County Office of Education
SEP	Secretaría de Educación Pública / Education Ministry
SPNS	Special Projects of National Significance
SRE	Secretaría de Relaciones Exteriores / Foreign Ministry
SUCCESS	United Chinese Community Enrichment Services Society
SYHC	San Ysidro Health Center
VCC	Vista Community Clinic